God's W

WOMEN A

God's Woman Revisited

WOMEN AND THE CHURCH

GARY T. BURKE

LUMINARE PRESS

WWW.LUMINAREPRESS.COM

Printed in the United States of America

Cover Design: Claire Flint Last

Luminare Press
442 Charnelton St.
Eugene, OR 97401
www.luminarepress.com

LCCN: 2019937212
ISBN: 978-1-64388-077-8

ACKNOWLEDGMENTS

For the far-too-often underappreciated contribution of our sisters to the Kingdom of God on earth.

For the courageous reopening of the matter of women in the church 80 years ago by C. R. Nichol, whose book, God's Woman, has been both the inspiration and impetus for this book.

For the invaluable assistance of the following brothers and sisters during the writing and editing of this manuscript: Kent Blake, Mike Gilliland, John Griffiths, Dennis Lacoss, Deb and Rick Rossing, and Steven Webb.

For the contribution of Philip Slate, whose critical read of the completed manuscript and helpful suggestions significantly improved the quality of the final product.

TABLE OF CONTENTS

CHAPTER ONE
God's Woman

CHAPTER TWO
The Current Impasse

CHAPTER THREE
What Disciplined Bible Study Looks Like

CHAPTER FOUR
The Creation Narrative

─────────────── **CHAPTER FIVE** ───────────────
New Testament Use of the Genesis Creation Narrative

─────────────── **CHAPTER SIX** ───────────────
Women in the World Of Jesus

─────────────── **CHAPTER SEVEN** ───────────────
Jesus and Women

─────────────── **CHAPTER EIGHT** ───────────────
Galatians 3:28 and Ephesians 5:21-33

CHAPTER NINE
I Corinthians 11:2-16

CHAPTER TEN
I Corinthians 14:34-35

CHAPTER ELEVEN
I Timothy 2:8-15

CHAPTER TWELVE
The End of the Matter

Foreword

*J*ack P. Lewis was approached by "a talented student, who was occupying a pulpit in size far in advance of others of his years" and who asked him a question about the Holy Spirit. When Jack gave him his answer, the student responded, "Is that the position our brothers have always taken?" Jack's typically condensed reply was, "I have never seen 'What our brothers have always taught' as the way to solve biblical questions." He held that one should go to Scripture and handle it correctly in the effort to answer biblical questions. It is in this vein that Gary Burke has brought together many years of painstaking exegesis to produce this work on women and the church.

The different views and practices among religious groups regarding the place of women in the life and work of the church vary enormously. One can observe a huge spread of beliefs and practices from highly restrictive male chauvinism to the no-restrictions approach that results in lesbian Bishops in a few churches. These variations have different causes, of course, but among those who seek to give a rationale for their practices it is clear that they operate from very different bases. The author of this volume, however, is chiefly interested in seeking answers to biblical questions by going through a responsible exegetical process. It is chiefly for the level at which he pitches his effort to answer biblical questions that I highly commend this work.

The author comes from a faith heritage that for two centuries in North America has stressed the importance of appropriate respect for and handling of Scripture, hermeneutics if you please. Since there are some differences in his own fellowship about the "interpretation" of Scripture, Burke lays out in detail the method of interpretation he has employed in handling all the critical passages on the position and work of women--from Gen. 1-3 to 1 Tim. 2:12. His approach includes an awareness and management of one's biases and assumptions when coming to a text. Two groups of people in particular will find appreciation for his approach to Scripture: preachers/teachers and missionaries.

As a Missiologist who has worked cross-culturally, for twenty-seven years trained students to engage in that kind of work, and evaluated disciple-making work in multiple countries, I know the value of digging into Scripture responsibly when issues emerge in another culture that one has previously never considered. Many missionaries simply opt for the answers Protestants, Roman Catholics, and independents worked out before them, but that is not good enough for people who are committed to following Scripture seriously. They need to know, of course, why and how others reached their conclusions, and then do their own hard work of exegesis and application. Burke gives a good model for such a procedure.

The other interest is in expository preaching/teaching. For people who hold a high view of Scripture, all good preaching and teaching should arise from a careful understanding of the text. Since Burke interacts with the exegetical work of several Evangelical scholars, they should find his work engaging. Understandably, the author uses his own fellowship, the Churches of Christ, for his "case study" and basic appeal since he knows best their history and thought. Indeed, "his jumping off" place is an older study, now largely forgotten, *God's Woman,* a 1938 work by a formidable Bible student, preacher, teacher, and debater, C. R. Nichol (1876-1961). That is the rationale for the title of his book, *God's Woman Revisited: Women and the Church.* Although he demurs from Nichol on several points, Burke consciously and appreciatively "stands on his shoulders" while doing his own exegesis of the critical passages and subjects.

While collected works like the two volumes of *Essays on Women in Earliest Christianity,* edited by Carroll Osburn, are very useful, one value of a single person's dealing with the whole gamut of biblical teaching on a subject is his or her ability to engage in intertextuality. He can do his own work of relating the Genesis materials to texts in the New Testament that use them. Thus, there is a wholeness involved in the sweep of Burke's work. In addition to his work on the classical texts, the illuminating chapter on the teaching of Jesus makes a good contribution to one's understanding.

This book is not a product of one who sits in an ivy-covered tower, largely out of touch with the life of a local church. He has served as a shepherd/elder in two congregations. He holds a high view of the church, is passionate about its unity and ministry, and is prudent about introducing any kind of substantive changes without appropriately processing with the congregation the grounds of such a change. In other words, he is not a radical "young Turk," as the saying goes; he has lived long enough to understand people and their feelings, recognize faulty reasoning, and to note the difference between closed and inquiring minds and hearts.

This book is a welcome effort to advance responsible biblical thought on a sensitive, potentially divisive, but unavoidable question about the ministry of Christian women in the local church, especially in its assemblies and educational work. The author has disagreed with himself from time to time, and all readers have the right to disagree with him on various points. Nevertheless, this is a stimulating volume that beckons a reading by those who have not done all the thinking they intend to do on the subject; it has the promise of new insight on several of the classical biblical texts on women.

C. Philip Slate
Retired professor, author, and former
Dean of Harding School of Theology

Introduction

*A*nother book on women! How could there possibly be a need, given the massive amount of attention this topic has received in the last 50 years since the revival of the women's movement in the West? Although several reasons can be cited, the short answer is that in the Churches of Christ in North America we have reached a dangerous impasse on this subject. The rift that has resulted threatens to become an unbridgeable chasm that imperils our unity, as once again we have allowed ourselves to become swamped by another "issue." Countless books, articles, tracts, and sermons on the topic have failed to bring us closer together. Much of the discussion has been in response to the concepts and terminology of modern Sociology. Where the Bible has been at the center of the discussion, far too often traditional interpretations have trumped those flowing from fresh, careful exegetical work on the biblical text. Perhaps there is some merit in another attempt to deal with this matter, free from the encumbrances of reading modern concepts and centuries of tradition into the Bible. So, this book has been written to engage fellow members of the Churches of Christ in a fresh consideration of whether or not limitations on women that are common in most of our congregations rest on a firm biblical base.

The impetus for the book came from the groundbreaking book, *God's Woman*, written in 1938, some 80 years ago as of this writing, by the respected evangelist, educator, writer, and debater, C. R. Nichol. Nichol was troubled by what he believed to be unbiblical limitations on women in the church, especially on their teaching men in group settings. Breaking with traditional interpretations, he did a fresh study of the Bible in which he arrived at some conclusions that troubled certain of his contemporaries. Others, including his friend, N. B. Hardeman, applauded his work, stating that it would become a textbook at his college. In the decades to follow, the influence of *God's Woman* waned, and those favoring the more traditional limitations on women in the church prevailed. With the coming of the women's movement in the last third of the twentieth century, positions and practices in certain portions of the Churches of Christ in North America even hardened and, in some cases, became more extreme.

This book is an effort to try again what Nichol attempted to do 80 years ago. Like *God's Woman*, it seeks to peel away layers of tradition and examine the relevant biblical passages exegetically, avoiding as much as possible the overlay of both tradition and modern concepts. In the spirit of our commitment to the principle that our practice be governed by what we find in the Bible, this book will attempt to draw its conclusions only from what the Bible actually says, rather than what its interpreters think it implies. It will then attempt to apply generally accepted best practices in interpretation to those biblical statements. The goal is to shed some new light that will help bring us closer together in our understanding of the way we should be treating women in the church.

Timeliness of This Topic

CHANGE IS DIFFICULT. MOST OF US ARE CONSERVATIVE AT heart in the sense that our natural reaction to change is to resist. We need to be convinced that the need for change is compelling enough to get us out of our comfort zone. This is doubly the case when it comes to matters of our religious faith. We require reassurance that any change does not go against God's will, since we measure our beliefs and practices against our understanding of that will as revealed in the Bible. This is particularly the case when we feel the pressure of the world around us urging us in a direction that is new to us. We rightly feel compelled to stand our ground on what we believe the Bible teaches. However, sometimes that urging from our culture turns out to be right and we have been behind the curve, as in the case of race relations in many of our congregations and Christian colleges. This book is being written in the conviction that another of those moments in our history has arrived. Just as with race relations, where reexamination of the Scriptures on the topic, though prompted in part from external influences, was what led to needed change, the same "back to the Bible" stance must characterize us as we respond to external pressures on our practice concerning women in the church. The costs of getting this one wrong are so great that avoiding a serious reexamination of what the Scriptures say on women in the church does not seem to be a safe option any longer. If we or any other individuals or churches who also have a high view of Scripture have been wrong in the way we have limited our sisters in their participation in the work and worship of the church, consider these four consequences of continuing to do so.

Alienating Our Young People. As we have all noticed, large numbers of our young people have moved on. They are casualties of the culture wars raging in our society. Many a young Christian woman has lamented the fact that the only place in her world where she has restrictions placed on her because of her gender is the church. Large numbers of our young Christian men feel her hurt and likewise are becoming estranged from the faith of their parents. As a campus minister for twenty years, I saw this happening over and over as young people tasted the freedom that college offered. Thankfully, many of them later came back to the Lord and the church because they reconnected with the values and beliefs that had been instilled in them earlier in life. However, it is different this time. What they see as unjustified discrimination against women runs counter to the values they now so firmly hold. If we have been right on women in the church, of course we should hold the line. But if we are wrong on this one, we run the enormous risk of pushing our young people away, unnecessarily. We must make sure we get this one right!

Alienating Our Culture. Historically, the teachings of Christ have been the impetus for virtually all the improvements in morality and ethical treatment of others in Western culture. Through the years Christians have been persecuted and even killed because their choice of the higher road reflected so poorly on those who chose the lower path. The influence of Jesus on education, science, government, our legal system, and on virtually every other facet of our lives and culture has been to elevate them for the good of our world. On the matter of women in the church, however, the traditional Christian practices are seen in our culture as archaic and oppressive. This current culture views itself as taking the higher road and we the lower. They see themselves as our ethical superiors, so our influence on them has been weakened significantly. Again, if they are wrong, we should not flinch in staying our course, but if they are right, we are doing inestimable, unnecessary damage to our ability to reach them with the gospel. We must make sure we get this one right!

Failure to Use Many of the Gifts of Half of Our Members. Many who have written on this subject have understandably resisted the argument that if a person has a gift from God, we should not place restrictions on its use. In countering this, it has been pointed out, I think correctly, that if those restrictions come from God, they override our freedom to exercise them. After all, tongue speakers and prophets were restricted in the use of their gifts in the Corinthian assemblies (I Cor. 14:27-32). But what if the restrictions we have placed on women do not actually come from God, but rather from our *mis*understanding of the relevant biblical passages? In that case, we would be putting restrictions on half of our members that are human and not divine, and we would continue to be much poorer for it. We must make sure we get this one right!

Limiting the Freedom of Half of Our Members. Limiting another's freedom in Christ is a very serious matter (see Gal. 2:4, 5:1). Often the argument is made that when choosing between two courses of action where the proper choice is not clear, we should follow the safer path. I have been an elder in two congregations. For some or all of the time in those congregations we have limited women's participation in the assembly in ways I no longer believe are biblical. Do you think, as one who must give an account for my shepherding (Heb. 13:17), I want to stand before God having wrongly restricted the freedom in Christ of half the members in my congregation? I do not regard that as the safer course of action. We leaders must make sure we get this one right!

Importance of This Topic

Questionable Assumptions. In addition to the above-mentioned impasse we have reached on this issue, other considerations underscore its importance. First, a whole host of problematic assumptions permeate the literature on women in the church. Assumptions are premises that we use to draw other conclusions. We do not feel obligated to support or try to prove them, either because we consider them self-evident or we believe they have been sufficiently established elsewhere. We all make assumptions and reason from them. The problem comes when we allow our assumption to become fact to such an extent that we are either unaware of them or are unwilling to reconsider them. Here are a few of the questionable assumptions about the teaching of the biblical text relating to women in the church that will be addressed in this book. The reason they need to be challenged is not just that their validity is doubtful but also that they frequently become part of the foundation used to support other points.

- God made man (Adam) a protector of woman (Eve).
- The concept of male spiritual leadership is found in the Genesis creation narrative.
- The teachings of Genesis 2-3 apply to women and men in general, rather than to wives and husbands.
- Wives' submission to husbands as found in Gen. 3:16 was later transferred to women's submission to men in the church.
- Leading is by its very nature domineering or a lack of submission.
- Teaching by its very nature has authority attached to it.
- Serving in some capacity in the assembly is assuming an unbiblical leadership role.
- Women in general are to be in submission to men in general in the church.
- Gal. 3:28 is Paul's Magna Carta for women and is primary to any other Pauline texts on women.

Inconsistencies. Second, in writings on women in the church, several inconsistencies appear and need to be noted. For instance,

- How is it that the creation story in Genesis 2-3 is interpreted as supporting the subordination of women to men in general or in the church when the chapters are clearly discussing the husband-wife relationship?
- How is it that women are prevented from praying out loud in the assembly based simply on an *inference* in I Tim. 2:8-10 when the *clear teaching* of I Cor. 11:5 is that they did so in the Corinthian assemblies?
- How is it that some use the reference to the creation story in I Tim. 2:13-14 to insist that I Tim. 2:12 applies the same way today as it did in first-century Ephesus,

but they do not interpret the reference to the creation in I Cor. 11:8-9 as requiring women to wear a head covering today?

- How is it that some take almost all of the 40 verses of I Corinthians 14 as not being applicable today but insist that two verses (34-35) are?

Keeping the Bible at the Center. Much of the discussion among us and the rest of the biblically-focused Christian world has either been a reiteration of traditional interpretations or a nod to our culture. Too often a study of the relevant biblical texts in their own contexts, done without the pressure applied by either of these two influences, has languished in the background. This book is an attempt to examine these passages in the belief that according to our Restoration heritage, serious biblical exegesis is the best, indeed the only, way to provide the true foundation we need for determining current practice in our modern setting. This topic has been one of the few that has occupied me throughout my adult life, but unfortunately its pursuit has been in fits and starts. For years I thought I was about 85 to 90 percent there in my understanding. What caused me finally to commit the time to complete the study was not only concern for our young people but also for the church at large. It seemed in reading some of the stories of congregations that had changed their practice, especially around what women were allowed to do in the assembly, that as much or more influence had been exerted by culture as by serious Bible study. Whether or not this was true, my own congregation was at a crossroad. We had studied the issue on multiple occasions but had not changed our practice, because we were determined not to change until we had completed studying the matter comprehensively. We did that, coming to some surprising conclusions about what the Bible actually taught on the topic. Having achieved consensus, we changed our practice. The important point here is that the impetus to do this was neither the urging of our sisters nor pressure from our culture, but the result of many, many hours of Bible study by both the elders and the congregation as a whole. My hope is that readers of this book, whether they agree with me or not, will be able to see that although a wider role for women in the church meshes with the broader culture, the case for it either stands or falls on the Bible itself.

Practical Matters

Target Audience. When I gave the first chapter to one of my readers for her critique, she appropriately asked me whether it was to be a scholarly or a popular book. The answer is both, but primarily the latter. It has attempted to be scholarly in the breadth and method of research and in thinking through the issues but popular in the way its ideas are presented. So, the book has been written primarily for the serious, intelligent, non-specialist whose approach to the Bible is still more one of wonder and a desire to learn than it is to find evidence to support what he/she already believes. These features are provided for this reader:

Theological jargon and acronyms that are so prevalent in this field of study have been kept to a minimum. Thus, for example, the Greek Old Testament has been spelled out as Septuagint, rather than using its normal abbreviation, LXX. For clarity's sake, a few terms are defined in a Glossary.

Greek and Hebrew words are transliterated, rather than presented in their original characters.

Any reader should be able to follow the complete flow of thought by reading only the text. Certain notes, however, are provided for the non-specialist to clarify some possibly unfamiliar words and other references in the text. The reader, however, is cautioned that at times the complexity of a topic under discussion will necessarily require a rather technical treatment, especially in chapters five, eight, and eleven, the longest chapters. When you come to points like these, you may find it helpful to slow down and break the reading into multiple sessions. Most of the time this should not be necessary. For readers with more theological training, extensive footnotes have been provided. Also, several excurses are included to present a more detailed look at specialized topics related to specific chapters. Indices at the end are furnished for those more used to theological research.

Avoidance of Labels. The book has attempted to avoid, as much as possible, loaded terms and labels. These "hot button" words are frequently found in writings about women in the church, but their net effect is often negative and in some cases can enflame the reader. Labels like "traditionalist" or "egalitarian" or "hierarchalist," though more direct than more wordy descriptive language, can actually inhibit understanding. For the sake of clarity, I have tried in this book to avoid the uses of labels, choosing instead a more neutral, though less concise, approach. Thus, for example, instead of "traditionalist" you will find wording like "those who support the traditional restrictions on what women may do in the assembly." This more verbose language offends my sensibilities as a writer, as it may yours. However, I believe it is a necessary concession to ensure clarity and avoid the baggage certain labels have acquired in writings on this subject.

Approach. Because this book has been written within a fellowship that like many in the Christian world at large has a high view of Scripture, it is basically an exegetical study of the relevant biblical passages relating to women in the church. Much of it engages with my own fellowship, the Churches of Christ, but it does much more than that. These issues are being felt keenly in many religious traditions. To reflect this, the current study has extensively drawn on and greatly benefitted from works from the broader Christian community. Hopefully readers from this wider Christian audience will also find some value here.

Flow of the Chapters. The first three chapters form the basis for the rest of the book by examining the way members of the Churches of Christ, principally in North America, have used the Bible to support a plethora of conflicting views on women in the church and by proposing a healthier exegetical framework that is used throughout the rest of the book in interpreting the relevant passages. Most treatments of this topic both among Churches of Christ and in the Christian community at large begin and frequently end with Paul, but in doing so we have unwittingly and unnecessarily narrowed the possible outcome. As Christians, Jesus is our basis for understanding everything about our faith, including Paul. And Jesus, in teaching on the important topic of marriage and divorce, went back even farther—to the creation of the first married couple. The Garden of Eden is where the biblical story begins, and Paul merely writes some of the concluding chapters. But Jesus, our Lord, is our interpreter for all of it. So, the part of the book that examines the relevant biblical passages (chapters four through eleven) begins with the creation narrative, moves next to Jesus and finally to Paul. The last chapter then attempts to pull it all together. The intent of this approach is to enable the reader to reexamine this important topic in a systematic and productive way.

Chapter one, which follows immediately, details how the move to widen the participation of women in our assemblies by respected interpreters in the Churches of Christ in North America began well before the rise of the modern women's movement in the last third of the twentieth century. In fact, the most notable writer to do so in the first half of the century was none other than C. R. Nichol in his groundbreaking 1938 book, *God's Woman*. This is where our journey begins.

CHAPTER ONE

God's Woman

*T*here is a common misconception among many in the Churches of Christ that the move to broaden the participation of women in congregational assemblies is rather recent. The assumption is that this development flows more from the influence of popular culture than a commitment to Scripture as our guide in religious matters. This book will seek to correct that misconception. In point of fact, serious challenges to the traditional limitation on women's roles in Christian assemblies were issued decades ago by highly respected Bible students based on serious examination, even re-examination, of the relevant biblical passages. Perhaps most notable among these is *God's Woman* written in 1938 by C. R. Nichol.

C. R. Nichol[1]

As this chapter was being written, it had been almost 80 years since the publication of this groundbreaking book. The

---

1   The ultimate source for numerous accounts of C. R. Nichol's life and work is Maude Jones Underwood, *C. R. Nichol: A Preacher of Righteousness*. Reuel Lemmons' obituary in the *Firm Foundation* ("C.R. Nichol Passes Away," 450) is also a good source, as are the two volumes of Batsell Barrett Baxter and M. Norvel Young's *Preachers of Today*, vol. 1 (1952), 249-50 and vol. 2 (1959), 316. The funeral notice, "The Life of C. R. Nichol," on http://www.therestorationmovement. com/nichol.htm contains a good summary of bibliographical details, as does Nobel Patterson's tribute to Nichol at the 2004 Freed-Hardeman University Lectures. The latter is also found on http://therestoration-movement.com./nichol.htm. Finally, the research paper by Charles H. Wilson ("Biography of Charles Ready Nichol" [July 20, 1962]), housed in archives of the Center for Restoration Studies at Abilene Christian

author was well respected by his peers both for his grasp of the
Scriptures and his dedication to his religious heritage. He served
for decades as an educator, evangelist, writer, and especially
debater. In fact, he held his first debate at age 22,[2] and by the
time he was 28 years old he had already conducted 60 of his
more than 300 religious debates.[3] For a more detailed account
of Nichol's life, work and impact, see *Excursus 1: C. R. Nichol*
at the end of this chapter. Two or three statements later in this
chapter and in that Excursus will suffice here to underscore his
significance. The full references can be found there.

In his death notice in the *Firm Foundation*, Reuel Lemmons wrote, "We seriously doubt whether any man since
Alexander Campbell has so influenced the destiny of the
church in America." At the 2004 Freed-Hardeman University lectures Nobel Patterson called Nichol "one of the most
important and influential figures in the growth of New Testament Christianity of the past 125 years." Finally, in 1938 in
the *Gospel Advocate* N. B. Hardeman not only endorsed the
content of *God's Woman*, he stated that "this book will serve
as a text at Freed-Hardeman College."

God's Woman

GOD'S WOMAN WAS ONE OF NICHOL'S LAST PUBLISHED
works. It was published in 1938 during his ten years in Seminole, OK. M. O. Daley wrote in the Introduction that the
book was the culmination of several years of study.

> The conflicting theories in the religious world touching
> the work of women in the church, brought the author face
> to face with the question: "What does the Bible teach on

University, though heavily dependent on Underwood, contains some
helpful primary material.
2   David R. Kenney, "Nichol's Pocket Bible Encyclopedia," 8 (also
found on http://drkenney.bolgspot.com/2008/02/nichols-pocket-bible-
encyclopedia.html, 2.
3   Baxter and Young, vol. 1, 249.

this subject?" Impelled by his love for the truth he made a long and careful survey of the subject as treated in the Bible; not with a desire to defend any theory extant on the subject; nor to attack any position held, save only as the truth when fully presented uproots any and every error concerning the subject matter treated.[4]

While the book addresses many issues relating to women in the Bible, reduced to its most basic point it contends that the Bible does not in either the Old or the New Testament forbid women to teach men. What she is not allowed to do is usurp authority over men or fail to be subordinate to them. So, when she teaches men in a way that she remains subordinate to them she is following God's design. Although many, including this writer, would question some of the finer points of interpretation Nichol uses to reach his conclusion that women are free to teach men, especially in his discussion of I Tim. 2, the combined weight of his reasoning was ground breaking. A statement in his chapter on "Women at Work" will suffice to illustrate the boldness of his claim.

In Old Testament times men went to women for instructions, and God inspired women to impart the instruction and information the men needed. Women *must not* usurp authority over the man in the meeting house, the store, the automobile, or on the field of battle. But there have been conditions under which woman taught a group of men, including high priest, by God's authority, without usurping authority over man, and she can do the same today. (47)

What follows is a synopsis of Nichol's key points as he progresses through the book.

Women Teachers/Leaders in the Bible. In the Old Testament Nichol pointed to Miriam (Ex. 15:20; Mic. 6:4), Deborah (Judg. 4:4-14; 5:7) and Huldah (II Ki. 22:14-20; II

---

4 *God's Woman*, "Introduction," 1.

Chron. 34:22-28) as examples of women who taught and/or led men. Miriam was the first prophetess in the Old Testament. Of Deborah he wrote, "Deborah… was at the time Judge in Israel; and she was also a prophetess (Judges 4:4-14; 5:7). She served not only in religious affairs, but in civil matters also. She was a prophetess and communicated God's will to the people." He further saw Deborah as an example of "the fact that teaching and helping a man in any work assigned him by Jehovah, is not usurping authority over man; nor do women in such work fail to show themselves to be in subjection to man." From Huldah's example he is even more direct:

> A woman can teach a group of men, even the men who occupied the highest positions in the land, without usurping authority over them. Surely if a woman can teach people things pertaining to the destiny of nations, without usurping authority over them, she can teach men about the destiny of their souls without usurping authority over them! If within the heart of any one there arises the question of the righteousness of the course of Huldah teaching the group of men, let it be remembered that she was inspired by Jehovah to do the teaching! God does not inspire people to do wrong. (28)

In applying this to today, Nichol concluded, "This woman, Huldah, taught a group of men without usurping authority over them, and women can teach men today without refusing to be in subjection to men." (30)

In the New Testament he singled out as examples the prophetess Anna (Luke 2:36), the deaconess Phoebe (Rom. 16:1), Priscilla (taught a man – Acts 18:26), women helpers in Philippi (Acts 16; Phil. 4:2-3), and Philip's daughters (Acts 21:9). He further noted that "It is a matter of Old Testament prophecy that women would be teachers in the New Testament times; and it is a matter or [*sic*] record in the New Testament that they did teach (Joel 2; Acts 2; 21:9, I Cor. 11)." (30-31, 45)

The Dress of Women. In the first of his chapters dealing with subjection, Nichol concludes that custom alone, not God, dictates women's hair length and adornment and their head covering. As far as men's hair length is concerned, it comes down to custom as well. "There is no legislation on the actual length of the hair by Jehovah. Legislation on the style of dressing the hair is not found in God's word." (59)

Subjection. In this chapter Nichol recognizes that in the real world of families the husband may not be as fit to lead the family as his wife. He offers two possible courses of action for the wife. First, "under such lamentable conditions it most needs be that the wife strive to lead through the husband— that she steer him and the children into proper paths." Secondly, a more extreme deficiency in the husband may call for a more extreme response by the wife. "Not infrequently the wife outranks the husband in every desirable thing, except physical strength. When such conditions exist, if the family functions to its best interest, and proves itself to be a godsend to society it may be necessary to ignore the lead of the husband." (88)

Nichol is also sensitive to the fact that some husbands may improperly exercise their leadership. So, "though the injunction is for the wife to be in 'subjection' to the husband, such is not to be interpreted as meaning she is to submit to harsh, ruthless, tyrannical rule." Further, "though the husband is the head of the wife, and she is under the necessity of being in 'subjection' to him, she is not to slavishly obey him. If needs be she must rebel against him, if he would prevent her serving Jehovah, or demand that she engage in acts of wickedness." (83, 93)

Within the confines of the husband's overall leadership of the wife, Nichol strongly emphasizes mutuality in the way the home is run. He sees both the husband and the wife as ruling the home.

The divine order is that the husband rule the household, and too, it is the order of heaven that the *wife* rule the household. In the home it is not "one man rule." Together the husband and wife build the home, and jointly they are to direct the affairs of the home; rearing the children and in an orderly manner conducting the discipline and details necessary in all things pertaining to the home. (100) He argues that men have a long history of being intoxicated by power and asserting themselves over others. This is not the way headship or subjection are to work in the Christian home. "For a man to feed on the fact that he is the *head* of the household, and that the wife is to be in 'subjection' to him ... he does not know what the 'subjection' of the wife to the husband means." (101) He even applies mutual subjection to the home. In commenting on Eph. 5:21, he writes, "But we are to be in 'subjection to one another,' that is, have regard for the rights of others, seek to serve others. In the same way the wife is to be in 'subjection' to her husband, and the husband is to be in 'subjection' to the wife." (110)

I Corinthians 11:4-5. Nichol sees the matter of women's head covering and hair length as simply Corinthian custom and nothing to do with what is right or wrong per se. (120) On women praying he opposes the idea advanced by some that (1) women were praying silently and/or (2) were only to do it privately. On the first he shows the inconsistency of claiming silent prayer, when the same cannot be said of prophesying. He notes that the purpose of prophesy was to edify, and women could only edify if heard. As to the second point, he argues that the distinction between public and private activities in worship is not biblical. Concluding that the argument that women were only allowed to pray out loud in private comes from a misinterpretation of I Cor. 14:34-35 about women's silence, he asserts that in neither I Corinthians 14 "or in any other inspired statement" is there "a prohibition against women speaking in public, *on the ground that it is public*." (121-23)

I Corinthians 14:34-35. Nichol is quite forceful in his denial that the assembly being discussed in I Corinthians 14 has anything to do with today. It is giving instructions for assemblies where spiritual gifts were being exercised, and since those assemblies do not exist today, the passage offers no instructions for our day. In fact, he does not believe the passage applies even to the regular Sunday assembly in Corinth, but rather to a "teaching service" where those inspired by the Spirit could supply needed inspired instruction in the absence of people like Paul. (134-35) He is emphatic in stating, "Let no one by [sic] guilty of perverting the scripture by trying to make the prohibition prescribed in that church binding on any congregation today!" (137) For this reason he rejects any attempt by people today to use I Cor. 14:34-35 to limit what women may do in the assembly, including forbidding women to pray out loud in the assembly. (121)

I Timothy 2:8-14. For Nichol this passage is crucial. The central message of his whole book is correcting what he regarded as a common misunderstanding of the prohibition of women's teaching in 2:12. It is difficult to follow or accept his reasoning at certain points, but the underlying point is that women are to be in subjection to men. Hence, he takes "in every place" (2:8) in the most literal way possible. It includes "not only the church when assembled, but the home, yes, every place where prayers are said." "The passage in I Tim. 2 … has reference to the relationship of the husband and the wife, as well as the relationship of women in general to men in general, under every possible relationship—in every place!" (146-47)

This being said, he then argues forcefully that the passage does not prevent women from praying in the presence of men or teaching them. First, he asserts that the fact that men are directed to pray (2:8) does not imply that women are not to pray. (146) As far as teaching is concerned, he believes he has proven that women may teach men in all sorts of settings, so the prohibition in 2:12 has to do with the manner in which they teach men. "It is not *teaching* that is forbidden, but teaching 'over a man.'" (153) Put another way, he writes, "I insist *there is not a prohibition* found in I Tim. 2:12 against a woman teaching a man!" Further, as he had earlier in his chapter on I Corinthians 11, Nichol rejects the public versus private teaching distinction. Finally, since the key point is that women are to be in subjection to men, how would they be considered in subjection if they were capable of giving a man information, but refused. "If I seek information of a woman, and she gives it, it is my pleasure; it is not the woman usurping authority over me, and if she imparts information, if she teaches me, she has not violated God's word." (151)

The Deaconess. Although the issue of whether women occupied a formal position as deaconesses in congregations in the first century is beyond the scope of this present study, since Nichol treats the matter, I will briefly address his position here. He believes the "women" in I Tim. 3:11 were deaconesses, not wives of the deacons. Here is part of his reasoning for this conclusion.

> To me it seems absurd to contend that Paul when discussing the qualifications of a deacon would turn aside abruptly and mention the character of the deacon's wife; but makes no reference to the character of the bishop's wife, when in the same connection he had discussed the qualifications of bishops, but did not say one word about the qualifications of the bishop's wife. In truth, verse eleven in the passage does not have reference to the wife of a deacon." (161)

He lists several ways in which such women could have served the first century church as well as our own. "It should be known in every congregation that Sister Phoebe, Sister Priscilla, and Sister Dorcas are deaconesses in the congregation, and that when their assistance is needed they are to be called." (165)

God's Woman's Reception

IN *GOD'S WOMAN* NICHOL FOUND HIMSELF AT ODDS WITH David Lipscomb, his esteemed teacher at Nashville Bible School. Earlier some of Lipscomb's views on women in the church and those of Nichol were more compatible,[5] but by the time Nichol attended the school in Nashville, Lipscomb's position had hardened somewhat.[6] In some respects Nichol was reclaiming old territory that had been lost. In others he was breaking new ground. G. C. Brewer, in an article written only four years before the publication of *God's Woman*, noted that earlier in his life he had heard women pray publicly, a practice no longer common. He questioned whether some of the restrictions on women's participation in worship had become custom and perhaps should be reexamined.[7] This is exactly what *God's Woman* did.

---

5   In an article in the *Gospel Advocate*, ("Queries," [1876], 1111) he held that Paul wrote nothing that "forbids a woman reading or singing or joining in any other worship of the brethren" and singled out prophecy in particular as something women did in the worship. See Bill Grasham, "The Role of Women," 216. In another article ("Woman's Work," 449), he wrote that a woman may "teach a class in a meeting-house" when others are doing the same.

6   Lipscomb later stated that although in the New Testament period women prophesied in the presence of both men and women, they did not do it in "promiscuous assemblies." ("Woman's Work in the Church," 6). Grasham postulates reasonably that the prevalence of women speaking in public in the woman's suffrage and temperance movements, which opened the door more for women preachers, may have influenced that hardening. (219) Lipscomb's opposition to women preachers was consistent throughout, but his view of the connection between women preachers and the women's movement of the time becomes apparent from such statements as, "the habit of women preaching originated in the same hotbed with easy divorce, free love, and the repugnance to childbearing." He was opposing a practice just beginning in some northern congregations, and he pleaded that "unless we guard against the first steps to set aside the word of God, infidelity will spread among the churches." ("Should Women Preach Publicly?," 486).

7   "Women Praying, 1020. See also Grasham, "The Role of Women," 227-28.

The book received a mixed reception when it was first published. John T. Lewis was quick to oppose the book, particularly
its author's contention that the head covering in I Corinthians
11 was merely local custom.[8] Lewis' accusation that the motivation for the book was to please the women in the church
"severely hurt" Nichol.[9] Perhaps the most notable criticism
came only a few months later from Nichol's close friend, Foy
E. Wallace Jr.[10] It also received enthusiastic endorsements.[11] M.
O. Daley stated in the Introduction that "'God's Woman' is not
'just another book,' but is one, which in its field of endeavor,
and the character of its content, will 'fill a long felt want' in
the prayerful study of God's word." (11) In a publication notice
imbedded in W. E. Brightwell's "News and Notes" in an issue
of the *Gospel Advocate*, he wrote further,

> "God's Woman," a new book, by C. R. Nichol, is a painstak-
> ing search of the Bible to learn all the truth about woman's
> work under God. I know of no book that so thoroughly covers
> the subject. False doctrine is exposed, and the truth is made
> to stand out. The arrangement for class work adds much to
> its value. I predict for the book a hearty welcome, and a wide
> circulation.[12]

---

8 "Death in the Pot," 12-13, 19. The article begins with a respectful,
even conciliatory, tone, but it quickly becomes harsh and biting. For a
fairly complete reconstruction of Lewis' opposition to Nichol's views in
God's Woman on women's head covering in I Corinthians 11, see Morris
D. Norman, "The Role of Women," 115-19.
9 Private correspondence of Pryde E. Hinton reported in Wilson, "Biography," 18-19.
10 "God's Women Gather," 40. He states that, although there were
"good things in the book," "taken as a whole the interests of the church
would have been better served if it had never been written." He expresses the belief that Nichol's book "has released and given impetus
to a dormant, pent-up ambition on the part of women in the church
to overstep divine restrictions placed around their work in the church."
11 Lewis ("Death in the Pot," 12) alludes to "commendations" to the
book that were already appearing.
12 "News and Notes," 1040.

Probably the most notable and enthusiastic endorsement came in the same section of the journal two weeks earlier. N. B. Hardeman, President of Freed-Hardeman College, wrote,

> I have read carefully 'God's Woman.' This is a most thorough discussion of what the Bible says about women. The arguments are clear, logical. The author does not evade such difficult passages as 1 Cor. 14:34, 35 and 1 Tim. 2:11, 12. He does not share the opinions held by many commentaries. I verily believe he has gone to the heart of what Paul had in mind and brought forth the truth. This book will serve as a text in Freed-Hardeman College. I commend the book to all interested in learning about 'God's Woman.'[13]

Other Voices of Dissent

THE NEXT CHAPTER WILL SURVEY THE ENORMOUS DIVERSITY of interpretation among those in the mainstream of the Churches of Christ who hold to the traditional limitations on women in the assemblies of the church. In spite of this wide range of views on individual points, the vast majority seem to agree on the following.

1. From creation God intended that women be subordinate to men, as is evidenced by the fact that (a) the woman was created second and came from the man (Gen. 2:21-22; I Cor. 11:8-9; I Tim. 2:13), (b) the woman was created to be the man's helper (Gen. 2:18), and (c) the woman, not the man, was deceived by the serpent (Gen. 3:13; I Tim. 2:14).

2. The prohibition of women speaking in the assemblies of the church (I Cor. 14:34) is absolute in both (a) the universality of its application (all regular congregational assemblies in every place for all time) and (b) the totality of their silence (although few, if any, would argue that this totality would prohibit women from speaking [Eph. 5:19]

---

13   "News and Notes," 992.

or teaching [Col. 3:16] when they sing in the assemblies).

3. Women are not permitted to teach men (I Tim. 2:12), although they may do so privately in the company of their husband (Acts 18:26).

4. Women are not permitted to be in leadership positions over men in the church (I Tim. 2:12b – "exercise authority over man").

As has been noted above, Nichol argues forcefully against some, though not all, of these propositions. Others who would require some or even most of these traditional limitations on women's participation in the church, nevertheless, like Nichol, disagree on certain key points. Here is a sampling of dissenting interpretations of those who wrote before the latest woman's movement in the last third of the twentieth century. They have been chosen because their views were not influenced in any way by the recent changes in our culture.[14]

Women prayed and prophesied out loud outside the assembly when men were present: David Lipscomb[15]

Women prayed out loud in the regular assemblies: Moses Lard[16]

Women prophesied in the regular assemblies: J. W. McGarvey[17]

I Cor. 11:3-16 refers to the regular congregational assembly: McGarvey, J. W. Roberts, Guy N. Woods[18]

I Cor. 11:3-16 is primarily concerned with the wife's

14   On the importance of this point, see Smith, *Men of Strength,* 14.
15   "Woman's Work in the Church," 6.
16   "Care of the Churches," 106-07.
17   *Commentary,* 142-43.
18   McGarvey, *Commentary,* 108; Roberts, "Veils," 184; Woods, "Exposition," 6 and "'Principle or Custom'?," 7.

subjection to her husband (not to men and women in general): McGarvey, Clarence C. Gobbel, Roberts[19]

The headship of man in I Cor. 11:3 refers to the husband's headship of his wife (not to men and women in general): Roberts[20]

I Cor. 14:34-35 states the rule for women's silence in the assembly, but the rule had exceptions in the first century (e.g., I Cor. 11:5), and it does today: McGarvey[21]

The women in I Cor. 14:34-35 were wives with Christian husbands: J. W. Chism, George W. DeHoff[22]

Women's not speaking in I Cor. 14:34-35 refers to their not dictating to or usurping authority over men, not absolute silence: J. C. McQuiddy[23]

According to I Cor. 14:34-35, women may teach in the assembly, as long as they do not usurp authority over a man: DeHoff[24]

I Cor. 14:34-35 may refer only to Greek churches, like those in Corinth and Ephesus: B. W. Johnson[25]

Since spiritual gifts were being exercised there, the type of assembly reflected in I Cor. 14:34-35 does not exist today: DeHoff[26]

---

19 McGarvey, *Commentary*, 109-11; Gobbel, "Principle or Custom," 7, 14; Roberts, "Veils," 191, 196.
20 *"Veils,"* 185-6.
21 *Commentary*, 142-3.
22 Chism, "Woman's Work," 450-51; DeHoff, *Sermons on First Corinthians*, 98-99.
23 "Women's Work," 1265.
24 *Sermons on First Corinthians*, 99-100.
25 *People's New Testament*, 119.
26 *Sermons on First Corinthians*, 98.

Only the customs of the age made it shameful for a woman to speak in church (I Cor. 14:35). That is no longer the case: McGarvey[27]

Women may teach in a way that does not usurp authority over a man and fulfil the requirements of I Tim. 2:11-12: Dehoff[28]

There are no limitations in the New Testament on women praying in private: Lipscomb[29]

Women are free to teach men in private, and this includes teaching a class in the meeting house, as long as others are doing it as well: Lipscomb[30]

Finally, although the matter of whether the first-century church had female deacons in a formal ministry alongside their male counterparts is outside the scope of this current study, it has relevance for the point at hand. For the most part, the leaders of the Restoration Movement in the nineteenth century, beginning with Alexander Campbell himself,[31] were uniform in their answer in the affirmative.[32] G. C. Brewer in the twentieth century can

27 *Commentary*, 143.
28 *Sermons on First Corinthian*, 99.
29 "Women Preachers," 452.
30 "Woman's Work," 449.
31 Campbell addressed the issue multiple times in his writings, but his translation of the two relevant passages in the New Testament also make his position clear: Rom. 16:1: "I recommend to you Phebe, our sister, who is a deaconess of the congregation at Cenchrea" and I Tim. 3:11, "The women, in like manner, must be grave, not slanderers; but vigilant, faithful in all things."
32 An issue of the on-line *Stoned-Campbell Disciple* provides the citations for several nineteenth-century leaders of the Restoration Movement who believed that the early church had deaconesses in the formal sense of the word. In addition to Alexander Campbell, they include Robert Richardson, Walter Scott, Robert Milligan, Talbert Fanning, Moses Lard, B. W. Johnson, and J. M. Barnes. Http://stonedcamp-

be added to their number.[33]

A Way Forward

AT THE VERY LEAST, THESE EXAMPLES DEMONSTRATE THAT
serious Bible students in past generations have come to vastly
different conclusions from the hardened ones today. They
wrote decades before the social change brought about by the
woman's movement and other factors in the last third of the
twentieth century. Their conclusions can hardly be attributed to these societal forces. Numerous more recent writers
have suggested that the current disagreement with what has
become the traditional position on women in the church is
motivated by something other than serious examination of the
Scriptures. This judgmental view fails to account for people
like Nichol and Hardeman. Anyone who reads *God's Woman*
can sense Nichol's passion to lift some of the burdens men
have placed on women and correct some practices that, in
his opinion, have arisen from a careless reading of the Bible.

In his own chapter at the end of *God's Woman*, M. O.
Daley speaks about how we are so indebted in our knowledge
of the Bible to what we have learned from those who have
gone before. He asked a minister "who was widely known to
have a general knowledge of the Bible far above the average
minister" how he obtained such a vast knowledge of the Bible.
His humble response explains a lot. "My fund of information,
be it great or small, is but the accumulation of the conclusions of other men added to my own, drawn as a result of
something they have said, or that suggested it." (174) In other
words, we all stand on the shoulders of former students of the
Bible. They have taught us what they have learned so we can
begin at that point and learn even more. So it is with *God's*

belldisciple.com/2011/09/29/voices-on-female-deacons-in-the-stone-
campbell-movement.
33   *The Model Church*, 101-05.

Woman. On certain key points my own study diverges from Nichol's understanding, but many of the conclusions of the book have provided a starting point for further study. What a pity it is that what Nichol has to teach us has somehow gotten lost, leaving us to wrestle with questions decades later as if some of the answers being given today were somehow new.

In a sense, then, the present study is a revisiting of *God's Woman* as a reminder that some of its conclusions are not new. That ground was broken some 80 years ago, and we need to acknowledge with gratitude and affection the one who did it. Standing on the shoulders of Nichol and others, I propose to do exactly what he did. This book reflects fresh study of the Scriptures over the course of many years. Though the conclusions are mine, the debt I owe to others for their help in reaching them is immense.

Excursus 1: C. R. Nichol. Charles Ready Nichol was born on March 26, 1876 in the hamlet of Readyville, TN, twelve miles east of Murfreesboro. He was the first son in a large family of eleven children. He was an excellent student in high school and began making talks in religious gatherings while still a teenager at home. When the time came for college, he studied under David Lipscomb and James A. Harding at Nashville Bible School, working at the Gospel Advocate office to support himself. His education also included course work at Vanderbilt University in Nashville, Southwestern Kentucky College in Hopkinsville, and Transylvania University in Lexington, KY. He earned a B. S. degree at Central Texas College in Walnut Springs, TX.[34]

Educator. Nichol served as both a college teacher and administrator. His two years as President of Thorp Springs Christian

---

34   Patterson "C. R. Nichol," 2; "Life of C. R. Nichol," 1.

College beginning in 1916 resulted in the school's gaining Junior College accreditation.[35] He taught briefly at both Harding College and Abilene Christian College.[36] While serving as preacher for the Vermont Avenue Church of Christ in Los Angeles he taught for two years (1944-1946) at George Pepperdine College.[37]

Evangelist. Nichol served nobly as an evangelist for 62 years—from age 20 until 1958, when he was confined to his home due to failing health.[38] He was in great demand for both preaching and debating. From the time he left the congregation in Clifton around the turn of the century until 1934, when he moved to Seminole, OK, he averaged 25 gospel meetings a year.[39] Estimates of how many people he baptized run as high as 30,000, but this apparently includes people who were baptized following his evangelistic sermons, not merely people he personally baptized. A resume written between 1938 and 1944 gives the precise number as 10,664, presumably the number he had personally baptized by that time.[40]

During his active ministry Nichol served as evangelist for four congregations. The first was in Corsicana, TX, where he went to visit a former classmate immediately after graduating from Nashville Bible School. There was no group meeting there at the time, but he found some members who had not been meeting and from that meager beginning built a congregation. He was 21 at the time and supported himself as a printer at the local newspaper. The next year he held his first debate.[41]

After a little more than two years in Corsicana he moved

35   Patterson, "C. R. Nichol," 6.
36   Baxter and Young, vol. 1, 249.
37   Patterson, "C. R. Nichol," 6; "Life of C. R. Nichol," 1.
38   Underwood, *Possibility of Apostasy*, 3; Wilson, "Biography," 22.
39   Baxter and Young, vol. 1, 249; Wilson, "Biography," 19.
40   "C. R. Nichol Biographical Notes."
41   Patterson, "C. R. Nichol," 5; Wilson, "Biography," 7-8.

to the church in Clifton, TX, where he also stayed two years. Two things of note occurred during this first brief time in Clifton: (1) he met his future wife, and (2) his notoriety as a preacher and debater grew to such an extent that he decided to be a traveling evangelist full time. Later, in 1946, he moved back to Clifton, where he continued evangelistic work until his health failed. Upon his death on July 7, 1961 he was laid to rest in the Clifton Cemetery.[42]

During a hiatus in his meeting schedule in 1934, Nichol determined to use the winter for study and writing. The church in Seminole, OK invited him to spend the three months with them with preaching as his only duty. During those months, while traveling to a debate in Kentucky, Nichol became seriously ill and had to undergo major surgery in Memphis. The church in Seminole suggested that he stay on during his recuperation, asking only that he preach when he felt well enough. The three months turned into ten years. It was during his time in Seminole that he wrote *God's Woman*. When he moved to Los Angeles in 1944, the local newspaper wrote this about his evangelistic success: "Dr. Nichol has been in Seminole ten years and under his direction his congregation has grown constantly. Almost his entire membership at the present time are persons whom he has baptized into his church since his ministry began here."[43]

In 1944 Nichol moved to Los Angeles, CA to work with the Vermont Avenue church and teach at George Pepperdine College. He was there for two years, after which he moved back to Clifton, where he spent the rest of his life.[44]

Writer. Nichol was a prolific writer. On the aforementioned resume, sixteen published books are listed. Three are debates. *Sound Doctrine*, which he co-edited with R. L. Whiteside,

---

42   Patterson, "C. R. Nichol," 5; Wilson, "Biography," 22; Lemmons, "C. R. Nichol Passes Away," 450.
43   Wilson, "Biography," 19-20.
44   Baxter and Young, vol. 1, 24; "Life of C. R. Nichol." 1.

contained four volumes. He did not collaborate with White-side in his later fifth volume. *God's Woman* is the last book listed.[45] Not on the list is *The Possibility of Apostasy*, which he published in 1951, and at least four other books.[46] *Bible Notes on the Holy Land* (1927) and *Sound Doctrine* in five volumes, published from 1921 to 1951, are two of his most popular works. Various volumes in the latter set have been translated into at least four languages.[47] The most noteworthy accomplishment in his publishing success is the fact that *Nichol's Pocket Bible Encyclopedia* (1926) is the only book written by a member of the Churches of Christ to have sold more than a million copies.[48] I obtained my copy while a Bible student at a Christian college decades ago, and it is still in print and use today. Nichol was also active as an editor on various brotherhood publications. For the *Firm Foundation* he served as front page editor and later general editor. In his younger years he was in charge of the Texas Department for the *Gospel Advocate* and later served on its editorial staff. For a while he was book review editor for the *Gospel Guardian*.[49]

Debater. Nichol has engaged in more public debates by far than any other member of the Churches of Christ.[50] His resume, dated between 1938 and 1944, listed precisely 363, which included debates with representatives of 27 religious groups, Materialists, Socialists, Agnostics, and Atheists.[51] *The Encyclopedia of Religious Debates* (online) lists by name

45   "C. R. Nichol Biographical Notes," 2.
46   This is consistent with a total of 21 books, according to "Life of C. R. Nichol," 2.
47   Ibid.; Underwood, *Possibility of Apostasy*, 3.
48   Lemmons, "C. R. Nichol Passes Away," 450; Baxter and Young, vol. 2, 316.
49   Baxter and Young, vol. 2, 316; "C. R. Nichol Biographical Notes," 1; Patterson, "C. R. Nichol," 6.
50   Underwood, *Possibility of Apostasy*, 3; Lemmons, "C. R. Nichol Passes Away," 450.
51   "C. R. Nichol Biographical Notes," 1.

of opponent and usually by date and location 70 debates.[52]
He held his first debate right out of Nashville Bible School
at age 22 just before the turn of the century and the last one
on December 1-4, 1953, when he was 77.[53] Ben Bogart, his
opponent in seven debates, said of Nichol, "I have never taken
Mr. Nichol by surprise in an argument; nor have I ever seen
him at a loss as how to proceed. He was always prepared."[54]

Tributes. Of the many tributes Nichol received after his death,
perhaps the most notable one was what Reuel Lemmons penned
in his death notice in the *Firm Foundation*. "We seriously doubt
whether any man since Alexander Campbell has so influenced
the destiny of the church in America." He went on to write,
"He was universally considered a safe, conservative, teacher,
preacher and writer."[55] Another death notice put it this way: "In
the passing of C. R. Nichol the churches of Christ lost a powerful preacher, an able defender of the faith, a great example of
faithfulness to the end."[56] In 2004 Patterson said, "One of the
most important and influential figures in the growth of New
Testament Christianity of the past 125 years was C. R. Nichol."[57]

Many more accolades could be added to these. And this
is the person who wrote *God's Woman*. Certainly Nichol
has earned the right to be heard, even when the fruit of his
extensive study on women in the church runs counter to the
mainstream opinion.

---

52   Http:www. ptc.dcs.edu/teacherpages/tthrasher/listings/n.htm.
53   Ibid.; Wilson, "Biography," 8.
54   Patterson, "C. R. Nichol," 5.
55   Lemmons, "C. R. Nichol Passes Away," 450.
56   "Life of C. R. Nichol," 2.
57   "C. R. Nichol," 4.

CHAPTER TWO

The Current Impasse

*T*he first chapter detailed some of the significant challenges to the traditional teachings on women in the church that occurred before the women's movement in the last third of the twentieth century. This chapter will begin by examining the great diversity of opinions on this topic among those who oppose widening the participation of women in our assemblies. What this will show is that while there was no consensus among these earlier interpreters, there is even less now. Positions have actually been hardened again, as they seem to have been in the late nineteenth century. We will then consider the question of why we have been unable to agree on our understanding of the key biblical passages.

Lack of Consensus

STUDIES IN OUR BROTHERHOOD ON THE TOPIC OF WOMEN in the church are a vast wasteland. Whether it is books, articles, sermons, or lectures at conferences and lectureships, interpretations are all over the place. This has not been our finest hour. And this is not limited to one side or the other on this whole topic. For a fellowship that prides itself in "speaking where the Bible speaks and being silent where the Bible is silent" and "calling Bible things by Bible names," lapses on this subject are far too common. There is the invention out of thin air of terminology or concepts not found in the text, like "male spiritual leadership" or "designated spiritual protector," and their subsequent use as evidence for conclusions drawn later. There is the proof texting of verses like Gal. 3:28 or I

Cor. 14:34a, pushing them far beyond the bounds of their context and reading into them ideas not found in the text. There is pontification about the meaning of words or phrases with little or no evidence or reasoning to support it. There are arguments more at home with the conclusions and methodology of modern Sociology than with serious biblical criticism. There is the reading of modern church practices into the New Testament (NT) period as if they were present among the first-century Christians. There is what can only be described as careless or at least highly suspect interpretation of relevant Old Testament (OT) passages. And the list goes on.

But possibly the most troublesome in our treatment of women in the first-century church has been the enormous diversity of opinions coupled with the confident assertion of the interpreters that their understanding is the one that is most faithful to the biblical text. How can the same Bible be the source of such divergent, contradictory views if we students of the Scriptures are simply letting the Bible speak to us? Perhaps some of our methods of Bible study are flawed. Or is it possible that sometimes what we get out of a text is more influenced by what we bring to it than what we find in it?[1] Maybe we have held to some conclusions so long that we find it difficult truly to look at a passage with fresh eyes.[2]

---

1   On this tendency see, Paul L. Watson, "Some Pastoral Implications," 160. "We should come to listen and to learn, not to inject the text with our own predispositions and preformed judgments, nor to find ammunition with which to shoot down the views of others." See also Nichol, *God's Woman*, 121: "The effort should be made to learn what the passage teaches, without regard to what you may have concluded about some other passage."

2   On the problems associated with this tendency see Brewer, "Women Praying," 1020. See also Woods, "Exposition," 6: "There is the type of mind that leaps to a conclusion without weighing carefully all the issues involved and is not open to reasonable appeals. When any Scriptural subject is broached, he has already decided what it teaches, and his mind is closed to additional evidence." Burton Coffman (*1 and 2 Corinthians*, 179) makes a similar point.

Can it be that we are sometimes like the Jews of whom Paul said, "to this day whenever Moses is read a veil lies upon their heart"? (II Cor. 3:15)

Many would have us believe that what a woman may or may not do in the assembly and other gatherings of Christians is crystal clear in the NT. Yet, as we have noted, these interpreters cannot agree among themselves. I have reviewed hundreds of pages of writings from authors in the Churches of Christ, including books, articles in our journals, lectureship and conference transcripts, blogs, and sermons. *Excursus 2: Diversity in the Interpretation of the Three Key Pauline Passages* at the end of this chapter presents a substantial list of these differing, often contradictory, opinions. They are all expressed, I believe, by Christians who thought they were being faithful to the biblical text. Each one comes from a person who supports the limiting of what women may do in our assemblies and/or other settings. It would be much longer and more diverse if it also contained the views of those who believe the Bible supports the wider participation of women in these situations. Here is just a sampling of these wide-ranging interpretations of the three key Pauline passages.

I Corinthians 11:3-16

- The type of assemblies where women were praying and prophesying was (1) the regular congregational assemblies, (2) house church meetings, or (3) non-regular public assemblies where men were present.

- The head covering for women or the lack of it for men was (1) a piece of clothing, (2) their hair, (3) both, or (4) either (for women).

- Paul's instructions on head covering are (1) God's will for all time or (2) culturally bound.

I Corinthians 14:33b-35

- The passage refers to (1) all women in the Corinthian

assemblies, (2) certain wives only, (3) wives of the prophets, or (4) women who possessed spiritual gifts.

• On the women's actions Paul is prohibiting: women were (1) questioning their *own* husbands, (2) being disruptive by asking questions or otherwise interrupting a prophet or men speaking, (3) addressing the assembly, (4) praying, (5) exercising their spiritual gifts, (6) speaking in a leadership role, or (7) disobeying, dictating to, or usurping authority over men.

• On the meaning of "shameful," (14:35b): shameful (1) in that culture only, (2) shameful in God's eyes, or (3) either is possible.

I Timothy 2:8-15

• On the meaning of "in every place" where some interpreters assume that women are excluded from praying: (1) in the assembly only, (2) any situation, public or private, where men are present, (3) religious assemblies only where men are present, (4) includes devotionals where teenage boys are present, (5) includes at home where wives may not pray in the presence of their husbands or sons and daughters may not pray in the presence of their fathers or brothers, (6) women may pray in the family, (7) includes even one woman in the presence of one man, (8) includes older Christian women praying with Christian boys present, or (9) women leading prayer in the presence of *adult* males.

• On what I Tim. 2:11-12 prohibits women from doing: (1) assuming a leading role when men are present, (2) teaching men in a formal setting, (3) having authority over men in a formal setting, (4) teaching men in an authoritative way, (5) teaching and leading prayer in the presence of men, (6) preaching, (7) leading public prayer, (8) baptizing, or (9) leading singing.

• On the meaning of Eve's being deceived in 2:14:
Genesis is being used (1) typologically, (2) by analogy,
or (3) archetypically.

I rest my case. We have to do better. Such disarray among
Bible students who presumably believe that what they are
writing is correct because they are faithfully representing the
Bible can lead only to the conclusion that this is not a matter
that is as cut and dried as some try to present it. It is time to
exercise a little more humility, a lot more discipline in our
Bible study, and more charity toward each other.

Why So Much Disagreement?

WHY IS IT THAT WE DISAGREE SO MUCH ON HOW WE
understand and apply biblical passages? It is not because truth
is unknowable or is not objective. No one who would be reading this book believes that. Though some may approach the
text with impure or insincere motives, as some have suggested,
again I will assume that does not apply to readers of this study.
More constructive is the suggestion by Alan Highers that,
while much of the Bible is rather straightforward and easy to
understand, some passages are simply difficult.

> The Bible is a book, or volume of books, written at several
> different levels.... Some [parts of the Bible] are quite simple
> to understand; others require more study and diligence. In
> short, the Bible is not a book one can pick up and read and
> be done with it. It invites a lifetime of study.... The point here
> is that God has given us enough in his word to challenge us
> and to engage us all of our lives. We continue to study and to
> learn.... We must learn to grow in knowledge.... The Bible is
> the story that never grows old. We can read it again and again
> and discover something each time we read.... Yes, the Bible can
> be understood, but not all teaching is on the same level. Some
> things are readily understood, and hard to be misunderstood....

Whatever is required by God for salvation is presented in the scriptures with the utmost simplicity. Other matters are given in the scriptures for our growth and study so that we will continue to learn and advance all of our days, but they are not made conditions of salvation.[3]

Our disappointing track record on interpretation of passages on women in the church is ample evidence that this is one of the more difficult issues to understand.[4] But why are some passages so difficult that we have trouble coming to agreement on their meaning? Some of the reasons are internal to the individual interpreter, while others flow from a lack of knowledge that is inherent in our modern setting. Before considering these, though, we need to acknowledge the great advantages modern interpreters have over Bible students in the past. The gap in our Bible knowledge is narrowing.

Text of the New Testament. In the last 150 to 200 years enormous advancements have been made in our knowledge of the text of the NT. Some previously unknown uncial manuscripts are now available for textual scholars to study. These include one in the British Museum dating from the first half of the fourth century that is the earliest copy of the entire NT in one volume. More than 100 papyrus manuscripts of portions of the NT have been discovered during this time. Most of them predate the manuscripts available to the translators of the King James Bible in 1611. The earliest of these, a fragment of the Gospel of John, has been dated to early in the second century.

World of the New Testament. Our knowledge of the world of the NT grows every year with the discovery of new texts,

---

3   "Understanding the Bible," 2.
4   Neil R. Lightfoot ("Women in Religious Services," 129-30) makes this exact point about the three key Pauline passages on women in the church. He asserts that "there are several factors that make these passages difficult to understand" and proceeds to develop two of them.

papyrus documents, inscriptions, and other primary sources. The archaeology of the Mediterranean world, not to mention biblical archaeology in particular, constantly enriches our knowledge of the world into which Christianity was born. Among the most significant finds have been the Dead Sea Scrolls and the Nag Hammadi manuscripts, but these are merely the more well known of many.

Language of the New Testament. The NT was written in the common Greek of the Hellenistic Period. Some of it, such as Hebrews, resembles a more literary style, like that exhibited in Greek and some Jewish authors of the period. Most of it reflects the every-day language of commerce, personal affairs, and private correspondence. The wealth of secular papyrus documents that have been found in the dry sands of Egypt has greatly increased our understanding of the language of the NT, both its style and its vocabulary. The Greek NT is also heavily dependent on the Greek OT or Septuagint, and significant advancements have been made is this field of study.

Tools for Bible Study. A trip to any religious bookstore or examination of a catalog of religious books and digital materials like that of the Christian Book Distributers is enough to showcase the massive amount of helps available for the serious Bible student. We are blessed with more and better concordances, Bible dictionaries, lexicons, Greek grammatical tools and translations than in any other time in history. Many of these and other tools for the study of the Bible and early Christianity are readily available in full-text form on the Internet. Digital, easily searchable versions of these tools at minimal cost provide modern Bible students with a significant advantage over their counterparts only half a century ago. All of these save us countless hours of study time, enabling us to learn much more in the same amount of time.

Some Reasons for Disagreements

Reasons Beyond the Interpreter's Control

Some passages are inherently difficult to understand.
Although he did not express it this way, this was basically
Highers' point a few paragraphs back. Peter even said that
about some of Paul's writings (II Pet. 3:16), to which we can
say a hearty Amen. In the vast majority of cases, however,
the meaning is plain and straightforward, even 2,000 years
later. The Bible was not written to confuse us. It is there as a
guide, not an obstacle. Matters that are key to our salvation
are well documented by many texts. However, probably about
five to ten percent of the passages are particularly difficult to
understand. Honest, well-disciplined Bible students are going
to disagree. Unfortunately for us, most of the NT texts dealing with women in the church come from Paul and fall into
that five to ten percent.

*The original readers had some obvious advantages we do
not have.* Basically, compared with them, we have a knowledge
deficiency. Our disadvantage in understanding the NT is in
our distance in time from the world in which it was written
and originally read.[5] Among other things, this limited familiarity with their world has to do with language, culture, and
common experience.

Language. As noted above, the NT was written in the Greek
of the Hellenistic Period. The common expression, "something got lost in translation," often applies. More than any
other time in history we are blessed with wonderful translations and tools for understanding what the original Greek

---

5   Nichol (*God's Woman*, 71) recognized this: "Too many of us do not
have a knowledge of the conditions and customs of the people in the
first century of the Christian religion to whom the letters in the New
Testament were written, hence some expressions and references may not
be fully appreciated."

meant. But no living person has the Greek of the period of the NT as his or her native language. The best we can do is study it from a distance. Most of the time the translations are clear enough and the texts straightforward enough that those who know Greek have no advantage over those who do not. I usually have my Greek text open when we are studying a NT passage in an adult Bible class at church. I rarely find it useful to comment on the Greek during the discussion. Usually when I am asked, "What does the Greek say,"? my response is "the same thing as the English." However, sometimes the greatest of Greek scholars have to throw up their hands and say, "I don't know what it means" or "This is the best I can do for now, but I don't know for sure." We are all at various stages of ignorance, because the language of the NT is not ours. Many examples of this could be cited, but one obvious one is the precise meaning of *authenteō* (having something to do with domineering or exercising authority) in I Tim. 2:12. We can never overcome the disadvantage of not sharing a common language with the first-century Christians.

Culture.[6] If I were to mention "Heaven's Gate" or "Branch Davidian" or "Jonestown," most would know that I was referring to religious cults of the late twentieth century in which the believers died a violent death en mass. Two hundred years from now if a person were to read one of my letters and found a reference to one of these in it, what are the chances he/she would recognize the allusion? They would not be good, but they would be a lot better than we have in figuring out exactly what the women and men's head covering was in I Corinthians 11. When the Corinthians read this they understood instantly what Paul meant. It was a part of their culture, their experience, their world. Many statements in the NT that the

6   See Lightfoot, "Women in Religious Services," 129-30. He states that "we do not know the customs of the time and of the ancient world as well as we would like" and uses the veiling of women in public as an example where "there is a paucity of firm historical information."

original readers understood readily are obscure to us because we live in a different time and culture. Surely the Corinthians knew who the people were that were baptizing for the dead and why they were doing it (I Cor. 15:29), but we don't. Or Timothy certainly knew what Paul meant when he spoke of being saved through childbearing (I Tim. 2:15), but we can only make an educated guess. We can minimize this disadvantage through study, but we can never overcome it.

Common Experience.[7] Somewhat related to the above, especially in the NT letters, the writer and the recipients shared a common experience. Thus when Paul writes in I Cor. 7:1, "It is good for a man not to touch a woman," his readers would know whether he was quoting and commenting on one of their slogans, as some have suggested, or it was his own comment. The same thing applies to the statement, "All things are lawful," in I Cor. 6:12, 10:23. Was it a slogan, and if so, whose—the people who took pride in their spiritual gifts, Paul's opponents, whose? They would also know which of the issues Paul addresses were on their list of questions to him (7:1). Further, they would know what he wrote in the previous letter he alludes to in I Cor. 5:9. The reference to the many who are weak and ill or have fallen asleep in I Cor. 11:30 would also have been clearer to them than it is to us. We can never overcome the disadvantage of not sharing their common experience.

Lest the impression be left that the first-century Christians had all the advantages and we have none, we should acknowledge one huge advantage we have over them. We have the entire NT, and it is readily available to us. They had only bits and pieces, a letter here, a gospel there. The ability to mass

---

7   Ibid, 130. Lightfoot points out "that we do not have enough information about the nature of the specific problems at Corinth and at Ephesus (where Timothy was when Paul wrote 1 Timothy). At best, what we have are a few clues that we can pick up with a careful reading of these passages."

produce written material brought about by the invention of printing makes the Bible so much more accessible to us than to them. Further, although most of the books that are in our NT were widely recognized as authoritative as early as the second century, the NT canon was not settled until much later. The earliest list we have of all the books in our NT to the exclusion of any others comes from the second half of the fourth century. While Paul could be concerned about people circulating counterfeit letters purporting to come from him (II Thess. 2:2), we have the benefit of the hard work done by Christians in the first few centuries to validate the apostolic documents. It is hard to overemphasize how significant this advantage is for our ability to do serious study of God's word.

Reasons Within the Interpreter's Control. In the profound words of the cartoon character, Pogo, "We have met the enemy, and he is us." More often than we would like to admit, *we* are the obstacle to properly understanding the Bible. This has been particularly the case on the topic of women in the church. It has become such a lightning-rod issue that we often don't apply the same careful methods of Bible study to these passages as we do to others.

For instance, it is sometimes argued that the act of teaching or preaching has authority inherently connected with it, so a woman may not do that in the assembly because it would mean she would not be submissive to the men present. Let us apply that reasoning to another relationship--that of a teenage son to his parents. According to the argument, teaching or preaching has authority inherently connected with it. A teenage boy would be violating his obligation to be submissive to his parents if he were to preach or teach when they are present. This is a more compelling obligation for the child and his parents than for a woman (or wife) and man (or her husband), because there is more in the Bible about the former than the latter. It is even addressed in one of the Ten Commandments, and certain types of parental disrespect were a capital offense under the Law (Ex. 21:15, 17).

In Ephesians 5-6 the wife is to be submissive to her husband (5:22, Col. 3:18), but the even stronger word, "obey," is used of the children for their parents (6:1, Col. 3:20).

Why would someone make such a careless argument? Perhaps it is because what women may do in the assembly is such a hot, emotional issue that we sometimes let our guard down. We lower our standards of biblical interpretation, because we feel so strongly about it, and the "truthfulness" of our understanding is so self-evident to us. Lest anyone think I am pointing my finger at others who do these things without realizing that I, too, have been guilty, let me give myself as an example of this careless use of the Bible.

When Pat and I got married, it was common for the bride's vows to include, "love, honor and obey." My wife's brother, who performed our ceremony, wanted to remove the word "obey" from the vows, but I held firm that I thought it should be there. It was not that I had any interest in ordering Pat around in our marriage or in requiring her obedience. It was because I believed that Paul's words to Christian wives in Eph. 5:22-24 should not be watered down simply because our society at the time seemed to be pushing us in that direction. Then for many years I used the word "obey" in the vows of weddings I performed. I was certain that I was on firm biblical ground in this and did not even consider that I might be wrong. Many years later I read an article on Eph. 5:21-6:9 in which the author pointed out that children and slaves were required to "obey," but not wives.[8] I was horrified that I was so wrong and so careless as to import into Eph. 5:22-24 an element found in the other two passages but not there. This, by the way, was after I had taught Ephesians two or three times at both the undergraduate and graduate level in college. My students, many of whom were preachers for congregations in

---

8   Everett Ferguson noted this same point in *Women in the Church*, 57.

the area, trusted me to teach them right, and on this point I let them down. Somehow for decades "a veil lay over my heart" (II Cor. 3:15) whenever I read Eph. 5:22-24. I had made up something that was not in the text, in my mind had inserted it into the text, and had patterned my erroneous practice on this fabrication. There is enough of this sort of thing going on in all of us that it should both humble us and cause us to rededicate ourselves to the careful, disciplined type of Bible study we know we should be doing all the time.

Flawed Methodology

JUST AS WITH COMPUTERS, IT IS "GARBAGE IN, GARBAGE out." If we approach the biblical text with faulty assumptions, closed minds, or questionable methods of interpretation, the quality of the result is doomed from the start. What are some of the types of flawed methodology that we find in writings on women in the church? What follows are some of the more common ones. In order to keep the focus on the issue at hand, rather than whose faulty method is being discussed, I will not identify the individuals involved. The references are all from publications within the Churches of Christ. They are in my files and can be made available to anyone who needs one.

1. **Proof texting**. We all know we should not do this, but it happens all the time. One of the quickest ways to misuse or misconstrue a statement is to separate it from its context. Proof texting involves taking a statement out of its context and applying it to another setting in a way that is either inconsistent with its meaning in the original context or does not account for the differences between the two contexts. As mentioned earlier, many who write on this subject are guilty of proof texting Gal. 3:28 or I Cor. 14:34a. This book will later deal with these two texts in some detail in their contexts.

   In another example, several authors proof text Tit. 2:15

to argue that women may not preach or serve as an evangelist, because Paul directs evangelists to "reprove *with all authority.*" Whether or not their conclusion is correct about women preaching, Tit. 2:15 hardly has anything to do with it. The argument goes like this: I Tim. 2:11-12 forbids women from exercising authority in religious matters in any way. Tit. 2:15 teaches that evangelists must "reprove with all authority." Preaching involves the exercising of authority. Therefore, a woman may not preach or evangelize. There are multiple problems with this line of reasoning, even beyond its proof-text methodology. First, the verse says nothing about evangelists or preachers. Rather it is Paul's instructions to one of his emissaries.[9] It also says nothing about preaching or evangelizing. Reproving can be done in various ways, not just through preaching. Finally, not all preaching involves reproving. Even if 2:15 were talking about preaching, how would it exclude preaching that does not involve reproof?

2. **Failure to Take Proper Account of the Context.** This is closely related to proof texting, but interprets a statement without due consideration of its literary (the text of the Bible in which the statement is situated) and historical (the setting to which the statement is addressed) contexts.[10] One example, which could be discussed either here or as a

9   Though Titus may very well have been an evangelist, he is not called one in this epistle. In fact, the only reference to an evangelist (*euaggelistēs*) in the Pastoral Epistles is in II Tim. 4:5. Titus was, however, Paul's representative in Crete, operating under Paul's apostolic authority (1:5), not his own.

10   Ferguson, (*Women in the Church,* 40) notes that "exegesis has to do with determining the meaning of a text in its literary and historical context." See also Carroll Osburn (*Reclaiming the Ideal*), 101), who correctly observes that "one must read each text according to appropriate method that recognizes literary and historical contexts.... Both 'proof-texting' and deconstruction attempt to read texts apart from their historical setting and [sic] are unacceptable."

proof text is the assertion by one writer that "the Law" in I Cor. 14:34 refers to anywhere in the OT. He then uses I Sam. 2:1-10 to demonstrate that "the Law" provides an example of a woman praying in the presence of a man. The context, however, shows that Paul's reference to "the Law" here is meant to restrict, not permit these wives' actions. In another example a writer argues that the *anēr* ("man" or "husband") in I Tim. 2:8 might be gender inclusive (both men and women). However, he fails to recognize the contrast set up by the use of *gunē* ("woman" or "wife") in 2:9. The context shows that *anēr* and *gunē* are used in their normal gender-specific sense here. Unfortunately these examples are only the tip of the iceberg in studies on women in the church.

3. **Uncritical Use of Background Evidence.** A common mistake by interpreters is to take a piece of evidence from background material, such as a quote of a Greek or Roman author, and apply it uncritically to a specific situation discussed in the NT as if it were the precise background against which a NT author wrote. It is uncritical because it fails to take proper account of such factors as (1) the actual *context* of the statement, (2) *provenance* in time and place, and (3) how *representative* the statement is of ancient views on the subject it is addressing.[11] It is a common failing of those who have a limited acquaintance with the primary sources in question, but unfortunately, any of us can fall into this trap.

An example of the uncritical use of Rabbinic background

---

11   On matters of how representative background sources are and their provenance, see Russ Dudrey, "'Submit Yourselves,'" 31-2. On the issue of provenance, Richard Oster ("Archaeological Evidence," 67) notes the "old-fashioned innocence" of certain modern writers on I Corinthians who "still try to interpret Paul with texts whose provenance cannot always be determined historically, geographically, chronologically or culturally."

material on women is the oft-repeated statement by Rabbi Eliezer that "if any man gives his daughter a knowledge of the Law it is as though he taught her lechery."[12] This citation is frequently used as *representative* of the Rabbinic attitude toward women at the time of Jesus and Paul. For several years I did so myself, until I actually read the words in *context*. Out of context, the comment sounds absolute, but in context it is clear that the speaker had a limited situation in mind. This tractate of the Mishnah (*Sotah*) deals exclusively with the interpretation of Num. 5:11-31, where a wife is suspected of adultery. R. Eliezer is talking about a woman who has been charged with adultery who seeks to use this passage in the Torah in her defense. In this case, to teach a daughter this specific law would be to give her the ability to escape the full consequences of her sexual sin, so the father might as well teach her lechery. Obviously the quotation has nothing to do with the general Rabbinic attitude toward women, as I used to think, along with many others, but with a specific issue.

The matter of women's head covering and men's lack of it in I Corinthians 11 is another good example. While numerous expositors make absolute statements about the practice in first-century Corinth, they either fail to provide evidence or refer to evidence that does not fit Corinth of that period. Everett Ferguson's excellent article on the topic in the *Restoration Quarterly* is the definitive study on the subject.[13] It is also a model of how to use background materials to throw light on biblical texts. He shows great sensitivity both to how representative background evidence is and to its provenance. For example, he suggests that the situation

---

12   Mishnah, *Sotah* 3.4.
13   "Of Veils and Virgins" (2014), 223-43. See also Oster's comprehensive study on the issue of men's head covering in I Cor. 11:4 ("When Men Wore Veils," 481-505).

seems to have been different in Ephesus, because women there were not required to wear the head covering.[14]

4. **Uncritical Use of Lexical Tools.** Dealing with the language of the Bible is tricky, because words have multiple meanings.[15] Lexicons or dictionaries of NT words are excellent tools, but for the serious Bible student, nothing is more useful than a good concordance. How we use these tools, though, is key to getting a good result. For instance, using an English dictionary to define a word in an English translation can lead to invalid conclusions. How could anyone possibly understand the correct meaning of the Greek words behind the English word "church" or "baptism" or "saint" by using an English dictionary? Yet we still see people do that, although more in sermons than in serious written exposition of the biblical text.

One of the most common uncritical approaches to determining the meaning of a Greek word in a specific passage is to pick one of several possible meanings in a Greek lexicon and assert without further evidence that it is *the* proper meaning in that passage. For example, one expositor used Thayer's lexicon to defined the meaning of the Greek word for "teach" (*didaskō*) in I Tim. 2:12 as "deliver didactic discourses." Although this is only one of about ten shades of meaning Thayer gives for the word, it became useful for the writer to single out this one because the word "discourse" in the definition enabled him to

---

14 "Of Veils and Virgins," 242.
15 Though it is not common, the same Greek word can even have two different meanings in the same passage. For example, in Heb. 9:15 the writer seems to use the word "covenant" (*diathēkē*) the way it is used in Jer. 31:31 of an agreement between two living parties. Then in 9:16-17 the word shifts in meaning to "will" (also *diathēkē*), a provision that only takes effect *after* the death of the person who made it. The two meanings are entirely different; yet they served the purpose of the Hebrew writer in the theological point he was making.

make the leap that Paul is talking about preaching as well as teaching in the passage. This is why serious Bible students should use a concordance to supplement the views expressed in lexicons. It is too easy to find the meaning that best supports the point the expositor is trying to make and build an argument around that nuance of meaning alone. Concordance study allows us to level the playing field by testing our own conclusions about specific word meanings against those of a lexicographer. After all, dictionaries don't define words; word usage does. Dictionaries merely draw conclusions from actual usage, and we can and should do the same.

In another example a writer, who had a limited knowledge of Greek, misconstrued what Thayer wrote about the Greek words "if" (*ean*) and "whenever" (*hotan*) and applied that to their usage in I Cor. 14:24 and 26 respectively. Misunderstanding the meaning of the subjunctive in Greek, he erroneously contended that Paul's use of these particles "shows uncertainty as to when the assembly will take place." He then concluded that this must not have been a regular assembly of the church. Not only does he fail to understand conditional sentences in Greek and the force of the subjunctive mood, his argument falls apart when we look at what he acknowledges as a regular assembly in I Cor. 11:17-34. Here Paul uses the subjunctive, including the particle "*ean*," in a similar way that he employs it in chapter 14. Greek lexicons are useful tools, but as with any tool, they must be used correctly.

5. **Demonizing Those Who Disagree**.[16] This is a particularly destructive activity. We ought to know better. It has to do with pushing or crossing the line between attacking a brother's position and attacking the brother himself.

---

16   On this practice see Watson, "Some Pastoral Implications," 160.

Examples of the latter are all too common. One author in an article on women in the church in describing a person's disagreement with a point he was making wrote that it was "selfish, arrogant, and illustrates the damnable 'will worship' loathed by the Almighty." He is not alone in calling others arrogant. Another wrote, "If there is a unifying spirit that characterizes the new 'left wing' of the current church, it is that of arrogance." He went on to say, "Such egotism is hardly consistent with the feigned humility that is so often touted by the 'new left.'" Or again, "The essay is grossly arrogant in tone, it smacks of pragmatic conformity to modern religiondom, and it is theologically liberal in disposition." On the other side, one writer characterized Christian men who hold the traditional view on women in the church as "so enraptured with their authority, so enamoured of their self-serving responsibility, so blinded by their insecurity, so weakened by their shallow love."

Others push the line very hard. You be the judge of whether they have crossed it. Note the epithets some use for their opponents: "architects of innovation," "digressive," "theologically liberal in disposition," "our progressive brothers," "change agents," "feminist theologians," "liberal," or "denial of the inspiration of the Bible." Those with whom they disagree are said to subscribe to women's liberation, they are the proponents of false doctrine, or they no longer respect biblical authority. One writer even accused those who support a broadening role for women in the church as "abandoning faith in the absolute authority of the scriptures in favor of a leftist reading of the scriptures in order to conform to the demands of contemporary culture." It is not a pretty picture.

Whether or not these descriptors are accurate is irrelevant in determining the validity of the points made by those to whom they are applied. Statements are true or false, regardless of who makes them. All this begs two questions. First, what kind of opinion of their readers do these writers and their editors have if they think personal attacks on and labeling of their brothers and sisters will influence their views on the issues addressed in the articles? Secondly, how strong is an argument anyway if it needs to be buttressed by this kind of name calling? We see enough of this in political rhetoric. We don't need it in the church. Surely there is "still a more excellent way" (I Cor. 12:31b). Here, again, my esteemed teacher, Everett Ferguson, provides us a model of brotherly behavior. In discussing his differences with Carroll Osburn over some of the conclusions in his book, *Women in the Church*, he writes, "Both he and I are committed to the authority of scripture, to its historical literary interpretation, and to this issue not becoming one that breaks fellowship."[17] Would that we follow his example in the way we interact with each other on this topic.

6. **Reading Elements into the Text That Are Not There**. This is done in various ways. One is what some call eisegesis, as opposed to exegesis. While exegesis involves extracting the original meaning from a text, eisegesis has to do with introducing to the text issues not found there. Another is the failure to approach a passage with as open a mind as possible. Rather, we saddle the text with preconceptions that inhibit discovery of a passage's meaning. Finally, some writers are actually guilty of manufacturing ideas and concepts not found in the text and treating them as if they were.

Modern Ideas and Experiences. One example that is often cited is the practice of interpreting the slave-master passages in the NT in light of slavery as it was practiced in the United

---

17   *The Christian Chronicle* (Sept. 2001), 31.

States in the pre-Civil War South. There were significant differences between the two. More to the point of writings on women in the church is the practice of interpreting both OT and NT texts on the relationship between men and women within the framework of modern Sociology. Words like patriarchy, matriarchy, egalitarian, or complementary are thrown around as if they were in the Bible. Modern positions on the issue are characterized by such descriptors as "Evangelical Feminism," "Patriarchalism," or "Hierarchal Complementarianism." Those whose approaches are so labeled can then be safely put away in a box and their conclusions on individual biblical passages dismissed. It is not that using the theories of modern Sociology or any of the other social sciences is without value. For some people they help bring into focus the *application* of biblical texts to our present situation. It is their interjection into the investigation of the *original* meaning of biblical passages where they can become anachronistic impediments to our understanding. We should allow the Bible to unfold its meaning to us before we start applying more recent non-biblical concepts to it. For that reason, unlike other books and articles on this subject, this study will not use those labels. The primary intent here is exegesis of the text of the Bible, and for that purpose we will attempt as much as possible to use only what we find in the world of the OT and NT.

Presuppositions. Presuppositions or assumptions are the premises we use to draw other conclusions. We do not feel obligated to support or try to prove them either because we consider them self-evident or axiomatic or we believe they have been sufficiently established elsewhere. That the Bible is the inspired word of God or that Jesus died on the cross to save us from our sins are assumptions we all make. They are assumptions because we are so certain of them that we feel no need to support them by reasoning or evidence. They become the foundation upon which we build other conclusions.[18] Where these presuppositions get us into trouble is when they have no biblical text that supports them. Previously we may have made an effort to establish them by stringing together a gaggle of Bible verses into a reasoned argument or even by making an argument without direct support of biblical texts, but no actual biblical passage supports them. They then become the premises upon which we base other reasoned arguments.[19]

Writings on women in the church are filled with these types of unproven or even unprovable assumptions. Nowhere does the Bible state what is being assumed by the presupposition, so the foundation of the subsequent argument is defective from the outset. Here is a concrete example of a faulty presupposition used to support a questionable interpretation of a NT passage. The writer is trying to show that I Cor. 14:34 forbids all women from speaking in church. His premise is that "all the teaching of the Bible is against women speaking in public," but his only support for this claim is I Cor. 14:31-37. Here he is assuming what he sets out to prove. Further, the premise is false. Nowhere in either the OT or NT does the Bible teach "against women speaking in public." This is totally made up. Further, there are sufficient OT examples to disprove

---

18   On the role of presuppositions in biblical studies, see Osburn, *Reclaiming the Ideal*, 97-102.
19   F. LaGard Smith (*Men of Strength*, 39), using the Genesis creation story as his example, writes this about the pull of what we already believe on our interpretation of the biblical text: "In trying to understand the implications to be drawn from the story of Creation, we are likely to see in the Genesis account what we have always believed. Tradition has a way of putting colored glasses over our eyes, so that we miss details we've never seen before." See also the citation by Watson in note 1 above.

the claim, as Nichol amply shows in *God's Woman*. Other frequently encountered examples of assumptions for which there is no biblical support include:

+ Leading is by its very nature domineering or a lack of submission.

+ Teaching by its very nature has authority attached to it.

+ The teachings in Genesis 1-3 apply to women and men in general.

+ Wives' submission to husbands as found in Gen. 3:16 was later transferred to women's submission to men in the church.

+ Women in general are to be in submission to men in general in the church.

+ Serving in some capacity in the assembly is assuming an unbiblical leadership role.

+ Gal. 3:28 reflects Paul's view about women in the church, and any other Pauline texts are secondary to it.

This book will challenge all of these assumptions. The Bible simply does not support them.

Inventing Terminology and Concepts. Possibly most disappointing of all is the practice of making things up as if they were in the Bible.[20] It is disappointing because this comes from people who pride themselves in not adding to or taking away from the Bible. For example, into the interpretation of the Genesis creation narrative some have inserted concepts like "male spiritual leadership" or Adam

---

20 See Woods, *Questions and Answers* (1986), 43. In opposing the practice of forbidding mothers to teach the Bible to or pray audibly in the presence of their Christian sons at home, he asserts, "It is a grave sin to make laws where God has not—to speak where he has not spoken."

as Eve's "designated spiritual protector." Then there is the complete fabrication that one of Adam's two sins was "failing to exercise spiritual leadership." It is bad enough to have the Genesis text polluted by concepts and terms not found there, but these inventions are repeated so often that they are easily used as premises for later reasoned arguments.

In the NT other examples abound. Two should suffice to make the point here. One writer asserts that "First Timothy 2:8 forbids women to pray audibly *in the presence* of men in religious assemblies." Note the three foreign elements he adds to the text: (1) "forbids" (the only thing forbidden in the verse is anger and arguing, and that pertains to men, not women); (2) "women" (the verse is talking only about men, not women); and (3) "in the presence of men" (nothing in this verse or in the next two, where women are actually talked about, is said about the presence of men). This is all made up; it is plucked from the air. Finally, referring to I Cor. 11:2-16, another interpreter states that "Paul emphasized that the Christian women of Corinth ought not to appear on the streets... without veils." Of course the passage says nothing about women's conduct "on the streets." It is no wonder that there is such great disagreement on what the Bible says about women when so much of the discussion centers on what is not even in the Bible.

7. **Asking Modern Questions of the NT.** In an effort to apply what is found in the NT to our current situation, often people ask modern questions that the NT cannot answer. For example, "Does God approve of human genetic engineering"? Or, "Is it a sin for a Christian to smoke cigarettes"? It is not that the NT does not provide us any direction for making decisions on these types of issues. It just does not and cannot give us *specific* direction, because these situations did not exist in the first century or they

are not specifically addressed in the NT. Neil Lightfoot's remarks apply here.

> As we look at the New Testament texts from the vantage point of the twentieth century, we may raise questions that are not New Testament questions at all. Often we may be able to detect some general guidelines, but we must acknowledge at the same time that on some problems we have no specific New Testament solution.[21]

This seems obvious enough, but on the topic of women in the church these types of questions abound. "May girls pray in mixed devotionals"? "May women *lead* prayers in the assembly"? "Is it Scriptural for a woman to act as a translator in an assembly"? "May a female pass a communion tray in the assembly"? What we need to remember in dealing with questions like these is that they have to do with the modern-day *application* of NT teachings, not with what specific NT texts actually meant in their original setting. Thus we need to be careful about confusing our answers (application), though informed by Bible study, with what the NT actually says and what exegesis of its text shows it actually meant in the first century.

Finally, in his book on *Women in the Church*, Ferguson proposes two additional "mistaken strategies in interpretation" he finds in some of the studies by those calling for a wider role for women in the assembly. They are worthy of our consideration.

Limiting "the apostolic directions to the circumstances that gave rise to the correction."[22] For Ferguson, the problem comes not from trying to reconstruct the setting in order

---

21 *Role of Women*, 10.
22 See also Everett and Nancy Ferguson, "Women in the Assembly," 30 and Jack P. Lewis, " Analysis of 1 Timothy 2:8-15," 37.

better to understand the text. It comes when moving from this exercise in exegesis to hermeneutics, that is, the modern application. What he sees some interpreters doing is applying the passage today only to the extent that our modern situation matches the original setting. Ferguson rightly points out that the flaw in this methodology is that although all Scripture is certainly written to a specific situation, much of what is written has to do with general principles and teachings that apply beyond a particular setting. "We should apply the principles and the instructions revealed in given historical circumstances to our own situation today. The text itself is our authority, not our reconstruction of the context." (39) While Ferguson's corrective here is an important one, it does not, of course, negate the fact that certain elements of a text are not for all time. A part of the exegetical task is to ascertain what the culturally bound elements are and what the enduring truths are, as an aid to the task of hermeneutics or modern application. The exegete works within the various contexts (historical, cultural, linguistic, and biblical) to perform this work.

Identifying "what one perceives to be the trend or goal of biblical revelation and then to regulate one's interpretation by that principle." Here also Ferguson makes a compelling point about a great deal of modern NT interpretation and its contemporary application. In dealing with the matter of women in the Bible, on the one side some writers conclude that egalitarianism is God's ultimate goal, and they find proof texts to support their understanding. On the other side interpreters come to the same conclusion about subordination, and they marshal their own Scriptural evidence. The problem comes when "the principle is then absolutized so that everything else is either interpreted in terms of the chosen principle or ignored as temporary or irrelevant." He then rightly concludes, "This approach leaves our theology or our interpretation as the authority, not the words of scripture. Certainly, it is appropriate to try to determine the great biblical doctrines and give central importance to them in interpreting Scripture, but the biblical texts themselves must continue to guide us in doing so." (40) All this is similar to #6 above and the interjection of modern Sociological terminology and concepts into interpretation of the biblical text.

Conclusions

Our record in research and writings on women in the church has been less than stellar. It is characterized by massive disagreement and sometimes unbrotherly accusations. This is one of those topics where the biblical evidence is difficult and capable of multiple interpretations. It begs the question of whether consensus is possible and if so to what degree. Flawed methodology stands firmly at the center of the differences in our understanding of the relevant biblical passages and their modern application. But this actually offers a ray of hope. If we can identify lapses in our methods, commit ourselves to a more disciplined Bible study, and become more charitable to those with whom we disagree, there is a reasonable expectation we can learn from each other and move closer together. This chapter has dealt primarily with our differences and some of their causes. The next will offer suggestions for what that more disciplined Bible study might look like.

Excursus 2: Diversity in the Interpretation of the Three Key Pauline Passages. Earlier in this chapter three examples of diverse, conflicting interpretations from each of the three key Pauline passages were presented. The list is much longer than could be presented there. What follows here is a number of additional examples, all coming from people who support the limiting of what women may do in our assemblies and/or other settings.

I Corinthians 11:3-16

- In 11:3 and in submission-related statements later in the passage, the reference is to (1) wives' submission to their husbands, (2) women in general being submissive to men in general in the church or (3) women in general being submissive to men in general outside the church as well.

- In this assembly where women were praying and prophesying, (1) only women were present or (2) men were also present.

- On the assumption that a head covering is required today, (1) a woman's hat would satisfy the requirement or (2) it would not.

- The angels referred to in 11:10 are (1) angels present in the assembly or (2) fallen angels.

- The reference to "nature" (*phusis*) in verse 14 is (1) universal, not cultural, (2) cultural (customary), or (3) the native sense of propriety.

- On the apparent conflict between I Cor. 11:5 and 14:34 on the silence of women: (1) I Cor. 14:34 is primary and I Cor. 11:5 must be interpreted to agree with it, (2) I Cor. 11 merely describes what was happening without approving or disapproving it, whereas I Cor. 14 commands women to stop speaking in church, or (3) the two passages are not in conflict.

I Corinthians 14:33b-35

- On the words, "as in all the churches of the saints" (14:33b), (1) they refer to what comes after, (2) they refer to what goes before, (3) the question is moot, (4) they go with both what precedes and what comes after, or (5) it doesn't impact the interpretation of 14:34-35.

- On the words, "let the women be silent in the

churches" (14:34a), they refer (1) to all women in every congregation for all time, (2) only to women endowed by the Spirit to speak, or (3) to specific circumstances in Corinth.

• The restriction on women speaking in church refers (1) only to the regular Christian assembly or (2) only to special assemblies where miraculous gifts were being used.

• On the meaning of "keep silence" (14:34a): (1) absolute silence or (2) not absolute silence.

• On the meaning of "the law" (14:34): (1) Gen. 2, (2) Gen. 3:16, (3) the creation narrative in Genesis, including Gen. 3:16, or (4) Num. 30:3-16.

• On what the passage prohibits women from doing in our modern assemblies: (1) nothing, (2) praying out loud in the presence of men, (3) leading the thought of men, (4) speaking out loud in the assembly, (5) being a foreign language interpreter in the assembly, or (6) being a foreign language interpreter in the assembly not prohibited.

I Timothy 2:8-15

• The passage refers to (1) all women in every congregation for all time or (2) special circumstances in Ephesus.

• On the meaning of "in every place" where men are to pray (2:8): (1) regular church assembly only, (2) not referring to every public or private setting, or (3) every public or private setting.

• Women are (1) not permitted to word an audible prayer in the presence of their husband or son in the home or (2) women are permitted to do both.

• On the meaning of "pray" (2:8): (1) *leading* prayer, (2)

nothing said about *leading* prayer, or (3) there is no NT example of anyone *leading* a prayer.

- On the meaning of "silence" in 2:11-12: (1) quietness, not absolute silence or (2) absolute silence—the absence of sound.

- On the meaning of women teaching and exercising authority in 2:12: (1) teaching "over" men prohibited but not teaching in the presence of men, (2) teaching in the presence of men, (3) exercising authority over men prohibited, but public roles with no inherent authority attached, including reading scripture and passing the Lord's Supper, permitted, or (4) any behavior that involves a woman leading, directing, presiding, or addressing in an authoritative capacity a mixed group participating in worship.

- On women's susceptibility to deception: (1) women are more susceptible to deception than men or (2) women are not more susceptible to deception than men.

- On the meaning of "saved" in 2:15: (1) from the stigma on woman from the fall, (2) from despair, or (3) accepting one's God-given role.

- The subject of "saved" in 2:15 (1) is Eve or (2) is not Eve.

- On the meaning of "childbearing" in 2:15: (1) synecdoche, a figure of speech or (2) through a woman (Mary) the Savior was born.

CHAPTER THREE

What Disciplined Bible Study Looks Like

*C*hapter two surveyed several of the types of flawed Bible study methodology that have been prevalent in writings on women in the church. It ended with the promise that this chapter would offer suggestions for what a more disciplined Bible study might look like. This will be done in three different ways. First, we will look at what the opposite of the flawed methods discussed in chapter two teaches us about good methodology. After that will be a few suggestions by some in our brotherhood who are widely recognized for their expertise in biblical interpretation and have written books on the topic. Finally, I will propose an approach that pulls all this together.

The Opposite of Flawed Methods

HERE ARE THE TYPES OF FLAWED METHODOLOGY IN BIBLICAL studies mentioned in chapter two and the sound methods their opposite implies.

Awareness of Assumptions. If approaching a passage with faulty assumptions or a closed mind can lead to misunderstanding of that passage, how can we correct that? Certainly we cannot totally free ourselves of our assumptions or presuppositions. Carroll Osburn's discussion of presuppositions in biblical studies is helpful here.[1] He correctly states outright

---

1   *Reclaiming the Ideal,* 97-102.

that "although some appeal for an allegedly neutral, unbiased approach, presuppositions are involved at every level of biblical research." He continues, "Presuppositions cannot be avoided. However, they must not be allowed to dominate the text, but to serve as guiding principles that are continually adjusted in terms of interaction with the text." In fact, he says, we *should* approach the text with certain presuppositions and lists several of them that we share in common, such as that "the supernatural exists and God is ultimate." This is much like Alexander Campbell's seventh rule of biblical interpretation: "We must come within the understanding distance."[2] We approach the biblical text with certain presuppositions about God and the Bible, and these can and should influence our reading of the text. Where the rub comes is when presupposition turns into prejudice. Here Osburn notes that "If one's prejudice is so deep-seated that one reaches a conclusion before the evidence is considered, then prejudice renders the accurate understanding of a text impossible." So what are we to do? Perhaps the best we can do is repeatedly remind ourselves that we do not approach the text as a blank slate, but bring our assumptions, presuppositions and, on our worst days, prejudices with us. To supplement this, asking for feedback from someone who disagrees with our conclusions can provide a needed reality check.

Faithfulness to the Context. The flawed method being discussed here expresses itself in either (1) interpreting a statement or verse out of its context or (2) the stringing together of individual statements or verses because of a common thread running through them with little regard to what they meant in their original contexts. All biblical statements need to be considered in their various contexts (the passage, the book, the author, the NT, the Bible), but the point being made here is the necessity of interpreting a verse or statement in its

---

2   *Christian System*, 4.

immediate context.[3] For instance, in I Cor. 14:34 what does the word translated "be silent" (*sigaō*) mean in its context?[4] How is it used elsewhere in the chapter? While a Greek lexicon may be of assistance here, we would probably get more help from a concordance, because it can tell us how Paul used the word in this particular instance. Or when Paul says in the same verse that it is not permitted for women "to speak" (*laleō*), what kind of speaking is he talking about? Does this refer to speaking of any type (like speaking while singing, Eph. 5:19) or would a careful look at the next verse help us reign in our wild speculation on this point?

Appropriate Use of Background Evidence. The most common flaws in this area are (1) quoting a pagan or Jewish author out of context, (2) failure to take proper account of the time and place of a piece of evidence, and (3) generalizing from a single piece of evidence (Greek, Roman, Jewish). Just as you can "prove" almost anything by the Bible, if you are determined to, so it is with background evidence. We first must check the context of a pagan or Jewish quotation to ensure that the author actually meant what we take him to have meant by his isolated statement. Next, since opinions varied widely in the ancient world in different places and times, we must establish the provenance of a statement to assess its relevance to the place and time of the biblical text

---

3 See, for example, Allen Webster ("Meaning of Galatians 3:28," 23), who in rightly appealing for the need to interpret Gal. 3:28 in context writes, "Good Bible students always look at context. They consider a book's purpose and examine closely the sentences around a verse in question. What is the purpose of Galatians? What problem is Paul addressing"?

4 See Highers, "Keep Silence," 24. Although his overall conclusion is questionable, Highers is right about the importance of context in correctly interpreting this verse. He writes, "It means they must 'keep silence' with respect to the matters under consideration; it does not mean they cannot utter a sound or otherwise participate in the activities of worship. So, likewise, with respect to women, they must 'keep silence' with regard to the *subject under consideration*."

we are interpreting.[5] This activity alone would clear up a great deal of the confusion about the background of Paul's statements in I Corinthians. Finally, since even in the same general place and time authors' opinions varied widely due to cultural differences and other factors (Greek, Roman, Jewish, slave owner, philosopher, pagan priest, government official, etc.), we must ensure that the evidence is representative enough of the background to illuminate our biblical passage. When it comes to the foreground, that is, pagan, Jewish, and Christian sources after the NT, the same principles apply. They also pertain to non-literary background evidence like inscriptions and art work. Everett Ferguson is a master of this type of careful use of background sources, and his article on the head covering in I Corinthians 11 is a model worth emulating.[6]

Appropriate Use of Lexical Tools. In biblical studies lexical tools are helps for determining word meanings. They include Hebrew and Greek concordances and lexicons (dictionaries). They also comprise special word studies found in articles and other books, such as biblical commentaries and theological dictionaries. The common failing of many interpreters in this regard has to do with defining the meaning of a word in a passage by selecting one of multiple definitions found in a Greek or Hebrew lexicon that most fits the point the interpreter is trying to make. As was pointed out in chapter two, dictionaries or lexicons don't define words; usage does.[7] That

---

5   See Ferguson's (*Women in the Church*, 42-43) application of this to the matter of women in the first century church where he notes that "The cultural context of the New Testament in regard to what was acceptable for women was not uniform and so offers no simple explanation for why the New Testament placed limitations on women's place in the churches." He continues, "No simple generalizations can be made about what was culturally acceptable or unacceptable for women in different places or in different times in the Greco-Roman world."

6   "Of Veils and Virgins" (2014), 223-43.

7   Campbell's rule 4 for biblical interpretation fits here. "*Common usage, which can only be ascertained by testimony, must always decide the*

is why a concordance and lexicon should be used in tandem. When a word has multiple meanings, we begin by examining usage of the word using a Greek or Hebrew concordance, then validate or modify our findings in a lexicon. If we go into a word study presuming a certain outcome, then use a lexicon to support our presumption, we have reduced significantly the likelihood of getting a correct result.

Chapter two also discussed the methodological flaws of **Reading Elements into the Text That Are Not There** and **Asking Modern Questions of the NT**. The opposite of these will be dealt with in the last section of this chapter.

Suggestions from Authors of Books on Women in the Church

IN SOME OF THE BOOKS ON WOMEN IN THE CHURCH WRITten by a few of our brotherhood's specialists in the field of biblical exegesis, the authors have offered several constructive insights on proper interpretive methodology. What follows is a synopsis of points culled from a few of them. The reader will find certain of their views more useful than others, and

---

meaning of any word which has but one significance; but when words have, according to testimony, (i.e., the Dictionary,) more meanings than one, whether literal or figurative, *the scope, the context, or parallel passages must decide the meaning*, for if common usage, the design of the writer, the context, and parallel passages fail, there can be no certainty in the interpretation of language." (*Christian System,* 4). Also see Highers ("Keep Silence," 24) where he writes, "The meaning of any New Testament word is determined not only by its definition, but also by its context." Lightfoot (*Role of Women,* 43) applies this principle of consideration of the context to determine a word's usage to a passage on women in the church. With reference to the argument that if a woman is to keep silent in church (I Cor. 14:34) she may not sing, he writes, "This is a supreme example of how some people have never learned that context determines the meaning of a word. 'The women should keep silence. For they are not permitted to speak....' The accompanying clause defines the kind of silence enjoined." Would that interpreters of this verse follow Lightfoot's logic on the meaning of "speak" (*laleō*) to determine the kind of speaking Paul has in mind.

there is understandable repetition both from what has been
written earlier in this chapter and among these writers themselves. They are presented here as principles or suggestions,
not as hard-and-fast rules of interpretation. They do have
value, though, in helping us consider the way we go about
our serious Bible study.

Everett Ferguson

IT IS FITTING TO BEGIN WITH EVERETT FERGUSON. HE
and his colleagues, Abraham Malherbe and J. W. Roberts,
were the teachers from whom I first learned how to do exegesis. Everything I have learned since has been based on the
foundation of that early instruction. They were my mentors.
It would be hard to overstate the positive impact Ferguson
has had on the later twentieth and early twenty-first century
Churches of Christ, not to mention the scholarly world at
large. His accolades for work in the world of early Christian
studies need not be enumerated here, but they are extensive
and impressive.

From his work as a first-magnitude specialist on early
Christianity he developed a methodology to approach theological issues that he has used at least three times in published
works, including in 2003 in his previously cited study, *Women
in the Church.*[8] This book is the culmination of his research
and publishing on the topic that spanned decades.[9] Just as
with C. R. Nichol, at key points my teacher's conclusions
and my own diverge, but his methodology and erudition

---

8   On the topic of early church music he used the methodology in *A
Cappella Music in the Public Worship of the Church* (1972), and on the
day for observing the Lord's Supper he wrote "The Lord's Supper and
Biblical Hermeneutics," (1976), 11-14, which appeared again as "The
Breaking of Bread," (1991), 52-55.
9   The earliest article on the subject I have been able to find is "Of
Veils and Virgins," *Christian Scholars Conference* (1985): 1-21, and the
most recent is a very different article but one on the same topic, "Of
Veils and Virgins" (2014), 223-43.

are sound. As will become obvious as this book progresses, his later views on the topic do not always agree with some of his earlier ones. This, of course, happens to all of us who continue to study an issue or a biblical text over many years. If that does not happen, it may be an indication that we have quit learning and become stagnant or worse. This is not to say that our later conclusions are necessarily better, because as our views on a topic become more set, the temptation to "reconsider" earlier conclusions to conform to our current understanding is strong. This happens to all of us and is quite evident in writings on this topic in particular.

Ferguson's three-stage approach for sound biblical interpretation is simple and direct.[10]

1. First, he performs exegesis on the relevant biblical texts.

2. Next, he studies the historical context (background) and "the early Christian development after the New Testament" (foreground). Into the first he places the results of his exegetical study of the biblical texts to ascertain "what was possible in the first century and how the New Testament is to be understood in its historical setting." Then, on the reasonable assumption that "the early Christian development is a witness to the apostolic teaching and practice and must be derivable in some way from it even when it departs from it," he examines the foreground evidence. For him, "this testimony from history is a control on whether one has read the biblical texts accurately and put them together correctly."

3. Finally he considers "the doctrinal significance and coherence of the conclusions" he has reached in the first two steps. He uses this activity as "a control on whether these practices were incidental to the texts or were culturally and temporally conditioned. Is there a doctrinal meaning for

---

10   *Women in the Church*, 5-6.

the practice that demonstrates its continuing relevance for the church"? He issues an important caution here that we not attribute a doctrinal meaning to a practice, but rather ensure that it is actually found in the text. "The theology must derive from the texts and be intimately associated with the practice."

Neil R. Lightfoot

IN HIS BOOK, *THE ROLE OF WOMEN: NEW TESTAMENT PERspectives*, Neil Lightfoot summarizes "the exegetical task" as "to gather together the relevant biblical texts, examine them linguistically and contextually, look at them historically, and by this means determine what these texts said to their first readers." (9) He is in perfect sync with Ferguson's first two steps at this point. While this activity may seem simple and straightforward, he reminds his readers that biblical interpretation is done by humans, and that interjects an element of variation into the process. He suggests two counter measures. First, "the exegete must put himself through a severe test of mind-clearing. Is he willing to put aside his partisan causes and pet ideas"? Then "he must recognize the complexities of his assignment." One of these complexities is the fact that at times texts on this topic appear to be in conflict. How do we deal with that? (9-10)

Finally, Lightfoot addresses what he calls "the hermeneutical problem," that is, "how the text translates to a modern setting and applies here and now." He offers no suggestion here, but later in the book returns to the issue. There, in discussing "how to distinguish between culturally-rooted ideas and lasting principles," he admits, "I do not bring with me any magic wand." The best he is able to do is provide the rather nebulous solution of "carefulness with the texts, with a good sprinkling of common sense." (36) Finally, he does add that where the OT is used as the basis of a Christian practice, we should assume that it is not culturally based. (37)

C. R. Nichol

IN HIS BOOK, *GOD'S WOMAN*, NICHOL DOES NOT ADDRESS BIBLIcal interpretation as a separate topic, but sprinkled throughout the book are little gems he throws in. There is nothing systematic about his treatment of them, as there is in Ferguson and Lightfoot, but to borrow Lightfoot's term, most can be characterized as "common sense." Here are some of those gems:

1. Note the point of emphasis. "Often one thing is denied that another may be emphasized, by contrast. Not that one thing is denied in the absolute, but denied to give stress to another thing." (62)

2. Be careful not to put too much weight on what is not said. "It is characteristic of writers and speakers, in discussing a subject with which the ones addressed are familiar, to omit many details, and matters generally known. You might discuss at length the character of those who can righteously eat the Lord's supper, without making comments on the elements used in that supper." (71)

3. Recognize that we do not know some of the background that was fully known to the original recipients. "Too many of us do not have a knowledge of the conditions and customs of the people in the first century of the Christian religion to whom the letters in the New Testament were written, hence some expressions and references may not be fully appreciated." (71)

4. Let a passage speak for itself. "The effort should be to learn what the passage teaches, without regard to what you may have concluded about some other passage." (121) This statement is in response to those who use what they assume I Cor. 14:34-35 means to conclude that women in Corinth must have prayed *silently* (I Cor. 11:5).

5. <u>Not all commands in the Bible apply today</u>. "To think that every commandment recorded in the Bible is applicable to yourself, or even to others now on earth, is a mistake for which there is no valid excuse." (129) This is the way Nichol begins his refutation of the common interpretation of I Cor. 14:34-35, and he uses several biblical examples to prove it.

6. <u>Consider the circumstances at the time of writing</u>. In writing about I Corinthians 14, Nichol says, "He who reads the chapter now under review, if he desires to know the truth, and is discriminating in his reading; will note carefully the conditions prevailing at the time the letter was written, as well as the purpose for which it was written." (133)

Carroll D. Osburn

CARROLL OSBURN FIRST PUBLISHED *WOMEN IN THE Church: Refocusing the Discussion* in 1994, then released a greatly expand second edition in 2001 under the title, *Women in the Church: Reclaiming the Ideal*. Because the latter book contains a fuller treatment of Osburn's proposed principles of biblical interpretation, we will follow it in the discussion here. Early in the work he suggests two elements of an approach. (4)

1. "<u>Cultivate a willingness to rethink the problem</u>." "Rethinking means that some change might result. So, we must have an honest willingness to change our views and modify our behavior if necessary."

2. "<u>Reexamine the biblical text</u>." We need to do this "instead of rummaging through the Bible to find texts that might support our pre-conceived notions.... I am suggesting patient exegesis (getting out of the Bible what the writer meant) as the basis for responsible implementation in contemporary life of ancient biblical principles and values."

Later in the book, in the section titled "*Reassessing Herme-*

neutics," Osburn argues that "proper biblical interpretation must begin with and be guided by the original, historical, contextual meaning of the text." (104) This means that "the 'meaning' of a text is the meaning intended by the author within a particular literary and historical setting." (104) "Since Christianity is a historical religion, it matters greatly what a statement meant in its original setting." (105) The rest of Osburn's discussion here is an exceptionally well-structured synopsis of some of the contemporary discussion over how to distinguish the culturally based from the eternal biblical teachings without being overly influenced by our preconceived notions. (104-108) This is so well done that the reader is encouraged to access Osburn's treatment directly, rather than depend on a summary here.

Each of these four who have written major studies on women in the church found it useful to include discussion of proper methods of biblical interpretation as they pertain to their endeavor. The methodology we employ has an enormous impact on the final results we produce from our study of a biblical topic or passage. So it is with this book. The final section of this chapter offers some closing thoughts on a disciplined approach to biblical interpretation in the hope that they will be useful as we move to the relevant texts themselves.

Say, Meant, Mean

In order to apply biblical teachings appropriately to our current situation, we need to ask three questions of a biblical text: (1) What does it say?, (2) What did it mean?, and (3) What does it mean? Most studies on biblical hermeneutics stress the importance of the second and third questions, but a failure to pay proper attention to the first often leads interpreters to make statements about what the Bible teaches that are either simply not true or cannot be established from the text itself. Further, these three questions are interconnected, with the second dependent on the first and the third dependent on the first and second. Because so much of the Bible is not difficult to understand,[11] most of the time we intuitively ask the three questions without being conscious of it. However, in those more difficult texts, where serious Bible students differ among themselves, a more disciplined and intentional use of the three questions is called for. It is my belief that were we to do this more often, the extent of disagreement on biblical passages would be reduced significantly.

What Does It Say? Here we are concerned with (1) establishing the correct reading based on the manuscript evidence and (2) avoiding the confusion about what we think the text meant with what it actually says. Only after we are satisfied that we are interpreting the best reading of the text and have limited ourselves to interpreting what the text actually says are we ready to answer the second question, "What did it mean"? Because word meanings in Greek and English do not correspond perfectly, in some cases we may have to answer this first question with the original Greek word rather than an English one. *Gunē* (woman or wife) and *anēr* (man or husband) are examples. To say that the text says "woman" or "wife" or "man" or "husband" is interpretation and answers the second question, "What did it mean"?, not the first. Thus to assert that I Cor. 11:3 says that "the head of the woman *is* the man" (KJV) or that "the head of the woman is man" (NIV) or that "the man is the head of a woman" (NASV) or that "the head of a woman is her husband" (RSV) confuses the two questions. Because of the ambiguity of the meaning of the two Greek words, each of these translations is interpretive and is not an adequate answer to the first question. There is also the lack of perfect correspondence between Greek and English on the presence or absence of the definite article. This ambiguity is reflected in the different translations above.

---

11   On this see the section, ***Some passages are inherently difficult to understand***, in chapter two.

What Did It Mean? This is the *exegetical* question. It seeks to learn what the original writer actually meant by his words and to a lesser extent how those words would have been understood by his readers. We do this by trying to put ourselves as nearly as possible in the shoes of the original readers, so we can derive the same meaning from a passage that they did. The exegetical question can only be answered correctly once the first question, "What does it say"?, has been addressed. Several factors go into answering this second, interpretive question. These include such things as (1) the original intent of the author and/or speaker, (2) the various biblical contexts (the passage, the book, the author, the NT, the Bible), (3) the meaning of the language used (words, phrases, grammatical constructions), (4) the literary form, and (5) the historical context (background and foreground).[12]

Unfortunately, if we are not careful, the distinction between the first and second questions can get blurred. One way this happens is the interpretive blunder of eisegesis, or reading our current situation or modern categories or terminology into a biblical passage. We can and should ask modern questions of ancient biblical texts, but we need to be clear that our answers are our own interpretations of the Bible, not what the Bible actually says.[13]

---

12   Sometimes the simplest explanation makes the point most directly. As pointed out in an article in his church bulletin ("Lifelines,") by Randall Caselman, my best friend while I was growing up in Northwest Arkansas, "Exegesis is simply the process of discovering the original author's intent, his real message to the recipient.... Proper exegesis means we determine who is speaking, who is being spoken to, and what the message meant in the life of the hearer. What is the context? You see, context is much more than just the verse before and the verse after. We need to consider: Who are these people? What kind of culture were they living in? What did this message mean to them"? On the importance of these types of issues for careful interpretation, also see Alexander Campbell's seven rules in *Christian System, 3-5.*
13   Examples of this kind of flawed methodology were enumerated in chapter two, especially in the section called **6. Reading Elements into**

Another way the distinction between the first and second questions gets blurred is by making an assumption that leads to the second question as if our interpretive answer is what the text actually says. These interpretations ("What did it mean"?) masquerading as answers to the first question ("What does it say"?) are usually easy to spot and quickly corrected. For example, on the cross Jesus uttered the words, "My God, my God, why have you forsaken me"? (Matt. 27:46=Mark 15:34). How many sermons have you heard about how the sin of the world on Jesus was so enormous that God had to turn away from him at that moment? The assumption behind that interpretation is that Jesus is crying out in despair in the utter loneliness of that hour. While that is certainly a possible interpretation (second question) of those words, we need to be clear that that is not what the text actually says (first question). Other interpretations of Jesus' words are possible, and if we assume what the text does not say (that God forsook Jesus in that moment), we may miss what Jesus actually *meant* (second question). For example, another possible meaning of his words is that Jesus is quoting the opening line of Psalm 22. In doing this, his purpose, far from expressing his belief that God had forsaken him, would have been to let those around him know that this Messianic Psalm referred to him. Challenging an assumption about the meaning of a familiar passage will often lead us back to what it actually says and open up possibilities we had not considered before. Only after this second question, "What did it mean"?, has been answered are we ready for the third and final one, "What does it mean"?[14]

---

the Text That Are Not There.

14   See F. LaGard Smith, *Cultural Church*, 151. He points out that "proper application always follows proper exegesis." Exegesis involves looking at the historical and literary context. "Get the context wrong, and you're bound to miss the point." In other words, if we get the second question wrong we are likely to get the third one wrong as well and, therefore, misapply the biblical text to our current situation.

What Does It Mean? This is the *hermeneutical* or application question. It seeks to apply what a passage meant (second question) to our specific modern situation. For those of us who believe that the Bible, and more specifically the NT, is the final authority for our current beliefs and practices, quite often the result of asking the second and third questions will be essentially the same. However, in many cases the results will be different. Simply because a passage meant something in the first century does not mean there is a one-to-one correspondence to our world. Here we consider such factors as (1) the original intent of the author and/or speaker, (2) the basis or reason for the author and/or speaker's words, (3) the recipients of the author and/or speaker's words, (4) how unique or specific the situation was to which the author and/or speaker addressed his words, and (5) the significance of any differences between our situation and that of the original readers and/or hearers.

Some examples of these might be Jesus' assurance of the apostles' ability to forgive or retain the sins of others (John 20:23), sounding a trumpet when giving alms in the streets or synagogues or praying in those settings (Matt. 6:2, 5), only enrolling widows who are at least 60 years old for church work and support (I Tim. 5:9), drinking wine in certain circumstances (I Tim. 5:23), elders anointing the sick with oil (James 5:14), having all things in common in the church (Acts 2:44), taking a Jewish vow (Acts 18:18), earnestly desiring the spiritual gifts, especially prophecy (I Cor. 14:1), not forbidding the speaking in tongues (I Cor. 14:39), advice to unmarried couples not to get married (I Cor. 7:25-27), advice to widows not to remarry (I Cor. 7:39-40), or instructions that younger widows should remarry (I Tim. 5:14). Clearly the adage that "it means what it says and says what it means" is not very useful if we are trying to be disciplined in applying the Bible to our situation.[15]

Let's look at an example of the use of these three questions in a matter relating to women in the church. Many have noted that Jesus appointed only men as apostles. To them it is evidence or proof of various conclusions, but all of them have to do with justification for limiting what women may do in the church. For example, one writer used the fact that the text says that Jesus appointed men ("What does it say"?) as evidence to justify his view that women in the church today ("What does it mean"?) may not lead public prayer and baptize.[16] For another it supports the opinion ("What did it mean"?) that women are limited as leaders and "Christ chose men to have places of authority in the church."[17] Two others related it to the doctrine of male spiritual leadership in the Bible ("What did it mean"?).[18] Finally, another saw it as a part of a biblical pattern of God's using men only for "the revelation, proclamation, and preservation of His Word" ("What did it mean"?).[19]

The point here is not to quibble with these interpretations, but to make it clear that they *are* interpretations, not what the text actually says. All these interpretations, though not uniform, go in the same direction and seem to be based on a common assumption not found in the text. That assumption is that the reason Jesus chose only men to be apostles was because it has always been God's intent that men lead and women follow. This means that Jesus was not at liberty to choose any women, if he was to be faithful to his Father's will. What this assumption fails to recognize is that the biblical

---

15   See also in chapter two the section on **7. Asking Modern Questions of the NT** for cautions relating to this third question dealing with the modern application of the Bible.

16   Burl Curtis, "Woman's Role," 15-16.

17   Phil Sanders, "Are Women Limited," 34.

18   Jay Lockhart, "Principle," 15; Flavil R. Yeakley Jr., *Why They Left*, 190.

19   Owen D. Olbright, "Women in the New Testament," 15.

text does not tell us *why* Jesus chose only men; it merely says *that* he did. In fact, the text does not make it a gender issue at all. Many other men and types of people besides women were not selected as well. Nichol, in his unique way, points out the weakness of this line of reasoning.

> The fact that there was not a woman in either of these groups is no proof that she may not do teaching, even public teaching. Had it occurred to you in this connection that there was not a Gentile in the group of the seventy, nor was there a Gentile in the school of apostles! Is it lawful to insist that because there was not a Gentile in either of the groups, it is therefore wrong for a Gentile to do teaching?[20]

So when someone asserts that women are limited in what they may do in the church in part because Jesus did not appoint any women as apostles, they are not stating what the Bible says (first question), but rather their human interpretation of what it meant (second question). Let's not put too much weight on our opinion of Jesus' intent when the text does not give us any information on that.

This current book is essentially an exegetical study of relevant biblical passages dealing with women in the church, trying to ascertain what the author or speaker originally meant. As such it is concerned primarily with the first and second questions. However, exegesis is merely an academic exercise if it does not serve the purpose of hermeneutics or modern-day application.[21] The third question will always be

---

20 *God's Woman*, 151.

21 Caselman ("Lifelines") makes this point well. Referring to modern-day application of the Bible as exposition, he writes, "Exposition is a must. Exposition is determining the proper application of the original text to our present circumstances without distorting the original intent of the message. New Testament exposition is a 20th century application of a first century message. Without application of the Bible text to life, all we have is knowledge, and '*Knowledge puffs up...*' I Corinthians 8:1. Knowledge alone doesn't impact life. Knowledge alone never compels us toward spiritual maturity. Facts are useless without application." See

in the background and sometimes will be addressed directly. It is my hope that the answers to the first two questions suggested in this book will help the reader answer the third for himself/herself.

---

also Osburn, *Reclaiming the Ideal*, 104: "The ancient meaning is not an end in itself, but must be brought to bear upon contemporary culture in a responsible way."

CHAPTER FOUR

The Creation Narrative

*M*ost Bible-based books and articles on the topic of
women in the church begin or at least concentrate
on key NT passages in Paul's writings. This is not surprising,
because no other biblical texts have had as much influence on
the position and role of women in the church as have Paul's.
Yet Paul's teachings are merely the end of a long biblical trajectory that goes all the way back to the creation of the first
humans. Further, Christianity did not begin with Paul, but
rather with Jesus Christ. Does it not seem reasonable to touch
base with Jesus before camping on Paul? This current study
will, therefore, begin with the creation story in Genesis 1-3,
move to Jesus, and finally deal with Paul.

There are at least three reasons for beginning in Genesis.
First, Jesus and Paul both draw on the creation account in
Genesis in their comments on men and women.[1] A correct
understanding of what the Genesis text actually says and what
it meant in its own context (the first two questions discussed
in chapter three) is an essential prerequisite to properly interpreting Jesus and Paul's uses of the Genesis account.

Secondly, among modern writers who do deal directly
with the Genesis account of human origins, there is a great
deal of disagreement on the interpretation of certain elements
of the text and their relevance to the question of women in the
church. For example, what, if anything, is implied by the fact

---

1   See, e.g., Matt. 19:4-5=Mark 10:6-8, I Cor. 11:8-9, II Cor. 11:3,
Gal. 3:28, Eph. 5:31, and I Tim. 2:13-14.

that Eve was fashioned from Adam's side as opposed to from the earth, as Adam was, or that Eve was given to Adam as his helper or that Adam "named" his wife? What one person sees as implied escapes another, and this reminds us that inferences are in the eye of the beholder.[2] To prevent us from drawing firm conclusions not justified by the text itself, it is imperative that we base them on what the passage actually says, rather than on what we think it implies.

This suggests the third reason for beginning with Genesis. It is an unfortunate circumstance that not a few studies on Genesis 1-3 introduce foreign terminology or concepts, such as "male spiritual leadership" or "designated spiritual protector," that are simply not found in the text. A careful examination of these chapters will quickly expose these inventions for what they are, so they can be disposed of when they reappear in NT discussions of women in the church.

One final point needs to be made before beginning an analysis of the Genesis text. In an effort to limit our study to what Genesis 1-3 says and meant in its own context, we must be careful not to introduce ideas that come from a later time, even NT times. Consequently, we will defer consideration of important NT references to the creation account to chapter five, where we can examine them in their own context. NT interpretations of OT texts are certainly relevant to us, but frequently they answer the third question, not one of the first two. Note, for example, as one of very many examples that could be cited, Hos. 11:1 and its use in Matt. 2:15. Matthew assigns an additional meaning to Hos. 11:1, answering the third question for his readers (what does it mean?), without denying the original meaning (what did it mean?). In the current chapter we are concerned with answering that second question to provide a proper foundation for considering the third later.

2　On the limitations and personal nature inherent in inferences, see Thomas Campbell's Proposition 6 in *Declaration and Address*, 46.

Examination of the Text

Prior to the Fall: Gen. 1:26-2:25

GENESIS I AND 2 PRESENT TWO COMPLEMENTARY accounts of the creation of humankind. There is an essential unity between the two, but the perspective is different.[3] Both use the word "humankind" or "man" ('adam), though differently. In Genesis 1 the word refers to both male and female, but in chapter 2 it designates a particular male individual. Further, both chapters discuss the origin of humankind as both male and female. Finally, each chapter presents male and female in relationship with each other, rather than as men and women in general.

First Account of Creation of Humans: Gen. 1:26-31. In contrast with the second account of human origins, this first account is notable for how straightforward it is and, therefore, how little disagreement it has elicited among its interpreters. Both the male and the female comprise humankind ('adam) without any further distinctions.[4] Both are created (bara') in God's image and after His likeness without any additional details as to the method or order.[5] Both are blessed (bērak) by

---

3   For a discussion of how the two narratives work together, despite their differences, see Rick Marrs, "In the Beginning," 4. On the unity of Gen. 1 and 2, see Richard M. Davidson, "Theology of Sexuality: Genesis 1-2," 12, n. 29.

4   See Marrs, "In the Beginning," 8: "In Gen. 1, male and female appear simultaneously with no mention of superiority or subordination." Davidson ("Theology of Sexuality: Genesis 1-2") notes that in Gen. 1 "there is no hint of ontological or functional superiority or inferiority between male and female." (7) He states further that " In Gen. 1:27 the generic term for humankind (ha'adam) includes both male and female.... The holistic picture of humankind is only complete when both male and female are viewed together." (8)

5   Marrs (*Embracing,* 39) captures this point well. "God has freely chosen to image himself not in one form, but in two—male and female. It is *humankind* that is created in the image of God." Everett Ferguson (*Women in the Church,* 61) puts it this way: "Genesis 1:26-27 establishes

God with the charge to populate the earth.[6] Finally, both are given specific dominion over all the various elements of God's creation on earth.[7] None of the many subsequent distinctions between men and women in specific situations or relationships come from this passage. Here they are merely male and female.[8] Note further that this text has already introduced the idea of men and women interacting with each other as couples, as the instruction to "be fruitful and multiply" (1:28) demands a sexual activity appropriately reserved to married partners.[9] Genesis 1 is not simply the story of the origin of the genders in humans; it is the story of the genders in personal relationship with each other.

Second Account of Creation of Humans: Gen. 2:4b-25

Exposition. What we now have is the beautiful story of the origin of the marriage relationship. No longer is it merely

the sexual distinction of male and female and the fundamental equality of human beings, male and female, all made in the image of God."

6   In commenting on v. 28, William W. Grasham, *Genesis 1-22*, 59) writes, "The blessing of sexual intimacy for the male and female, which is involved in procreation, is not an accident of nature or simply a biological phenomenon.... Procreation is set forth in a positive way as the divine purpose of marriage and part of God's will for man and woman, who are made in His image."

7   Owen D. Olbright ("In the Beginning," 7) makes this point succinctly: "God did not give greater rule over what He had created to men than He gave to women. The task and privilege to rule over everything was given to both men and women." Also see Katharine D. Sakenfeld, "Bane or Blessing," 224: "Both male and female participate equally in their assignment within creation. There is no dominion of male over female, but only of both together over the creation."

8   See Smith (*Men of Strength*, 33), who calls attention to "the equality between man and woman stressed in Genesis chapter 1." Also see James B. Hurley, *Man and Woman*, 206: "The interpreter may not read into the text any implications about headship, subordination or equality of the sexes."

9   Although a more thorough consideration of Jesus' allusion to Gen. 1:27 in Matt. 19:4=Mark 10:6 will occur in the next chapter, it can at least be noted here that Jesus applies the passage to married couples, not men and women in general.

alluded to in the passing reference to being fruitful and multiplying (1:28). Here it is full blown in its answer to human need for companionship (2:18, 20) and in the husband's joyous exuberance upon discovering that companion (2:23). It comes in response to the first time God concluded that something about His creation was *not* good.[10] The man was alone. He needed a helper fit for him (2:18, 20).[11] Though the text is not explicit, some have suggested reasonably that the fashioning of the woman was the crowning achievement of the creation, because in that act it went from incompleteness to completeness.[12] The man's own response was that here is a companion like him, yes even a part of him (2:23).[13] This allowed them to share an intimacy completely without shame

10 Six times in the first account of creation God noted that what He had done was good, and His conclusion about the entire effort, including the creation of male and female humans, was that it was *very* good (1:31).

11 The Hebrew word usually translated "meet" or "fit" or "suitable" (*neged*) literally means "before" (Grasham, *Genesis 1-22,* 100) or "alongside" (Speiser, *Genesis*, 17.) "The term carries with it the connotation of 'prominence' or 'being conspicuous'; but in 2:18, 20, it suggests that she 'corresponds to' the man." (Grasham, 100). See also Olbright, "In the Beginning," 8 and Rick Marrs, *Embracing, 47.*

12 Jimmy Jividen ("Glorious Woman," 149), for example, argues that the woman "was the last and most refined of all God's creation. She filled the only void that existed in God's newly created world. When God saw it was not good for man to be alone, he made woman. She is the completion of all God's plans in creation. She is the fulfillment of all that was lacking in man." See also Marrs, *Embracing,* 55 and "In the Beginning," 19 and John T. Willis, "Women in the Old Testament," 34.

13 Jon Paden ("Woman in Genesis 1-3," 20) captures this well. "The intimacy of the woman's formation from the man's rib, and not from the ground, cannot be overstated. Unlike the rest of creation, the man and the woman share the same nature.... The man recognizes in her a creature who shares his own nature ('my' bone and flesh)." See also Jay Treat ("Woman in Genesis 1-3," 7): "All the other times that a prospect had been presented, it had not proved suitable as a partner. But this time, at last, he has found a partner—the flesh of his flesh and bone of his bone."

(2:25).

Verse 24 is not a part of the narrative, but rather the author's comment about its significance.[14] Many have noted the oddity of applying this to a man leaving his family when he takes a wife, rather than a woman leaving hers, as was customary in the patriarchal society when this was written.[15] What the text says is clear enough; what it meant is not.

William Grasham's comments are the most helpful and plausible I have found.[16] If his interpretation is the correct one, it would be hard to overstate the elevated status on which God places human marriage. Grasham observes that in a patriarchal society the wife had already left her family when she married. God's requirement here is that the husband must do the same. In ancient society, much different from Western society in more modern times, a son's duty to his family was superseded only by his duty to God. God's intent in 2:24, however, is the shocking requirement that someone else, a man's wife, must now come before his parents. "While the husband must still honor his parents (Ex. 20:12; Deut. 5:16), he must now put his wife ahead of them." In this context, the force of the final words of verse 24 ("and they become one flesh") charges through. "Becoming one flesh with a spouse creates a bond closer than blood kinship, and the two find completion and fulfillment in their lives in a way that no other human relationship provides." What an exalted view of marriage!

From what the text of chapter two actually *says*, not what

---

14 Jesus attributes these words to the Creator Himself (Matt. 19:5).

15 For example, see Paul Watson, ("Exegesis of Genesis 2:24," 4): "This does not seem to square with the patriarchal customs of ancient Israel, whereby the wife broke far more completely from her family than the husband did from his." Marrs (*Embracing,* 47) similarly calls attention to the fact that "later social customs typically reflect a practice in which the woman left her family to join her husband's family." See also Jeanene Reese, *Bound and Determined,* 25.

16 *Genesis 1-22,* 105-08.

some have suggested it *implies*, two conclusions stand out. First, the entire focus of chapter two is on a husband and wife, not on men and women in general. Second, no hierarchy in the relationship of this married couple is in evidence. Pointing to the first is the fashioning of the woman to address an individual man's loneliness, the intimacy of the actual shaping of the woman from the one who was to be her husband, the man's delight at having his own companion, and the author's concluding application of all of this to future husbands and wives, including their sexual intimacy. The second conclusion has become more problematic in the interpretive history of this passage, not because of what the text actually says or does not say, but because of what certain interpreters say it implies. As noted earlier, what one person sees as implied escapes another, and this reminds us that inferences are in the eye of the beholder. Nevertheless, these suggested implications deserve to be noted and examined.

Examination of Proposed Reasons for Interpreting Genesis 2 Hierarchically.[17] Those who believe that from the beginning (before the fall) God intended man to be the leader generally support their convictions by implications they draw in one or more of the following areas: (1) *order* of creation, (2) *source* of creation, (3) *purpose* of creation, or (4) *naming* of the creatures.

Order of creation.[18] *It is argued that the man was created before the woman, which implies that he will be over her.* Were this the case, then the animals would be over man, but instead

---

17   See William J. Webb (*Slaves,* 127-31) for a balanced discussion of these issues.
18   The meaning of I Tim. 2:13 ("Adam was formed first, then Eve") will be discussed in chapter five. It is not a part of our consideration here, since the current chapter is concerned solely with what the Genesis text says and what it meant in its own setting, without interjecting opinions about how Genesis is used by later writers. This will come in due course.

man was given dominion over all the animals (1:26). You cannot have it both ways, that is, argue man's supremacy over the animals as the crowning and final act of creation while at the same time asserting the man's supremacy over the woman because he was created first. Note also the striking degree to which priority of appearance is no indication of ultimate status in the book of Genesis. Consider Cain, Abel and Seth; Isaac and Ishmael; Jacob and Esau; Rachel and Leah; Judah's sons; Ephraim and Manasseh; and Joseph and his brothers. Such an inference about dominion necessarily or even usually flowing from priority of appearance just does not work in Genesis.

Source of creation.[19] *It is argued that the woman was fashioned from the man, which implies his position over her.* On the contrary, note that the man was formed from "dust of the ground" (2:7). Who would argue that the earth is somehow over the man? Certainly after the fall, the man's relationship with the ground will become problematic because it is cursed (3:17-19), but that was not the case from the beginning. Far from indicating the woman's subordination, the fact that she was made for companionship with her husband (2:18, 20) and came from his side (2:21) suggests that intimacy between the man and the woman is the real point, not status relative to each other. How many times in Christian weddings have we heard this beautiful poem attributed to John Wesley:

> *Not from his head he woman took*
> *And made her husband to o'erlook;*
> *Not from his feet, as one designed*
> *The footstool of the stronger kind;*
> *But fashioned for himself a bride;*
> *An equal, taken from his side.*

---

19   Just as with I Tim. 2:13 above, opinions about the meaning of I Cor. 11:8 ("for man/husband is not out of woman/wife, but woman/wife out of man/husband") will be deferred to the next chapter.

Purpose of creation. *It is argued that the fact that the woman was created to be the man's helper implies her subordination to him.* This is such a curious notion, because all that is necessary to dismiss it is a simple concordance study of the Hebrew word translated "helper" (2:18, 20) (*'ezer*).[20] The word is used 19 other places in the OT, 15 of which refer to God, including all the 11 occurrences in the Psalms. Typical is Ps. 121:1-2: "I lift up my eyes to the hills; where does my help come from? My help comes from the Lord, who made heaven and earth." Are we to conclude that God is to be subordinate to us because he is our helper? Such an idea borders on absurdity, so much so that one wonders how such a distorted view of this word should ever have arisen. Rather, Moses' point relates to companionship. God noted that something was missing—"it is not good that the man should be alone"—and he gave him someone "fit for him" in a way none of the animals could be (2:19-22). Again, intimacy, not status, is the point.

Naming of the creatures. *It is argued that generally the leader names those under him, not the other way around. The man named the animals, over which he had dominion; so it was in giving the woman her name.* Aside from the fact that this interjects a notion into the text that is totally absent, what we have in 2:23 rather than a formal naming is a spontaneous expression of joy. Now at last here is someone like me ("bone of my bones and flesh of my flesh"). She is no less than my counterpart![21] This is indicated by the words for the two in

---

20   Where the notion could have come from, other than what the interpreter himself brought to the text, is a mystery. Even Smith (*Men of Strength*, 30-31) rejects it. See Ferguson (*Women in the Church*, 61): "'Helper' (Gen. 2:18) is 'one who gives help or support,' in this case a companion complementary to the man. Hence, there is a mutual relationship resulting from the undesirability of man being alone. No subordination is implied." Also see Jay Guin, *Buried Talents*, 32-35.

21   In discussing the man's naming of the animals (2:20) and the "naming" of the woman (2:23), Marrs (*Embracing*: 47) points out that "a close reading of the text shows that the grammatical construction

the verse: "man" (*'ish*) and "woman" (*'ishshah*). The formal naming of his wife occurs after the fall (3:20).

Thus, to repeat the earlier-stated conclusion, (1) the entire focus of chapter 2 is on a husband and wife, not on men and women in general and (2) no hierarchy in the relationship of this married couple is in evidence.

The Fall and Aftermath: Gen. 3:1-24

AN UNFORTUNATE FEATURE OF THE PROLIFERATION OF studies on Genesis 1-3 in the last several decades has been the introduction of numerous elements into the discussion that are either foreign to the text or are inconsistent with it. The culture wars over the role of women in the world and in the church that came to a head in the last third of the twentieth century have significantly colored the way in which commentators on both sides of the question have interpreted these foundational biblical chapters. It is impossible to escape the conclusion that far too often what a writer brings to the text is as influential on his/her interpretation as the text itself, often more. We saw this to an extent in connection with Genesis 2, but in chapter 3 it builds to a crescendo, reaching its climax in meanings assigned to 3:16.

This verse has become the crux for interpreting the account of the fall and aftermath in chapter three, and the views expressed are legion. It has become ground zero in the conflict over the impact of the Genesis creation account on the matter of women in the church. In the last 50 years or so it has been interpreted and reinterpreted ad infinitum, ad nauseam. As Gen. 3:16 goes, so goes the war. The verse has been so picked apart that one wonders if there is anything

---

changes between the two namings. When Adam names the animals, the grammatical construction reflects the traditional construction of defining, ordering, and controlling. When Adam names the woman, the grammatical construction changes and the element of exclamation appears." On this see also Webb, *Slaves,* 116-17 and Mary Evans, *Woman in the Bible,* 16.

that can be said about it for certain. Here are some of the questions that have emerged in the discussion: (1) whether it reflects a curse or punishment or consequence or natural result of sin, (2) whether it is prescriptive or descriptive, (3) whether the source of the consequences is God Himself or the natural result of their sin, (4) the interconnection among the three elements of the verse, (5) the meaning of "desire," and (6) the meaning of "rule."[22] All these will be considered in due course, but first, as always, it is important to address what the text actually says about the fall and its multiple consequences.

Exposition

Temptation and Disobedience. **(3:1-7)** The serpent's temptation of the woman involved the trickery ("the serpent was more crafty," 3:1) of changing God's command by only one word (from "you will surely die" to "you will *not* surely die") and adding the enticement of becoming like God by obtaining knowledge that only He had (3:1-5). Of the three characteristics of the fruit that drew her, it was "that it was to be desired to make one wise" that was the real temptation (3:6). Beauty and desirability for food were features of all the fruit trees in the garden (2:9). The writer ascribes none of this temptation to her husband. The text simply says that she gave him some of the fruit and he ate it. This experience of disobedience brought to them a knowledge they had not had before—that they were naked (3:7), unlike their previous state (2:25).

Confrontation by God. **(3:8-13)** After his sin, the pros-

---

22 See Marrs, "In the Beginning," 29 for a similar list of what he calls "difficulties and ambiguity which defy resolution." "1) What is the precise syntax of v. 16? What is the relationship of 16a to 16b? 2) How should v. 16b be translated? 3) What is the intended nuance and meaning of 'desire'? 4) How is this statement related to Gen 2? 5) What is the hermeneutical significance of this statement"?

pect of a further encounter with God also brought the man something he had not experienced before—fear (3:10), and it caused them to hide. Here also, for the first time since the formation of the woman, the man is singled out in the narrative.[23] "And the Lord God called to the man, and said to him...." (3:9)[24] God did not address the woman, the first to sin, at this point, nor both of them together, the reason for which the writer does not explain. At this point the blame game begins. The man tries to deflect the culpability from himself to his companion and by extension to God Himself (3:13). Now for the first time the woman has a solo direct encounter with God, and she tries to blame that crafty creature (3:1), the serpent, for deceiving her.

The Consequences. **(3:14-19)** Three general points deserve attention before looking at how God responded to each party: (1) curse or no curse,? (2) one or more punishments for each party,? and (3) "because you have."

Curse or no curse? One of the first things a careful reading of the text reveals is that there are only two curses in Genesis 3, and neither of them is on the woman or the man. Only the serpent (3:14) and the ground (3:17) are cursed (*'arar*), although the curse on the ground is for the man's sake. This is in stark contrast with much of the literature on this passage, where the word "curse" is thrown around in places where the writer never put it, especially with reference to the man and the woman. It is also an excellent example of how even normally careful interpreters impose their prior under-

---

23   Earlier Gen. 2:24 is written from the man's standpoint, but it is technically not a part of the narrative, but rather a follow up to the man's response to the woman in 2:23 and is oriented toward the future.
24   Unlike in chapter 1, *'adam* (man) refers to the male person as distinct from the woman in chapters 2 and 3. This is further seen in the pronoun, "to him," in 3:9. Note also how in their post-fall state the man is singled out for expulsion from the garden, not both of them (3:22-24). It is the one taken from the ground (3:23).

standing on the text to the detriment of recognizing what it actually says. So what do we call what happened to this couple as a result of their sin? "Consequence" probably has the least baggage associated with it and is widely used in the literature. "Punishment" is also faithful to the text, because it is God's response to their sin. To the woman God said, "I will greatly multiply your pain in childbearing...." (3:16) and to the man, "because you have..., cursed is the ground for your sake...." (3:17)

One or more than one punishment for each party? This issue has to do with whether the different elements of the consequences of the sin for each party are tied together or are independent punishments. Rick Marrs notes that "presently, the majority of scholars envision one punishment per party" but confesses that a decisive answer to how this relates to 3:16 "eludes us."[25] What does seem clear, though, is that the three elements of 3:16 make much better sense taken together than they do as independent consequences. Given the intensity of pain and perhaps even the great danger of death in childbirth, a wife might forego sexual intimacy with her husband, even to the point of disrupting God's original intent that humankind "be fruitful and multiply and fill the earth" (1:28). Her desire for her husband will override that instinct, but it will also include rulership over her by the one for whom she has the desire.[26]

"Because you have." In the case of the serpent and the man, God confronted them with the accusation, "because you have" (3:14, 17), but He did not with the woman. With the serpent His grievance was no more specific than "because you have done this." (3:14) With the man, however, God specified two aspects of his disobedience, one the actual disobedience ("you

25   "In the Beginning," 29 and n. 76.
26   On this see also ibid., 32 and *Embracing*: 52 and Irvin A. Busenitz, "Woman's Desire," 207-08.

have eaten of the tree of which I commanded you, 'you shall not eat of it'") and the other what led to it ("you have listened to the voice of your wife") (3:17). The fact that God did not specify the woman's sin has opened the door to speculation that goes beyond anything that the author actually wrote.[27] What is clear is that she knew of God's commandment not to eat of a certain tree (3:3) but that she succumbed to the temptation to be like God in knowledge and wisdom. (3:5-6).

Consequences for the serpent (3:14-15). The serpent's punishment contained the element of a curse. Henceforth he would go on his belly, eating dust (3:14). If the bruising of the serpent's head (3:15) is literal as a result of his being on his belly, then the two verses contain one punishment. If, however, the bruising of the serpent's head is figurative, as it has generally been viewed in Christian interpretation, 3:15 refers to a second punishment. Limiting ourselves to the first two questions (what does it say? and what did it mean?), there is not enough information in the text to decide.

Consequences for the man (3:17-19). As noted above, the man is not cursed directly, but the ground is cursed because of him. This is his punishment, and the vocation God had earlier given him to till the ground (2:5) or till and keep the garden (2:15) would now involve labor (the same Hebrew used of the woman in 3:16) and sweat because of the thorns and thistles the ground would bring forth.

Consequences for the woman (3:16). As noted above, the three elements of this verse are best seen as interrelated.[28]

---

27   For example, see Mike Willis ("Role of Women," 21), who asserts that part of Eve's failing was "to step outside her submissive role as wife and lead the family."

28   Busenitz ("Woman's Desire," 207) observes that in the case of both the serpent (3:14 and 3:15) and the man (3:17-19) the structure is the pronouncement of the punishment followed by an explanatory statement. It is, therefore, reasonable to conclude that the same applies to the woman in 3:16.

3:16a. In spite of the vigorous discussion in the literature over whether 3:16 is prescriptive or descriptive, observe that at least 3:16a is a punishment prescribed by God Himself ("I will greatly multiply your pain...."). The consequence of the woman's sin is more *pain* in childbearing, not the childbearing itself, because that was already a part of God's plan, as He indicated in His blessing to "be fruitful and multiply" (1:28). The word for "pain" (*'issabon*) is the same one translated "labor" in the judgment on the man in 3:17, an apt descriptor for the birthing experience.

3:16b. The key issue in this part of the verse is the meaning of "desire" (*tešuqah*), a word used elsewhere in the OT only in Gen. 4:7 and Song of Sol. 7:11(10). Though some find Gen. 4:7 as the closer parallel for deciding the word's meaning in 3:16b,[29] its use in the Song of Solomon of a bridegroom's desire for his bride comes much closer to the context of 3:16b.[30] Hence, the most reasonable interpretation of the nuance of "desire" in 3:16b is the woman's sexual desire for her husband.[31]

3:16c. In commenting on the phrase, "and he will rule over you," Marrs perceptively observes "not unexpectedly, how this passage is utilized in subsequent portions of Scripture

29   For example, Susan T. Foh,"Woman's Desire," 383 and Hurley, *Man and Woman,* 219.

30   See Janson C. Condren ("Battle of the Sexes," 227-45) for a detailed critique of Foh's article. Busenitz ("Woman's Desire," 211) presents three solid reasons for preferring the meaning in Song of Sol. 7:11 to Gen. 4:7: (1) the meaning is clear in Song of Sol. 7:11, whereas it is obscure in Gen. 4:7; (2) "desire" in Gen. 3:16 and Song of Sol. 7:11 has a literal meaning, whereas it is figurative in Gen. 4:7, and (3) both Gen. 3:16 and Song of Sol. 7:11 involve the relationship with the opposite sex, whereas Gen. 4:7 does not. Also see Richard M. Davidson, "Theology of Sexuality: Genesis 3," 129 and n. 27 and John J. Schmitt, "Like Eve, Like Adam," 6-7, n. 24.

31   So Marrs, "In the Beginning," 31 and *Embracing,* 56. The medieval rabbinic biblical commentator Rashi took the word as a desire "for intimacy" with her husband, which in context clearly refers to sexual intimacy (Eruv. 100b). See also Gilbert Bilezikian, *Beyond Sex Roles,* 55 and n. 12.

impacts greatly our reading of it in its original setting."[32] Opinions among the legion of interpreters of these words are so far reaching that simple exegesis in the context (i.e., asking the questions what does it say? and what did it mean?) does not exhaust the possibilities. Consequently, as with the rest of this chapter, the exposition here will be limited to the context, saving until the next chapter such issues as whether it is prescriptive or descriptive, to whom it applies in the rest of the OT, how it may or may not be used in the NT, and the extent to which it represents God's permanent will for the future husband-wife relationship. Answers to some of these questions may help us come back to 3:16 later and obtain greater clarity, but they cannot help us with the interpretation within the creation narrative itself, because they would necessarily add something not found in the text.

From an exegetical standpoint, the key issue in 3:16c is the meaning of "rule" (*masal*). By far the majority of interpreters rightly follow this meaning of the word,[33] but two minority opinions deserve mention. They are dealt with in ***Excursus 3: Alternative Interpretations of the Meaning of the Hebrew Word* Masal** below. That discussion finds the evidence for them lacking, leaving us with the widely attested meaning, "rule." God, in this verse, is telling the woman that her husband will rule over her.

Conclusions

GENESIS 1-3 TELLS THE STORY OF PARADISE GAINED AND paradise lost for the first married couple. The narrative moves from joint vocation without gender distinction (chapter one)

---

32   "In the Beginning," 33.
33   See the standard English language Hebrew lexicon, Brown, *Hebrew and English Lexicon*, 605b. Here the editors list 38 examples of the type of construction found in Gen. 3:16c and provide the definition "*rule, have dominion* over."

to companionship in paradise (chapter two) to the ugly effects of sin as that companionship is damaged and the gender distinction enters the relationship (chapter three). The text does offer a brief glimpse of the impact of the story on future humankind ("have dominion over…"—1:26, 28; "fill the earth and subdue it"—1:28; "therefore a man leaves his father and his mother…"—2:24). However, the story as it stands in Genesis 1-3 is one of a specific married couple and the effect on *them*. Subsequent biblical writers will return to this narrative and draw conclusions about its impact on future persons (answering the question, what *does* it mean?), but the writer of these chapters in Genesis does not, with the exception of the verses noted above. What is abundantly clear is that the entire narrative refers to a married couple, not to men and women in general. We must not lose sight of this fact as we move in chapter five to how Genesis 1-3 is used in the NT.

***Excursus 3: Alternative Interpretations of the Meaning of the Hebrew Word* Masal.**

To be like. Two alternative meanings to the prevailing definition of *masal* as "to rule" have been offered in the literature. First, John Schmitt has suggested that *masal* be read "to be like, similar," one of the three distinct meanings of the Hebrew root *msl*.[34] In this case 3:16c would be translated "and he will be like you [having such a desire]." Thus Schmitt would have God telling the woman that her sexual desire for her husband would be reciprocated. Schmitt's argument is very technical, is dependent on what would be an unusual linguistic construction in the original Hebrew, and has not been widely received. Richard Davidson's afore-mentioned article

---

34 "Like Eve, Like Adam," 1-22.

on Genesis 3 provides a useful critique of Schmitt's article.[35]

Harsh rule. A few interpreters assign a meaning to "rule" (*masal*) in Gen. 3:16c that involves a domineering, even sinful, harshness.[36] A blog by David Tarbet[37] lays out the evidence and reasoning for this conclusion. The argument begins with the premise that in Genesis 2 God assigned Adam "authority as protector and leader of his family" (something that is found nowhere in chapter two). Thus since Adam already had headship over Eve before the fall, "rule" in 3:16c must mean something other than headship. It indicates "the kind of rule which involves force, conflict or compulsion." Tarbet further describes it as "coercive, oppressive, self-centered and cruelty, causing woman pain." His evidence for this far-reaching conclusion is the fact that the Septuagint translates "rule" (*masal*) with the Greek word *kurieuō*, "which Jesus used to refer to pagan rulers who '**lord it over**' others (Luke 22:25)." The methodology of defining a Hebrew word by one Greek translation of it supported by a single example of it in the NT is questionable, to say the least.

Does *masal* necessarily "indicate the kind of rule which involves force, conflict or compulsion," as Tarbet suggests? Certainly not. A concordance study of the Hebrew verb in the OT shows that *masal* has a wide range of meanings, some of which are the opposite of the nuances Tarbet ascribes to it.[38] Note a few examples. In II Sam. 23:3 it refers to a king ruling justly with reverence for God. In Prov. 17:2 it refers metaphorically to the wise, compassionate "rule" of a slave over a son who acts shamefully. In Isa. 63:19 God's rule is seen in contrast with that of Israel's adversaries. In Zech. 6:13 it

---

35   "Theology of Sexuality: Genesis 3," 127, n. 18.
36   For example, Melvin D. Curry, "Male and Female," 180.
37   "Involvement of Men and Women," April 2013, 3.
38   See Robert D. Culver, "*Mashal* III," 534: "*Mashal* usually received the translation 'to rule,' but the precise nature of the rule is as various as the real situations in which the action or state so designated occur."

refers to the rule of "the Branch" who "will sit and rule upon his throne." Finally in Isa. 40:10, it refers to the good news of the Lord God as He shepherds His people.

> O Jerusalem, herald of good tidings, lift it up, fear not; say to the cities of Judah, "Behold your God." Behold, the Lord God comes with might, and his arm *rules* [*masal*] for him; behold, his reward is with him, and his recompense before him. He will feed his flock like a shepherd; he will gather the lambs in his arms; he will carry them in his bosom and gently lead those that are with young. (40:9b-11 -- RSV)

Next, what about the other places where the Septuagint translates *masal* by the Greek word *kurieuō*? *Kurieuō* is used 30 times in the canonical part of the Septuagint, and half of them render the Hebrew word *masal*. Certainly there are times where the rule in view was probably oppressive (e.g., Judg. 9:2, 15:11; Ps. 106 (105):41; Isa. 3:12, 19:4; Lam. 5:8; Dan. 11:3). In others the rule is neutral, and once God Himself is the ruler (II Chron. 20:6). The common thread through all of these instances is that *kurieuō* has to do with being in authority over someone, especially as a king or ruler over a nation or people. The character of that exercise of authority is entirely determined by the context.

This brings us to *kurieuō* in the NT. In addition to the example Tarbet cites in Luke 22:25, *kurierō* is used six times in the NT. In Rom. 6:9, 14 and 7:1 it is used metaphorically of the rule of death, sin, and the Law. In I Tim. 6:15 it is used in the usual sense found in the Septuagint of the exercise of authority by someone in a formal position of rulership. In II Cor. 1:24 Paul uses it of his refraining from lording it over the Corinthians' faith. Finally, in Rom. 14:9 it refers to Christ's lordship of both the dead and living. Thus, as with *masal* in the OT, *kurieuō* has a diverse range of meaning with the specific nuance in each case determined by the context. In his article in the *Theological Dictionary of the New Testament*, Werner Foerster defines the word as "to be or become *kyrios*" ["lord," GB] or "to act as *kyrios.*" Of the usage in Luke 22:25, Tarbet's example, he writes, "The reference here is to the use of power as such (not its misuse)."[39]

From all of this it is clear that neither the Hebrew word *masal* in the OT, nor the Greek word *kurieuō* in either the Septuagint or the NT carry with them any of the negative traits Tarbet ascribes to them in Gen. 3:16. They describe the exercise of authority or power associated with ruling, such as that done by a king, without making any value judgment about the manner of that rule.

Excursus 4: F. LaGard Smith's Treatment of the Creation Narrative in Genesis 1-3. This chapter has been an attempt to treat Genesis 1-3 exegetically without engaging in an extended dialog with those who have come to different conclusions. This excursus is different. It deals with F. LaGard Smith's treatment of the creation narrative as he develops it in the first three chapters of his *Men of Strength for Woman of God.* The reasons for this are twofold. First, in recent decades perhaps no book written by a member of the Churches of Christ has been as influential in defending the traditional limitations of women in the church as this one. This is certainly the case with his development of human beginnings in the garden. Terminology he creates and ideas he develops crop up in other people's writings to a significant degree.[40] Secondly, Smith's work provides an excellent example of a different methodology for dealing with the biblical text than the one proposed in chapter three of this book and followed in the current chapter. This excursus, then, will offer an examination of both Smith's method and certain of his conclusions that flow from it.[41]

---

39   "κυριεύω," 1097.
40   For example see Yeakley, *Why They Left,* 189-90, where he applies the "principle" of "male spiritual leadership" to women's conduct in Christian assemblies.
41   For a balanced, though critical, treatment of Smith's fuller de-

Although this excursus is a critique of Smith's discussion of the creation narrative, it must be noted at the outset that at a number of points his work is to be commended. Here are some of those strengths of his study.

1. It is obvious that Smith has read and digested a healthy amount of the literature on this passage. Much of what he writes is a dialogue with those with whom he disagrees and at numerous points his rejection of their positions is justified.

2. He recognizes the importance of starting with Genesis, rather than Paul. "Focusing on only a few key passages in the New Testament can distort the overall picture and cloud our conclusions." (17) He speaks of "retracing history to a point in time before any patriarchal structure existed, before any custom and culture whatever had developed— back to Creation and the first man and woman. It is there that our journey begins." (18)

3. In his analogy of the barricades in the play *Les Miserables* he captures many of the arguments on both sides of the question, though it more closely reflects the discussion in the larger culture than in the Churches of Christ. (10-15)

4. He rightly draws a distinction between speculation and what God has told us, i.e., "the known facts of Creation regarding the first man and woman." (29-30) (Unfortunately, as the book progresses he engages in a great deal of speculation and does not appear to feel at all limited to drawing conclusions only from what the text actually says.)

5. He is aware of the difficulty of reading a familiar biblical passage with fresh eyes. "In trying to understand the implications to be drawn from the story of Creation, we

---

velopment of his hermeneutical methodology in *Cultural Church*, see Jeffery S. Stevenson, *All People, All Times,* chapter 15.

are likely to see in the Genesis account what we have always believed. Tradition has a way of putting colored glasses over our eyes, so that we miss details we've never seen before." (39)

6. He does not fall into the modern trap of defining the Hebrew word for "helper" (2:18, 20) by what the English word means in some contexts.[42] He rejects the notion that the application of the word to Eve implies her inferiority. Smith sees Eve as on Adam's level "of equal position, not inferior." (30-1)

7. His contention seems right that more than just the reality of physical death came on this couple after the fall. (54-56) The man (3:17-19) and woman's (3:16) situation was different after the fall, and it came from God as a punishment for their sin. There is more than description here. Something changed, and God was the source of that change.

8. In "Same Text, Different Interpretation" he rightly rejects some of the more extreme interpretations of Gen. 3:16. (56-58)

In spite of these strengths, Smith's treatment of the creation narrative is seriously flawed because of his methodology for interpreting the biblical text. Rather than being an exegetical study, his methodology follows his training as a trial lawyer (39) who is forced to offer his own speculation to answer questions the evidence is incapable of answering. He even describes how as a law professor he taught his students the skill of formulating persuasive arguments to support a certain interpretation of the evidence (52-3).[43] Smith's chap-

---

42   See, for example, Coffman, *1 and 2 Corinthians*, 241; Dave Miller, "Role of Women," 22; and Charles Jones, "Genesis 2:18-25," 305.

43   I am quite familiar with this method of arguing a case, having spent four years on the intercollegiate debate team at one of our Christian colleges. At a typical debate tournament my partner and I would

ter three on Genesis 3 is even structured along the lines of a courtroom trial. This is not to say there is anything wrong with using such an extended analogy in the chapter. It actually made it rather interesting. But it underscores the fact that Smith repeatedly uses this method in his interpretation of Genesis 1-3. His sentences are liberally sprinkled with words like "possibly," "probably," "if," "clue," "may," "might," "guess," "hypothesize," "appear," "might tend," "speculate" and other qualifiers that enable him to suggest possibilities where the text is silent. These "possibilities," however, are piled on top of one another and in certain key cases are returned to as solid enough to establish other speculative points. The end result is the importation into the text of terminology and ideas that are not there but are treated as if they were.

While there are numerous individual questionable features of Smith's overall argument that flow from his methodology, attention here will be limited to the three on which he hangs most of the weight of his conclusions. They are (1) the phrase "male spiritual leadership," (2) the "principle of firstborn," and (3) Adam's role as "designated spiritual protector" of his wife. In his discussion they are deeply intertwined and interdependent. For that reason, it is difficult to treat here one without the other. Nevertheless, to provide as much clarity as possible, they will be dealt with individually, starting with the one most closely associated with Smith—male spiritual leadership.

Male Spiritual Leadership. Smith begins his discussion by acknowledging that the phrase "is not found in Scripture" but is his own creation "to summarize the many passages

argue the affirmative of the proposition at 9:00 a.m., defend the negative at 10:30 a.m. and return to the affirmative right after lunch, all with the same fervor and conviction of the rightness of our case. It can be a highly effective technique for "proving" a point and persuading others of a certain position. In the hands of a skillful practitioner it can also mask the truth.

which call for men to be in positions of either headship in the home or functional leadership in the church." (16-17) Here he does not explain why he interjects the word "spiritual" into the phrase, but in the next chapter he presents his rationale. He does it by connecting it with his so called "principle of firstborn,' which he says has "more to do with the spiritual than the material realm," referring to the consecration of the firstborn in Ex. 13:1-2. He then jumps to Abel's sacrifice of some of the "firstborn" of his flock as a way of introducing the principle of the firstborn into the creation story. To round off this circuitous argument he refers, without any justification in the text itself, to "Cain's role of spiritual leadership as firstborn son." (34) With this clever move Smith has been able to use Exodus 13 to justify the insertion of the word "spiritual" into the phrase "male leadership," creating a new concept, and interjecting it into the creation story. As bizarre as this argument may seem, this so-called principle will continue to grow and morph into something much more than this and become a faulty premise upon which much of his total argument rests.

Principle of Firstborn. Smith is able to import this foreign "principle" into the Genesis creation narrative by proposing that it is parallel to Adam's position as first created. He writes, "We are drawn, then, to the temporal priority of man's creation as being parallel with the principle of firstborn that is proclaimed later in the Bible." (33) In the next two pages he discusses several examples of his principle later in the OT, finally bringing them to bear on Adam with this statement.

> Adam's status as "firstcreated" suggests similar implications as with his "firstborn" successors—that is, that responsibility for family leadership befell Adam; that family headship was on his shoulders; that the guarantee of spiritual heritage to unborn generations should flow from his special consecration before God as the "firstcreated." (35-36)

It does not take a great deal of sophisticated critical thinking to recognize what Smith has done here. First, he has only stated but not proved that Adam's priority of creation is parallel to all the baggage associated with firstborn status in the rest of the Bible. After all, Adam was not born, and to connect "the principle of firstborn" to him is to go beyond what is written in the text. Secondly, to suggest that what was true of firstborn individuals later applied to Adam in this primitive situation in the garden, as he does in the quotation above, is at the very least anachronistic. It imports elements from later passages to interpret a text from a different time in a different setting, a cardinal error in exegesis. Finally, where in the creation narrative do we read of Adam's "special consecration before God as the 'firstcreated'"? This is a total invention.

Believing that he has established this "principle" as appropriately applied to Adam, Smith can now use the point to make further arguments. Thus, he employs it to postulate a second sin by Adam, one not found in the Genesis text, that of "failing to exercise spiritual headship." (45) Later he will go even farther to state, "Even before the Fall, as the 'firstcreated' person Adam had been given the responsibility of being Eve's spiritual protector." (60) This is a perfect illustration of how a questionable insertion into the biblical text (i.e., that ideas associated with the "principle of firstborn" belong in the creation narrative) can then be used to support other conclusions based on elements also not found in the text.

Designated Spiritual Protector. To conjecture that God intended Adam to be Eve's protector Smith assumes his character as a prosecuting attorney, "speculating" from "clues." He writes

> At this point I am back to *speculating* as to who shot whom and why. With *so little hard evidence*, one can only *hypothesize* regarding all the *implications* that *might* have been intended. But there are two *obscure clues* which are

often overlooked in this most famous of all cases. (45)
[Emphasis mine]

Is it possible for three short sentences to have more dis-
claimers for having any solid evidence to go on? And yet,
this is the start of Smith's argument that Adam was Eve's
"designated spiritual protector." Here is the way the argument
continues. The "two obscure clues" he develops are (1) "God
never told Eve directly not to eat of the forbidden fruit" and
(2) "sin entered the world through one man" (Rom. 5:12).
(45-6) In fact, Smith states about his second clue that "one
should not read too much into the structure of this passage
one way or another"; nevertheless, he follows this with his own
"guess." How one gets from these clues to Adam being Eve's
protector is certainly "obscure," to say the least. His argument
continues: "it appears that Adam's sin of disobedience may
have been compounded by his failure to exercise a separate
responsibility for protecting Eve from spiritual danger."
(46) He goes on, "as 'firstcreated' Adam was the *designated
spiritual protector* of his family." Finally, this time with no
"might" or "possibly," he asserts boldly, "had Adam faithfully
exercised his role as protector, neither he nor Eve would have
succumbed to the serpent's temptation." (46) Observe that
these conclusions flow from a situation where there is "so little
hard evidence," but instead "two obscure clues." Compare all
this with what the author of the Genesis creation narrative
actually wrote, and draw your own conclusions. My own were
not difficult to reach.

Certainly Smith is an enjoyable writer to read, and who
can question his stellar skills in formulating arguments to support a case he is developing? However, this brief look at some
of his key conclusions by examining his methodology in arriving at them has highlighted the weakness of doing biblical
interpretation by postulating theories to supplement what the
biblical text actually says. Disciplined biblical interpretation
asks first what the text actually says, which leads naturally to

explaining what it meant. Smith's treatment of the Genesis creation narrative is just one example of numerous ones that could be cited on both sides of the question of women in the church where the authors do not limit their interpretation to what the biblical writer actually wrote.

CHAPTER FIVE

New Testament Use of the Genesis Creation Narrative

*C*hapter four attempted to answer the questions "what does it say?" and "what did it mean?" in the Genesis creation narrative by interpreting it exegetically in its own context. This, of course, begs the question, "what *does* it mean?", as we consider the contribution of the rest of the Bible, especially the NT, toward gaining a fuller picture of how these three chapters should be understood. Much of the use of the OT by NT writers and speakers interprets OT texts in a literal, straightforward manner. However, a number of passages use interpretive methods that draw meanings that cannot be derived solely from the OT text itself. All of this flows from an underlying belief that in addition to the literal sense, for many OT passages God intended a secondary meaning. Words like "deeper," "spiritual," "allegorical," or "mystery" are commonly used to describe this meaning behind or below the literal one. This approach to interpreting the OT is most clearly understood in light of its use in contemporary Judaism and the church fathers. When we do this, we find that their use of the OT falls well within the standard methods at that time, but that NT writers and speakers avoid some of the interpretive excesses of the time that violate what we would consider norms of reasonableness. In this chapter we will look at how these writers and speakers used and interpreted the Genesis creation narrative in passages that are relevant to the matter of women in the church.

Types of References

NT REFERENCES TO THE OT COME IN THREE FORMS: (1) direct quotations, (2) verbal allusions, and (3) non-verbal allusions. T. R. France has helpfully suggested a more precise breakdown, but it still revolves around these three.[1] Whereas direct quotations are more straightforward, allusions are not. What one interpreter sees as a clear allusion to an OT passage another may not.

What follows is my own classification of all the NT passages relevant to this study culled from 37 clear and possible references to Genesis 1-3 found in 14 NT books.[2]

Direct quotation with introductory formula: Matt. 19:4, 5

Direct quotation without introductory formula: Mark 10:6-8a; Eph. 5:31

Clear verbal allusion: Gal. 3:28; I Cor. 11:8; II Cor. 11:3; I Tim. 2:13, 14

Possible verbal allusion: I Cor. 11:7; I Tim. 2:15

Clear non-verbal allusion: I Cor. 11:9; I Tim. 2:13

Possible non-verbal allusion: I Cor. 11:3; I Cor. 14:34; I Tim. 2:12

---

1   *Jesus and the Old Testament*, 259. He subdivides direct quotations into those with and those without an introductory formula. An example of this difference is Jesus' ascribing his quotation of Gen. 2:24 to the Creator in Matt. 19:4-5 versus Mark 10:7 without ascription. He also distinguishes between verbal and non-verbal allusions by whether they are "clear" or merely "possible."

2   Because it is based on the original Greek, rather than English wording, the list of clear and possible references to Genesis 1-3 that was used is based primarily, but not entirely, on the outer margins and page 772 of Eberhard Nestle, *Novum Testamentum Graece.*

This chapter will probe the use of the Genesis creation narrative in these passages, which means that the discussion will be limited to Jesus and Paul. *Excursus 5*, which follows immediately, discusses how their interpretive methods fit into their historical and literary context.

***

Excursus 5: Jewish Interpretive Methods during the New Testament Period. In Judaism of the general period in which the NT was written, in addition to the literal interpretation, there were multiple approaches to deriving secondary or fuller meanings from OT passages, but there were three principal ones: (1) Midrashic, used by the Rabbis, (2) Allegorical, used by philosopher-theologians, and (3) Rāz-Pesher, used by the community at Qumran. This does not mean that an individual interpreter limited himself to one approach. Paul, for example, used all three.

Midrashic. *Midrash* comes from the Hebrew word *darash*, meaning "resort to" or "seek," so by extension "read repeatedly," "study," "discuss," or "expound.[3] This approach was used by the Rabbinic Judaism (the Pharisees) of Jesus and Paul's day. It was the way Paul, as a star rabbinical student, was trained to interpret the OT. The great Rabbi Hillel[4] was most closely associated with the following seven "rules" for interpreting an OT passage:[5]

1. An inference from the less important to the more important

---

3   Brown, *Hebrew and English Lexicon*, 205a.
4   Probably the leading rabbi of his day, Hillel is thought to have been either the father (Hermann L. Strack, *Introduction to the Talmud and Midrash*, 109; Emil Schürer, *History of the Jewish People*, 363, n. 164) or grandfather (C. G. Montefiore, *Rabbinic Anthology*, 155; R. Travers Herford, *Pirke Aboth*, 36) of Rabban Gamaliel I, Paul's teacher. See Acts 5:34, 22:3.
5   See Strack, *Introduction to the Talmud and Midrash*, 94.

or vice versa.

2. Inference by analogy. Verbal similarities in different passages are used to bind those passages together for the sake of interpretation.

3. Constructing a family from one main passage. In a group of passages that go together, specifics that apply to the main passage apply to all.

4. The same as #3, except that the deduction is drawn from *two* main passages.

5. General to particular or particular to general. What applies generally also applies to a particular case or what applies to a particular case applies generally.

6. Something in a similar passage aids in the interpretation of the primary one.

7. Something is inferred from the context.

We find examples of some of these interpretive principles in both Jesus[6] and Paul.[7] This should not be surprising in Jesus' case, because by going to synagogue every Sabbath and attending synagogue school, these methods of reasoning from the Bible would have been in the air he breathed. In Paul's case, we would expect to find even greater familiarity with them, since he studied under the leading rabbi of his day, a direct and recent descendant of Rabbi Hillel himself (Acts 22:3).

---

6   #1 – Matt. 12:5-6; John 7:22-23, 20:34-36. He also used the lesser to greater argument in statements where the OT was not in view: Matt. 6:26 (=Luke 12:24), 6:30, 7:11 (=Luke 11:13), 10:25b, 28; Luke 18:2-8a. #2 – Luke 20:17-18.

7   #1 – Rom. 5:15-17, 11:12, 24; II Cor. 3:7-8, 11. Like Jesus, he also used the lesser to greater argument where the OT was not under consideration: Rom. 5:6-10; I Cor. 9:12a; I Tim. 6:2. #2 – Rom. 9:33; Gal. 3:10-13. #5 – Rom. 5:18-19, 13:8-10. #6 – Gal. 3:6-9. #7 – Rom. 4:10-11a.

The basic presuppositions of the rabbis who used these "rules" were that (1) every word of the OT was divinely inspired and (2) God was the source of both the written and oral Law. The impact of the first was that the OT could be interpreted atomistically, i.e., individual words and phrases could be interpreted apart from their context. This is particularly evident in rules #2, 3, 4, and 6. The second presupposition came from the rabbis' belief that when God gave the written law recorded in the books of Moses, He also gave a much more prolific set of oral laws that had been passed down through the centuries to the rabbis of their day. This allowed them to draw inferences that went well beyond what one could normally deduce from the written text itself, justifying them as part of this ancestral oral law. What is noteworthy about the way NT authors and speakers use similar interpretive principles is the comparative restraint and reasonableness of their conclusions when set alongside those of contemporary rabbinic Judaism and, of course, that that they reject the oral law.

Allegorical. Examples of the allegorical interpretation of the OT can be found among the Palestinian rabbis and the authors of the Dead Sea Scrolls, but the method is most closely associated with Greek-speaking Alexandrians. At least as early as the middle of the second century B.C. Alexandrian Jews were allegorizing the OT, but the philosopher-theologian most associated with the method was Philo, whose career fell in the first half of the first century A.D. These Jews borrowed the method from the Greeks, who allegorized the epic poems of Homer and Hesiod to address elements in them that they found offensive. Philo used his training in Greek philosophy to derive meanings below the literal interpretation of OT texts. Although he viewed this underlying allegorical meaning as superior to the literal, he, nevertheless, accepted the literal as well. For him, it was essential to follow the literal commands of the Law and accept the historical accounts, except where they reflected inappropriately on God, as in the case of anthropomorphisms. The allegorizing of the OT that Jesus and Paul would have encountered in first-century Palestine was different from that of Philo in its lack of a close connection with Greek learning.[8]

The Gospels contain no examples of Jesus' use of allegory to interpret the OT, but Jesus did provide allegorical interpretations of some of his parables.[9] In dealing with the OT, however, he did find himself referred to in the Scriptures in ways that were not obvious to the uninstructed reader.[10] So, even though Jesus may not have employed allegory in his OT interpretation in the usual manner of the day, these interpretations would certainly have gone beyond the literal to the underlying meaning of the text. Paul identifies his method of interpreting the story of Hagar and Sarah as allegory (Gal. 4:24), and his writings contain three other clear allegorical interpretations of the OT (I Cor. 5:6-8 [leaven], 9:8-10 [muzzling an ox], and 10:1-11 [the Exodus and wilderness wandering]). As will be seen in the section on Rāz-Pesher interpretation that follows immediately, in the case of both Jesus and Paul the source of these underlying meanings was not human intellect, but God Himself.

Rāz-Pesher. Until recently the manner in which NT authors and speakers viewed OT prophecies as being fulfilled in their own day was considered unique when compared with contemporary Jewish OT exegesis. Neither the rabbis nor the Alexandrian allegorists did this. However, not only did Jesus

---

8   For excellent discussions of these matters, see Harry A. Wolfson, *Philo,* 115-138 and Friedrich Büchsel, "ἀλληγορέω," 260-63.

9   Parable of the Sower (Matt. 13:18-23=Mark 4:13-20=Luke 8:11-15), Parable of the Weeds (Matt. 13:36-43), Parable of the Net (Matt. 13:49-50), and Parable of the Wicked Tenants (Matt. 21:43). In this last example Jesus uses Ps. 118:22-23 to support his interpretation of the parable.

10   Luke 24:27, 44-47 ("he opened their mind to understand the Scriptures").

find himself as the subject of OT prophecies (Luke 24:27, 44-47), but this same thread runs throughout early Christian evangelistic preaching and letters to established churches in the NT. The discovery of the Dead Sea Scrolls at Qumran in the mid-twentieth century changed all that. Here were found theological treatises and biblical commentaries written by a community who believed *they* were living in the end times and were the specific intended subject of OT prophesies.[11] It appears that the early church and the Qumran community had a common source for this type of OT interpretation—the Book of Daniel.[12]

In the dream interpretation narratives in Daniel, God's message came in two stages. God communicated both the dream/vision and the interpretation. Without the interpretation (*pesher*), the dream remained a mystery (*rāz*). The Greek word *musterion* always translates the Aramaic word *rāz* in the Book of Daniel, where it is uniformly used of a mystery concealed in a dream. Nebuchadnezzar caught the sense of this well in 4:9: "O Beltshazzar, chief of the magicians, because I know that the spirit of the holy gods is in you and that no mystery is difficult for you, here is the dream which I saw; tell me its interpretation." (RSV) In Paul's use of the Greek word *musterion*, he, like the Qumran community, affirmed that that second act of revelation, the interpretation, identified his own day as the time of fulfillment.[13] For Paul, however,

---

11   In explaining the end-time meaning of Hab. 2:1-2 the *Habakkuk Commentary* (1QpHab 7.1-5) states, "And God told Habakkuk to write down that which would happen to the final generation, but He did not make known to him when time would come to an end. And as for that which He said, *That he who reads may read it speedily*, interpreted this concerns the Teacher of Righteousness, to whom God made known all the mysteries of the words of His servants the Prophets." (Translation by G. Vermes, *Dead Sea Scrolls*, 236).

12   See G. K. Beale, *Handbook*, 75-78 and *John's Use of the Old Testament*, 215-20.

13   See, for example, Eph. 1:9-10, 3:3-11, Rom. 16:25b-26 and I Cor. 10:11. Peter makes the same point in I Pet. 1:10-12.

the source of the mystery was not in the Scriptures alone; it was also there "from the ages" (Eph. 3:9) hidden in God Himself. Nevertheless, this *musterion* could also refer to an OT text, as he showed in Eph. 5:31-32, a passage to which we will return later in this chapter.

The mystery is the first act of revelation from God, but what about the second act, the interpretation (*pesher*)? It is certainly true that any of Paul's allegorical interpretations of the OT would qualify, but we can go beyond that. Paul uses the Greek verb, *sugkrinō*, in I Cor. 2:13. It is in the same word family as the two Greek nouns that translate *pesher* in Daniel. The verb can mean "compare," as it does in II Cor. 10:12, but it can also mean "interpret/explain," as it does of Joseph's interpretation of the butler and baker's dreams in Genesis.[14] It seems hardly an accident that *sugkrinō* in I Cor. 2:13 follows closely on Paul's use of *musterion* in 2:7, joined in the same context as they are in Daniel. What Paul is saying here is that we speak God's wisdom in a mystery (*musterion*), wisdom that has been hidden and which God predetermined before the ages (2:7), and we interpret (*sugkrinō*) these spiritual matters with the aid of the Spirit (2:13). What was true of Joseph and Daniel is now at the end of the age true of inspired Christian teachers.

Whereas the Rabbis controlled their OT exegesis by adherence to certain rules or principles of interpretation, and Philo thought that only through much learning and experience could one exegete the OT at the deeper level, God inspired the Christian apostles and prophets (Eph. 3:5) to explain how it points to the time in which they were living. No longer does a veil obscure the end-time message of the OT, because "through Christ it is taken away" (II Cor. 3:14-16). Herein lies the uniqueness of the use of the OT in the NT.

---

14   40:8, 16, 22; 41:12, 13, 15 twice.

Jesus and Paul's Use of the Old Testament in Passages Relevant to This Study

Passages with Stronger Connection with the Old Testament

Direct Quotations

Matthew 19:4-5=Mark 10:6-8a. In both Matthew and Mark's version of Jesus' encounter with the Pharisees over divorce, Jesus connects a few words from Gen. 1:27 with a full quotation of Gen. 2:24. In Matthew he ascribes the words to God Himself ("the Creator"). Jesus treats both passages in a straightforward, literal manner and presents a specific interpretation of them, with application—"so that they are no longer two but one flesh" (interpretation) and "therefore what God has joined together, let man not separate" (application). The relevance of Jesus' use of Gen. 1:27 and 2:24 here is that he applies these verses to individual men and women in a marriage relationship with each other, not to men and women in general. This, of course, is obvious about Gen. 2:24, but his argument to the Pharisees about the applicability of these verses to divorce would make no sense if he did not also take Gen. 1:27 that way. In doing so, Jesus interprets both these passages in a manner that coincides with the conclusion about the meaning of Gen. 1:27-28 reached earlier in chapter four of this book.

Ephesians 5:31. Paul also quotes Gen. 2:24, but his use and interpretation of the verse could not be more different than that of Jesus. Whereas Jesus took the passage in a straightforward, literal way to support his opposition to divorce, Paul put forward an underlying interpretation in the manner of allegory. Because of his identification of the verse as a mystery (*mustērion*),[15] Eph. 5:32 has the earmarks of a *rāz-pesher* interpretation.[16] At the literal level, the verse has to do with the marriage of a man and a woman, but there is a mystery in those literal words pointing to a deeper meaning much more sublime than human marriage—that of Christ and the church. In Eph. 5: 22-33 Paul moves back and forth between the marriage of a man and woman to that of Christ and his bride. On the surface, then, Gen. 2:24 refers to human marriage, but Paul's interpretation for his purposes here is the prefigurement of the marriage of Christ and the church in God's institution of human marriage.[17] Paul's connection here of human marriage with Christ's to the church highlights the exceptionally high value God places on this human relation-

---

15 Of the six occurrences of *mystērion* in Ephesians, this is the only one that relates to the interpretation of a specific OT passage. Eph. 1:9, 3:3, 4, 9, and 6:19 refer to the mystery hidden in God from the ages (3:9), but now revealed to the holy apostles and prophets (3:5). Though the specific content of the mystery in these verses relates to the inclusion of the Gentiles based on Jesus' redemptive act, 5:32 interprets a mystery just as connected to Jesus' mission on earth. See Rom. 11:25-27 for the other example of where Paul interprets an OT text (Isa. 59:20-21 conflated with 27:9) as the explanation of a *mystērion*.

16 This is quite similar to the interpretive method in the early part of the Gospel of Matthew, where the author asserts that certain OT passages have a specific fulfillment in Jesus, without denying the meaning in the original context. For example, Matt. 1:23 and Isa. 7:14, Matt. 2:15 and Hos. 11:1, and Matt. 2:18 and Jer. 31:15. For an explanation of the *rāz-pesher* interpretive method and how it relates to Paul, see above **Excursus 5: Jewish Interpretive Methods during the New Testament Period**. On the identification of this as a *pesher* interpretation, see E. Earle Ellis, *Prophecy and Hermeneutic*, 161.

17 The words "but I say" (*egō de legō*) occur only here in Paul and elsewhere in the NT only in Jesus' six antitheses in the Sermon on the Mount (Matt. 5:22, 28, 32, 34, 39, 44). In Matthew Jesus draws on his authority (7:29) to reinterpret well-known sayings principally from the OT. Similarly, Paul draws on his apostolic authority ("but I say"; see Eph. 3:4-5) to provide a deeper interpretation of a well-known OT passage.

ship. It makes all the more understandable Paul's opposition to Christians getting a divorce (I Cor. 7:10-13, 27, 39) and links up with Jesus' own opposition to this action when he interpreted Gen. 2:24.

Clear Verbal and Non-verbal Allusions

Galatians 3:28. The words "male and female" (*arsen kai thēlu*) in 3:28 appear to be a verbal allusion to Gen. 1:27. This is clear from the fact that their structure breaks with the pattern in the other two pairs and reproduces the wording of the Septuagint in Genesis 1:27. "Jew *nor* (*oude*) Greek," "slave *nor* (*oude*) free" becomes "male *and* (*kai*) female" in the final pair.[18] What is not clear is Paul's reason for choosing this wording here. Interpreters have been all over the map in offerings possible explanations.[19] Unfortunately Paul provides us with no interpretive help in the immediate context or anywhere else in his writings.[20] He simply does not tell us why he

---

18   The older English translations from Wycliffe through the KJV uniformly obscured this fact by rendering the text by a form of "nor" rather than "and." Twentieth and twenty-first century English translation have been mixed, but the general movement is in the direction of "and." In line with this, the RSV had "nor," but the NRSV has "and." Likewise, as late as the 1984 edition of the NIV, that version had "nor," but the 2011 edition has "and."

19   They range from (1) a new creation based on Christ's redemptive work, returning to God's original purpose (Rick McKinnis, *Equally Yoked*, 179) to (2) a new creation where the gender distinction of Gen. 1:27 no longer applies (Richard B. Hays, "Letter to the Galatians," 273) to (3) a reminder that there is a place for a non-married person in Christ (Ben Witherington III, *Women in the Earliest Churches*, 77), to (4) a reference to "the general relationship between sexes and not the specific relationship between husband and wife" (Ronald Y. K. Fung, *Galatians*, 175), to (5) the end of all discrimination based on being female (Dorothy R. Pape, *God's Ideal Woman*, 203), to (6) an indication that the gender distinction is "no longer social but physical" (J. B. Lightfoot, *Galatians*, 150).

20   The only other possible reference to Gen. 1:26-27 in Paul is in I Cor. 11:7, but as will be seen, that it is a reference to Gen. 1:26-27 is open to question, and the point there is quite different.

reproduces the wording of the Septuagint here, so we have to be content with that, notwithstanding the wide variety of interpretive "guesses" that have been offered.

I Corinthians 11:8, 9. Verses 8 and 9 are clear allusions to Gen. 2:22-23 and 2:18, 20 respectively. In 11:8 there may even be a *verbal* allusion (*ex andros*, "out of man") to Gen. 2:23 (Septuagint: *ek tou andros autēs*, "out of her husband/man"), but not to 2:22 (Septuagint: *apo tou adam*, "from Adam"). Here Paul interprets these Gen. 2 texts in a literal, straightforward way to support his statement at the end of verse 7 that "the wife is the glory of the husband."[21] Thus verses 8-9 are parenthetical[22] in that they support 11:7c directly and Paul's point about "glory,"[23] rather than pertaining directly to his overall argument about head covering[24] and or headship.[25] This is seen by the conjunction "for" (*gar*) at the beginning of both verses 8 and 9, connecting back to what he has just asserted.[26] One final point needs to be made. As was shown in the discussion of Genesis 2 in chapter four, everything in that chapter has to do with a husband and wife, not men and women in general. Hence, any interpretation of Paul's use of Genesis 2 here that takes Paul's reference in a literal,

---

21   Literally the reading is "but the wife/woman is glory of husband/man." Only the context can determine whether the gender-specific words used here should be translated "wife/husband" or "woman/man."

22   The RSV even puts the two verses in parenthesis, as it does verses 11 and 12. See Joseph A. Fitzmyer, *First Corinthians,* 415 and Archibald Robertson and Alfred Plummer, *Corinthians,* 231.

23   See Mark C. Black, "1 Cor. 11:2-16," 210: "Vv. 8-9 are explanatory, offering the reasons for woman being the glory of man: the creation order and purpose." Richard E. Oster (*1 Corinthians,* 258) makes the same point: "By his use of the term 'for' (γάρ, *gar*) he offers 11:8 as an explanation of how woman is the glory of man."

24   Contrary to Roy Deaver, "Christian Women," 810.

25   Contrary to John MacArthur, *1 Corinthians,* 258 and Allen Black, "Paul's Use of Genesis," 301.

26   See Oster, *1 Corinthians,* 258 and Henry Alford, *Greek Testament,* 566.

straightforward way necessarily connects these as instructions to husbands and wives, not men and women in the church.[27]

II Corinthians 11:3. Here Paul makes a non-verbal allusion to the serpent's temptation of Eve in Gen. 3:4-5 and a verbal allusion to Eve's response to God in Gen. 3:13, "the serpent deceived me."[28] He does not use the reference to Genesis 3 to prove a point, as he does in references to OT texts in several other places, but rather to draw an analogy from Eve's deception by the serpent to the Corinthian church's risk of being deceived by the false apostles (11:13).[29] Paul interprets the Genesis narrative here in a literal, straightforward way.

I Timothy 2:13, 14. I Tim. 2:13-14 has become ground zero in the dispute over the traditional versus a wider role for women in the church. While 2:12 has probably had a greater impact on limiting what women may do in the church than any other passage in the Bible,[30] verses 13-14 have been employed as the coup de grace in the defense of the traditional view. Thus the question of how Paul uses the OT in these two verses is critical to the present study.

Verse 13 makes a verbal allusion to Gen. 2:7-8, 15 (*plassō, to form*) and a non-verbal allusion to the fashioning of Eve from a part of Adam in Gen. 2:21-22. Verse 14 is a verbal

---

27   On this point see Willis, "Role of Women," 21; Craig L. Blomberg, *1 Corinthians*, 211; Lightfoot. *Role of Women*, 35; Coffman, *1 and 2 Corinthians*, 173; and William F. Orr and James A. Walther, *I Corinthians*, 260.

28   The Septuagint has *apataō*, whereas Paul uses *exapataō*, but the two words are essentially synonyms. In Paul's other allusion to Gen. 3:13 in I Tim. 2:14, he also uses *exapataō* of Eve. For more on this, see the discussion of I Tim. 2:14 below.

29   See Craig S. Keener, *Paul, Women & Wives*, 117; Leonhard Goppelt, *Typos*, 131, n. 17, and E. Earle Ellis, *Paul's Use of the Old Testament*, 62.

30   While various interpreters view this differently, Osburn (*Reclaiming the Ideal*, 252) sees it quite negatively. He concludes his chapter on I Tim. 2:9-15 with "no biblical text has been so misused to legislate so many prohibitions that stifle so much service by so many people."

allusion to Gen. 3:13, where the woman made the excuse that the serpent had *deceived* her (*apataō, to deceive*, Gen. 3:13 ; *exapataō, to deceive* or *deceive utterly*, I Tim. 2:14). On the significance of the use of different words for "deceived" in 2:14, the evidence is mixed. Some see the compound verb for Eve's deception (*exapataō*) as a strengthened version of the word used of Adam (*apataō*).[31] Others make no such distinction, but note that *apataō*, the word used in the Septuagint at Gen. 3:13,[32] was becoming used less and was being replaced by *exapataō*.[33]Neither view affects the conclusion that there is a verbal allusion to Gen. 3:13 here, but it could impact whether or not Paul is intentionally contrasting Adam and Eve here by making a word play.

In considering Paul's point in these allusions to the creation narrative, many interpreters have observed correctly that he does not tell us what it is. He merely makes the allusions and connects them back to 2:11-12 by the word "for" (*gar*) in 2:13. For many, the point is self-evident. However, what is self-evident to one is not to another, because we bring our own presuppositions to the text. With this in mind, let us consider how self-evident the traditional interpretation should be.

2:13. The traditional interpretation of 2:13 is that Paul is making a point of primogeniture, the higher status of the

---

31   See Henry George Liddell and Robert Scott, *Greek-English Lexicon*, where *apataō* is defined as "to cheat, deceive" and in the passive voice "to be self deceived, mistaken, deceived into thinking" (181); but *exapataō* is defined "to deceive or begile, deceive thoroughly." (586) Also see G. Abbott-Smith, *Manual Greek Lexicon*, 159, where *exapataō* is said to be a "strengthened form of *apataō*."

32   *Apataō* is used 33 times in the Septuagint to translate four Hebrew words, whereas *exapataō* is not used in the Septuagint, except in a variant reading in Codex Vaticanus at Ex. 8:25.

33   See J. H. Moulton and G. Milligan, *Vocabulary*, 54. Neither Bauer (*Greek-English Lexicon*, 3rd edition) nor Albrecht Oepke ("ἀπατάω," 384-85) nor Armin Kretzer (*Exegetical Dictionary*, 117) distinguish between the two words.

one who is prior in time. Its normal application in the OT is to the birth order of brothers. Certainly if the reader puts the emphasis on the words *first* and *then*, that interpretation might make sense. But what if Paul's point in Adam's being first and Eve next is the original point in the Genesis 2 text itself, that of the companionship of this first married couple brought about by the way they were brought together? Seen this way, Paul is making an historical allusion to the creation account that shows that he is talking primarily about *married* women, i.e., women who are in a relationship like Adam and Eve's. *First* Adam was alone, and *then* the Lord God fashioned Eve and brought her to him to make them a married couple. In the context of I Timothy, where marriage was under attack (4:3), this would make perfect sense.[34] This interpretation is also more faithful to the Genesis account, where there is no hint of a hierarchical relationship between the two. Additionally, it addresses the observation of many interpreters going all the way back to Calvin,[35] that primogeniture is not a very strong argument in support of Paul's prohibition of these women teaching.[36] After all, primogeniture did not prevent women teaching other women (Tit. 2:3-5) or teaching or

---

34   See Thomas C. Geer, Jr.'s ("Admonitions," 295) application of this to Paul words in 2:12. When "the intended complementary relationship between man and woman is destroyed due to the domineering attitude of the women, Paul's appeal to remember that woman was created after man is not an appeal for a return to male dominance and female subjection, but to return to a complementary role."

35   *Commentary on I Timothy*, note on 2:13. Calvin's specific point was that Paul's reason "appears not to be a very strong argument in favor of her [woman's] subjection."

36   The problem with applying the principle of primogeniture to the Genesis creation narrative was discussed earlier in this book in chapter four, where it was noted that animals were created before Adam and that so-called primogeniture is frequently reversed in the book of Genesis. To these may be added the examples of (1) John the Baptist and Jesus and (2) the first Adam and the last or second Adam in I Cor. 15:45-47. For a list of about 20 examples of the reversal of primogeniture in the OT see Webb, *Slaves*, 136-39.

prophesying to men (Acts 2:17-18, 18:26, 21:9, I Cor. 11:5) elsewhere in the NT.[37] Finally, it fits the context of 2:15, where *married* women are in view.

2:14. Just as with 2:13, Paul does not tell us what his point is in verse 14. Until recently the rather uniform understanding of Paul's meaning in this allusion to the Genesis 3 temptation story has been that Paul is arguing that woman's ability to resist temptation is weaker than man's.[38] Thus she should not be allowed to teach or be in a position of authority over men (2:12). More recently interpreters on both sides of the question of women in the church have rejected the traditional interpretation, seeking to find an explanation of Paul's words that makes more sense and is less demeaning to Eve's successors.[39] So if the interpretation of Paul's meaning here that

---

37   If one begins with the presupposition that woman may not prophesy in mixed company, then Acts 2:17-18 and I Cor. 11:5 will not be seen as convincing support of this point. However, to limit the application of these references to women prophesying to women adds something that is completely foreign to the text. The word "prophesy" (*prophēteuō*) in Acts 21:9 is a predicative participle, indicating an activity in which Philip's four virgin daughters were engaged with Paul and his companions, not an attributive participle ("*who* prophesied," as almost all English translations imprecisely translate the participle; Young's Literal Translation is a notable exception: "and this one had four daughters, virgins, prophesying"). On this see Max Zerwick and Mary Grosvenor, *Grammatical Analysis*, 425 and Evelyn and Frank Stagg, *Woman in the World of Jesus*, 231. Lipscomb ("Woman's Work," 6) wrote of the activity of Philip's daughters in Acts 21:9 that "they in the presence of men and women – their brethren and sisters, among them Paul, prophesied."

38   Webb (*Slaves*, Appendix B, 263-68) produces an impressive list of authors who taught the greater susceptibility of women to deception going all the way back to the fourth century. Other commentators of note who interpret I Tim. 2:14 this way include David Lipscomb, *Commentary*, 144, note on verse 14; Burton Coffman, *1 & 2 Timothy*, 171-72; James W. Thompson, *Transforming Word*, 992; Luke Timothy Johnson, *Letters to Timothy*, 202; and Donald Guthrie, *Pastoral Epistles*, 77.

39   Just a few of the multitude of interpreters who reject the traditional view that Paul's point in 2:14 is woman's greater susceptibility to temptation than men's include Grasham, *Genesis 1-22*, 126; Ferguson,

has been self-evident for centuries must be reconsidered, with what is it to be replaced? While there are many variations, currently there are three general approaches to the meaning of 2:14, starting with the traditional one.

Full traditional interpretation. There are those who still support the two elements of the traditional interpretation, namely that (1) women are more susceptible to deception than men and (2) Paul's use of the creation narrative here means that the restrictions on women in 2:11-12 are timeless. While the traditional interpretation is possible, for several reasons it presents the interpreter with more problems than it solves, thereby rendering it improbable. First, it adds elements not found in the Genesis narrative. While, as we have seen elsewhere, Paul and other NT writers under inspiration do this from time to time, in those cases it is usually clear that a midrashic or pesher or allegorical type of interpretive method is being used. That is not the case in 2:13-14. This fact alone does not make such an interpretation impossible here, but at least it should be noted that serious exegesis of the Genesis text itself reveals no hierarchical relationship between the man and the woman before the fall, and it does not indicate a greater susceptibility to deception of the woman. The traditional interpretation goes against the flow of the Genesis narrative.

Secondly, it goes against the flow of the way women are viewed in the rest of the NT, beginning with Jesus himself. Chapter seven of this book will lay out the evidence from Jesus, but let us consider briefly several other NT references, especially in Paul. God gifted women to be prophets (Acts 2:17-18, 21:9), a gift higher than teaching (I Cor. 12:28, Eph. 4:11; cf. also the reference to higher gifts in I Cor. 12:31). Although some assert that women did not prophesy in the

Women in the Church, 35; Lewis, "Analysis of I Timothy 2:8-15," 37; Allen Black, "Paul's Use of Genesis," 304-5; and David M. Scholer, "1 Timothy 2:9-15," 211-12.

presence of men, no NT passage teaches that (see I Cor. 11:5, where the issue is not even raised), and Acts 21:9 suggests just the opposite.[40] So elevated were some Christian women in God's mind that as prophets they are actually in the foundation of the church along with Jesus and the apostles (Eph. 2:19-20). This means that in any number of congregations certain women would have had this lofty status even above elders who did not have the gift of prophecy. As an example of Paul's high esteem for women who served the church, ten women are highlighted in Romans 16, eight of them by name. Paul heaps high praise on some of them as fellow workers, one even to the point of being imprisoned with him (16:7). These and several others in the NT who could be cited are not mentioned here as proof that women taught or exercised authority over men, but merely to underscore the prominent position of women in the NT. While the traditional interpretation of I Tim. 2:13-14 is consistent with women's position in Judaism at the time,[41] it goes against the flow of the way women are regarded in the rest of the NT, especially in Paul's writings.

Thirdly, if Paul's use of the Genesis creation narrative in 2:13-14 is proof that the prohibition of women teaching and having authority over men is a universal precept, why does it show up so late in the Bible? Specifically, as C. R. Nichol pointed out (see chapter one of this book), how do we explain the women in the OT whom God raised up to do just that? Specifically God raised up Miriam (Ex. 15:20-21; Mic. 6:4), Deborah (Judg. 4:4-14, 5:7), and Huldah (II Ki. 22:14-20; II Chron. 34:22-28) as prophets and/or authority figures to or

---

40   See note 37 above.
41   See Mishnah, *Kiddushin* 4.13, where women were not even allowed to teach children: "An unmarried man may not be a teacher of children, nor may a woman be a teacher of children." B. W. Johnson (*People's New Testament*, 119, 262) suggests that the restrictions on women speaking in the assembly were possibly true in Greek churches only. They occur only in letters written about Greek churches—Corinth and Ephesus.

over men. In fact, it was Huldah's prophecy after the discovery of the book of the law in the temple that prompted Josiah's reform. If it is a *universal* precept based on Paul's words in I Tim. 2:13-14 that the Genesis creation narrative forbids such actions, it should apply backwards as well as forward. Should not the fact that God raised up these women to assume these roles give us pause about interpreting Paul's prohibition in 2:11-12 the way it has been interpreted traditionally?

In the fourth place, there are some significant difficulties with the first of the two elements of the traditional interpretation of 2:14, namely that women are more susceptible to temptation than men and therefore should not teach or have authority over men. If this is the case, how then can we explain the fact that Paul directs older women to teach younger women (Tit. 2:3-5) and he speaks favorably of women who taught the Scriptures to a child (Timothy; II Tim. 1:5, 3:15)? Is it reasonable to conclude that women may teach women and children, who are more vulnerable to deception, but not men, who are less so? Further, if Eve's deception is the theological basis of women in Ephesus not teaching men, how is it that Paul was not similarly disqualified? In Rom. 7:11 Paul acknowledges that he himself sinned having been deceived, and here he uses exactly the same verb for deception (*exapataō*) that he uses of Eve in I Tim. 2:14 and II Cor. 11:3.

Modified traditional interpretation. Some who view Paul's use of the Genesis creation narrative in 2:13-14 as evidence that he intended the restrictions on women in 2:11-12 as universal, rather than specific to the situation in Ephesus, have suggested a modified traditional interpretation. While rejecting the traditional position that women are more susceptible to deception than men, they have suggested other meanings that preserve the element of the traditional interpretation that sees Paul as making a universal statement. Two key alternatives have been proposed: that (1) Eve was the first to transgress or (2) Eve was guilty of role reversal.

Eve was the first to transgress. The idea here is that somehow the basis of the restrictions on women in 2:11-12 is the fact that Eve transgressed God's command before Adam. There are two key problems here. First, it is not at all apparent how the one supports the other. This alternative is generally just stated without explaining how Eve's priority in transgression logically supports the restrictions in 2:11-12.[42] Second and most important, although we know from Gen. 3:6 that Eve ate the fruit first, 2:14 says nothing about that. 2:14 talks about the woman's deception in contrast with Adam, not who transgressed first.[43] Inexplicably, here a key interpretation of 2:11-12 is based on something that 2:14 does not even say!

Role reversal. This interpretation is based on the assumption that Eve was already in a subordinate position to her husband at the time she ate the fruit.[44] If that is so, then Paul's point in 2:14 would be that the restrictions he places on women in 2:11-12 are based on the point that Eve stepped out of her subordinate role when she ate the fruit without consulting her husband and gave some to him. Dave Miller's exegesis of I Tim. 2:9-15 is a representative example of this line of reasoning. Of 2:14 he writes, "the allusion is to the crime of launching forth in a leadership capacity in a religious/spiritual matter while the male passively complied with her leadership."[45] This

---

42   For example, see Ferguson, *Women in the Church,* 35; Cecil May, "Woman's Role," 247; Nell Taylor, "A Woman's View," 17; and Roy Lanier, Jr., "Role of Women," 226.

43   On this see Timothy J. Harris, "Eve's Deception," 346: "This so-called priority in deception is not actually found in the text, for it doesn't say that Adam was not deceived *first,* but that he was not deceived, presumably at all."

44   See the exegesis of Genesis 1-3 in chapter four of this book, especially the section, **Examination of Proposed Reasons for Interpreting Genesis 2 Hierarchically,** for evidence to the contrary.

45   Dave Miller," I Timothy 2:11-15," 282-83. Other examples include Keith A. Mosher, Sr., "Biblical Positions for Women," 370; David L. Lipe, "1 Timothy 2:11-15," 299; and Lanier, Jr., "Role of Women," 226.

statement imports into the record in Gen. 3:6 three elements that are not there. First, Eve's "crime," according to Genesis was disobeying God by eating the fruit. Second, Miller's inferring that what the text records as a simple act of giving her husband some fruit is "launching forth in a leadership capacity" stretches this passage to the breaking point. Finally, characterizing this as "a religious/spiritual matter" introduces a distinction into the text of Gen. 3:6 that is simply not there. On the next page Miller continues, "Eve circumvented the divine arrangement of submission by taking the initiative in a spiritual matter and exercising authority over her husband." Here handing her husband a piece of fruit has been blown up into "exercising authority over her husband." And Miller got all of this out of Paul's simple statement in I Tim. 2:14, "Adam was not deceived, but the woman having been deceived became a transgressor." 2:14 simply talks about who was not deceived and who was and the consequence of that deception. Anything else is an inference only, an inference that is imported into the text, not derived from anything in the text.

Full rejection of traditional interpretation. Many interpreters find in the traditional understanding of Paul's allusions to the Genesis creation narrative in 2:13-14 a failure to properly recognize the role the specific circumstances in Ephesus may have played in Paul's choice of these two features of Genesis 2-3. Timothy was facing numerous challenges as he sought to help the congregation conduct itself as a household of God while he waited for Paul's arrival (I Tim. 3:14-15). It is impossible to determine with certainty precisely what elements of the situation in Ephesus are most relevant to understand what was going on in I Tim. 2:8-15, but it is reasonable to conclude that I Timothy was not written in a vacuum. While Paul writes a small amount about men, the emphasis in this passage is on women.[46] From I Timothy in particular and the Pastoral Epistles in general we learn that all was not well with some of the women.[47] Various reconstructions of the situation in Ephesus have been proposed as the relevant background for Paul's restrictions on women in 2:11-12. By far the most prevalent has to do with the *content* of their teaching. It is argued that certain women were either influenced by or a part of the heresy Paul opposes in I Timothy, especially pressure on marriage and the family. Thus certain women should be barred from teaching in the assembly.[48] The evidence for this view, however, is mixed.[49]

More probable is the view that Paul was concerned with the *manner* of their teaching.[50] The word in 2:12 translated

46   See Alan Padgett, "Wealthy Women at Ephesus," 22: "The author's thinking moves to and focuses on the women after only one verse about men, probably because the women were giving him trouble."

47   See James W. Thompson, *Equipped for Change*, 37-8 and *Transforming Word*, 992.

48   For example, see Thomas Robinson, *Community Without Barriers*, 93, 95 and Geer, "Admonitions," 295-96.

49   This will be discussed further in chapter eleven of this book, but a few remarks are in order here. Certainly II Tim. 3:6-7 can be read that way, but it does not refer specifically to Ephesus. The opposition to marriage by the false teachers is clear (I Tim. 4:3), but involvement of women with that is not. To the contrary, some younger widows were *desiring* to remarry, although their motives were questionable (I Tim. 5:11). While some of them were "saying what they should not" (5:13), the context shows that Paul's reason for that comment had more to do with their being gossips and busybodies than false teachers (5:13). At most, the emphasis on the domestic role for women in the Pastorals (I Tim. 2:15, 5:14; Tit. 2:4-5) reflects Paul's opposition to the heretical pressure on marriage, but there is no direct evidence in these passages of any women's involvement in the heresy. For a different, but well-articulated interpretation of the evidence, see Harris, "Eve's Deception," 348-50.

50   As noted in chapter one of this book, this was C. R. Nichol's understanding of 2:12. In fact the central message of his book (*God's Woman*) was correcting the misuse of 2:12 to prohibit women from teaching. See specifically p. 153. See also Gordon P. Hugenberger, "Women in Church Office," 358: "Paul's concern is to prohibit only the sort of teaching that would constitute a failure of the requisite wifely

"assume/have/exercise authority" or "domineer" in most modern English translations (*authenteō*) gets at the manner of teaching. It is the antithesis of "submission," "submissiveness," or "subjection" (*hupotagē*) in 2:11. These wives were teaching in a domineering way, which was not consistent with the proper submissiveness of women to their husbands, particularly in public.[51] This was disruptive to the tranquility Christians are to pray for in their lives (2:2)[52] and that should be characteristic of their assemblies. The dual use of *hēsuchia*[53] ("quietness") in the Greek text in 2:11-12 frames Paul's restrictions on women, showing that it is a, if not *the* key concern of Paul here. This is very similar to the issue of disruptive behavior of some wives in the assembly in Corinth (I Cor. 14:34-35).

So what does 2:13-14 have to do with Paul's limitation on women's behavior in 2:11-12? The original purpose of woman was to be a companion to her husband (Gen. 2:18, 20). To this end, Adam having been formed first, Eve was formed next to be with him. This is where 2:13 fits. However, "trouble in Paradise" came when through deception the woman became a transgressor (Gen. 3:6, 13; I Tim. 2:14).

'submission' to her husband (the very concern with which v. 11 concludes)."

51   The impact of the behavior of Christians on the reputation of the church on outsiders is a major concern in the Pastorals. See I Tim. 3:7, where the bishop is to "have a good reputation with outsiders"; 5:13-14, where the bad behavior of some younger widows might give an adversary the opportunity for slander; 6:1, where slaves are directed to behave in such a way as to prevent God's name and the teaching from being defamed; Tit. 2:5, where younger women are to be submissive to their husbands, "lest God's word be defamed"; and 2:8, where younger men are to behave in such a way as to prevent an opponent having anything evil to say "about us."

52   *Ēremos* – "quiet" or "tranquil" and *hēsychios* – "quiet" or "well-ordered."

53   Bauer (*Greek-English Lexicon*, 3rd edition, 440) defines this word as "state of quietness without disturbance, *quietness, rest.*"

This now becomes analogous to the situation with wives in the assemblies in Ephesus.[54] So here Paul uses an analogy[55] or negative or cautionary biblical illustration to support his restriction on these wives' teaching. This is much like he does in the fourfold cautionary analogy in I Cor. 10:7-10 (v. 7 – idolatry; v. 8 – immorality; v. 9 – testing the Lord; and v. 10 – grumbling). More to the point is II Cor. 11:3, where Paul uses Eve's deception as a cautionary analogy or illustration of what might happen to the men and women of Corinth if they listen to false teachers.[56]

There is no way to know for sure whether this reconstruction of the setting in I Timothy adequately explains what was behind Paul's instructions on women in 2:11-12 any more than any of the other interpretations of 2:13-14 that have been proposed. What is evident in reading the literature on this passage is that there is almost always a strong correlation between what a writer already believes about 2:11-12 and the conclusions reached on the meaning of 2:13-14.

For reasons that should be obvious from the above critique of the traditional interpretation, the analogy approach appears to me to be the most exegetically sound. Regardless, however, of which of the interpretive approaches one takes, a final, critical point remains. 2:13-15 demonstrates that Paul is not discussing Christian women in general in 2:13-14, but Christian wives.[57] The woman was formed for a particular

---

54 Even some who hold the traditional view on 2:11-12 see Paul's reference to Genesis in 2:14 to be analogy. See Lewis, "Analysis of 1 Timothy 2:8-15," 37.

55 Various terms have been used in the literature, all with the same meaning: analogy, illustration, example. For example, Osburn (*Reclaiming the Ideal*, 248) uses all three.

56 See the discussion in Padgett, "Wealthy Women in Ephesus," 26.

57 Among others who have noted this are Geer ("Admonitions," 290, n. 28), Duane Warden ("Conduct of Christian Women," 11), Oliver S. Howard, ("Women's Role," 8), and Edwin Broadus ("Role of Women (4)," 7).

man, her husband (2:13). The woman sinned when she was deceived by the serpent in the presence of her husband (2:14).[58] Among the consequences of the woman's sin was increased pain in childbirth (2:15), a result coming from an intimate activity between a particular man and woman. There is no justification for applying the Genesis creation narrative in general or the three references to it in I Tim. 2:13-15 to women in general in Ephesus. This conforms to the conclusions of the exegetical study of Genesis 1-3 reached in chapter four of this book. Since the formation of the first woman in Genesis 2 through the fall and consequences in Genesis 3, everything was about the relationship between a particular woman and a particular man. Ending this unwarranted misapplication of the Genesis creation narrative to women in general is long overdue.

I Timothy 2:15. Whether this is a possible or probable verbal allusion to Gen. 3:16 is an open question. The verbal similarity is clearly there. The word for "childbearing" in I Tim. 2:15 is *teknogonia*. In Gen. 3:16 the phrase "she will bear children" is rendered in the Septuagint by two words, the verb *tiktō* and the noun *teknon*. It is not a perfect verbal match, but the meaning is the same, thereby rendering it, in my judgment, a probable verbal allusion. To what "childbearing" refers, however, is one of the most disputed points in the entire epistle.[59]

---

58   A number of writers have drawn attention to the "with her" in the Hebrew text of Gen. 3:6, a detail of the text that is obscured by many English translations. On this point, see Smith, *Men of Strength*, 43; Marrs, *Embracing*, 49 and "In the Beginning," 25; Scholer, "1 Timothy 2:9-15," 210; and Thomas R. Schreiner,"1 Timothy 2:9-15, 145.

59   In the interpretive history, the key possibilities for the children who will be born are either Eve's children, the Christ child, or the children of Christian mothers.

Passages with Weaker Connection with the Old Testament

Possible Verbal Allusions

I Corinthians 11:7. The question here is whether 11:7b ("being the image and glory of God") is an allusion to the Genesis creation narrative or not. If it is, how do we explain it? Two factors point away from identifying the reference with Gen. 1:26-27: (1) although the word "image" (*eikōn*) is found in the Genesis narrative (1:26, 27, 5:1), the word "glory" (*doxa*) is not and (2) female is also in the image of God (1:27). With reference to the first, some see "glory" (*doxa*) as a reference to "likeness" (*homoiōsis*) in Gen. 1:26,[60] but this seems a stretch, since the Septuagint never translates the Hebrew word for "likeness" (*demuth*) in Gen. 1:26 with the word "glory" (*doxa*).[61] "Glory" is not found in either the Hebrew text of Gen. 1:26 or in the Septuagint translation. On the second point, the fact that both male *and* female are created in God's image (Gen. 1:27), the only way Paul's point in 11:7b ("being the image ... of God") could be a reference to Genesis 1 would be that he is using a midrashic interpretive method, where an element of the text is interpreted out of its context. It was a common rabbinic method to single out one word or phrase in a statement and interpret it in isolation from the rest of that statement.[62] In this case Paul would be referring to Gen.

---

60   See Antoinette Clark Wire, *Corinthian Women Prophets*, 120 and n. 6 and Black, "Paul's Use of Genesis," 301. Black's belief that in 11:7b Paul alludes to Gen. 1:26 appears to be based on a misreading of Wire. His statement that "the Septuagint sometimes translates the word here translated 'likeness' as 'glory'" is incorrect.

61   Hurley (*Man and Woman*, 173-74, 205) and Alford (*Greek Testament*, 55) develop the case against associating "glory" with "likeness" in Gen. 1:26 and firmly oppose the view that Paul alludes to Genesis 1 here.

62   On this see the discussion of the midrashic interpretive method above in **Excursus 5: Jewish Interpretive Methods during the New Testament Period**.

1:26, where "man" is made in God's image, but ignoring 1:27, where "man" being made in God's image is defined as both "male and female." Given the usual care and reasonableness of Paul's interpretation of the OT, it seems unlikely that he would be ignoring the context in this instance. A further difficulty for this interpretation is that in both the Hebrew text (*'adam*) and the Septuagint (*anthrōpos*) the word for "man" is the generic ("human being"), rather than the gender-specific one. Therefore, while it is still possible that 11:7b is a reference to Genesis 1, the above two considerations make it unlikely.

Excursus 6: The Meaning of Genesis 3:16 for the Matter of Women in the Church. The final three NT passages whose possible references to the Genesis creation narrative will be considered here are I Cor. 11:3, 14:34; and I Tim. 2:12. They are considered only *possible* allusions because the traditional interpretation of these verses has generally assumed the connection. Check almost any Bible's marginal references to verify this. Yet, there are no *verbal* allusions to the wording of Gen. 3:16 in any of these passages. Further, with the possible exception of the words, "the law," in I Cor. 14:34 Paul gives no hints that he is drawing on any of the OT at all.

This excursus, then, will consider first whether Paul or any other NT writer for that matter refers to Gen. 3:16 in a way that is relevant to the issue of women in the church. Then, as promised in chapter four of this book, by considering the third question, what *does* it mean?, the excursus will address some of the lingering questions that a simple exegesis of Genesis 3 in its own context could not answer.

Paul's Use of Gen. 3:16. As noted above there is a probable verbal allusion to Gen. 3:16a in the word "childbearing" (*teknogonia*) in I Tim. 2:15. The matter at hand here is whether

Paul alludes to the verse anywhere else in his writings. The belief that he does draw on Gen. 3:16c on the issue of the relationship of husbands and wives in particular, if not men and women in general, has been almost axiomatic among many on both sides of the question of women in the church.[63] Krister Stendahl's unqualified statement that Gen. 3:16 is "the decisive scriptural passage for the whole New Testament's instruction concerning the subordination of women" is a good place to start.[64] The only passages where some interpreters have proposed a possible non-verbal allusion to Gen. 3:16 are I Cor. 11:3, 14:34, and I Tim. 2:12. Only in I Cor. 14:34, where Paul refers to "the law" (*ho nomos*), is there any hint that some part of the OT may be in the background.[65] In I Cor. 11:3 and I Tim. 2:12 there is no introductory formula that often accompanies a reference Paul makes to something in the OT, there is no quotation from the OT, and there are no words or phrases indicating a connection with the OT.

Thus, that Paul may be alluding to Gen. 3:16 in these passages is merely conjecture. The apparent reason for this widespread speculation is that no other OT passage comes closer to some aspect of these three verses than Gen. 3:16.

---

63   Prior to doing the research for writing this book I was strongly convinced that Gen.3:16 was the basis of Paul's teaching about the subordination of wives to their husbands, although I recognized and still do that it could have nothing to do with the relationship of men and women in general in the church. I have to credit David Tarbet for first causing me to question my belief that Paul alluded to Gen. 3:16c in his writings.

64   *Role of Women*, 29.

65   Interpreters are deeply divided on what Paul meant by the words, "the law." While many see Gen. 3:16 as the probable reference, not a few are just as certain that it is not, citing the view that no OT passage, including Gen. 3:16, fits Paul's particular point here. Other OT references that have been suggested include Gen. 1:26ff., 2:21ff. and Num. 30:3-16. These, however, suffer from the same weakness as the proposal of Gen. 3:16 as Paul's reference. If "the law" refers to some portion of the OT, the allusion is so opaque that interpreters are reduced guess-work.

Spreading the net wider, nothing else in the NT points to Gen. 3:16. This, of course, begs the question of how solid the assumed connection of Gen. 3:16c is with the matter of women in Paul's writings and in the rest of the NT. Since Gen. 3:16 refers to the relationship of two individuals in a marriage, the most that can be said is that Paul *may* have had Gen. 3:16 in mind as the justification for his teaching about a wife's subjection to her husband. That possibility cannot be ruled out, but it should be noted that it is a conjecture without supporting evidence. Further, it would in no way support the supposed subordination of women in general to men in general in the church.

Lingering Questions

Genesis 3:16 in the rest of the OT. Having considered whether and to what extent Gen. 3:16 may have been alluded to in the NT, we now turn to the same question as respects the OT. Several writers have correctly noted the complete absence of references to the consequences of Adam and Eve's sin after Genesis 5 in the rest of the OT.[66] After Gen. 5:5, Adam is mentioned in two other places in the OT: in the genealogy in I Chron. 1:1 and in a possible reference to his transgression Hos. 6:7.[67] Eve is never mentioned again in the OT after Gen. 4:1. Certainly there are voluminous examples of patriarchy being the norm in the family and in society at large, as it was in other cultures in the ancient Near East. It is even found in the Law of Moses (see Num. 5:19-20, 29, 30:3-8, 10-16). However, nowhere does the OT connect this with God's intent in the creation, much less with Gen. 3:16.

---

66   See, for example, Bilezikian, *Beyond Sex Roles*, 267, n. 13; Carol L. Meyers, "Gender Roles," 342-43; and Katherine C. Bushnell, *God's Word to Women*, sect. 90.

67   Deut. 32:8 and Job 31:33 are also possible references to Adam, but translators do not agree on whether the Hebrew word *'adam* there is a proper noun or a general reference to man.

In fact, as Nichol so clearly pointed out in chapter one of *God's Woman*, there are some rather striking counter examples in the OT of where God raised up even married women as leaders and prophets to carry out His work.[68] Deborah, the wife of Lappidoth, prophesied (Judg. 4:4), judged Israel (Judg. 4:4-5), propped up a weak military commander (Judg. 4:9-10, 14), and actually co-led the army with Barak (Judg. 5:2, 15). God raised up Huldah, wife of Shallum and a contemporary of Jeremiah, to issue the prophecy that led to Josiah's reform (II Ki. 22:14-20, II Chron. 34:22-28). Isaiah's wife was a prophetess (Isa. 8:3).[69] The conclusion is inescapable. Other than a possible allusion to Gen. 3:16a in I Tim. 2:15, there is no clear reference to Gen. 3:16 in either the OT or the NT.

Genesis 3:16: Prescriptive or descriptive. Most broadly stated, the issue here is whether the consequences of Adam and Eve's sin for their descendants come from God (prescriptive) or whether they are simply what happened as a natural result of their sin without any intent by God that that is the way it must be (descriptive). Modern discussions of whether Gen. 3:16 as a whole or individual parts of the verse are prescriptive or descriptive are fraught with imprecision and confusion. The imprecision comes from the numerous words various writers use for the concepts of "prescriptive" and "descriptive," each expressing a different nuance.[70] The confu-

---

68   See Hollis Miller, "Women in Paul's Letters (3)," 7: "That O. T. prophetesses exercised their prophetic gift in the presence of men cannot be questioned. Huldah not only spoke the will of the Lord to men, she did so in the presence of the high priest."

69   Philip B. Payne ("Libertarian Women," 197) concludes that "examples such as these OT women leaders vitiate the allegation that women by their created nature are not suited to teach or have authority."

70   In connection with "prescriptive," various interpreters use words such as "penalty," "punishment," "command," "ought to be," "imperative," and "edicts." In connection with "descriptive," words like "preview," "predictive," "prophesy," "indicative," and "explanation" are used.

sion comes from differences in the understanding of God's role and will in bringing about the consequences of Adam and Eve's sin and whether he regards them as permanent. Is Gen. 3:16c ("he will rule over you") merely a consequence of Eve's sin (descriptive), or did God bring it on her in spite of His original intent for the marriage relationship (prescriptive)? And if it came from God, is it God's intent that it always be that way, or is this something that was reversed in Christ by returning to God's original intent?

It is difficult to provide a definitive answer to these questions here, because the gulf between the presuppositions behind them is so great. However, certain observations are possible. First, it is abundantly clear that Gen. 3:16a, the part about pain in childbearing, is not simply a natural consequence of Eve's sin. It came from God Himself. The Lord God told Eve, "*I* will greatly multiply your pain...." This is quite prescriptive. Yet, many view 3:16b and especially 3:16c as descriptive. It takes more than just the assertion that 3:16c is descriptive to make it so.

On the other hand, is it possible to view God as the source of the consequences of Adam and Eve's sin and at the same time seek to mitigate their effects? It certainly would seem so. First of all, note that this matter is an attempt to answer the third question, what *does* it mean? It is not a question that comes out of an exegesis of the Genesis text itself. It is a modern hermeneutical question that neither the author of the Genesis creation narrative nor any first century person could have asked in the way we can today. Numerous writers have noted the fact that modern advances in medicine and agriculture have made it possible to reduce the impact of some of the consequences of Adam and Eve's sin,[71] and most

---

71   Rebecca M. Groothuis, *Good News for Women*, 139; Mary Hayter, *New Eve in Christ*, 155; Evans, *Woman in the Bible*, 19; Webb, *Slaves*, 119; Treat, "Women in Genesis 1-3," 7; and David Parrish, "Submission," 18.

Christians today are quite open to taking advantage of them. Is it a violation of God's will for women in childbirth to use anesthesia to decrease or eliminate their pain (Gen. 3:16a)? If not, how is it a violation of God's will in Gen. 3:16c if a wife had a husband who chose not to rule over her? Or is it wrong to use herbicides to control the "thorns and thistles" that resulted from God's cursing the earth (Gen. 3:18)? If not, why would it be wrong for women to be in a marriage where, unlike it was in ancient societies, many men are choosing not to lord it over their wives? We could ask the same question about the consequence, "in the sweat of your face you shall eat bread" (Gen. 3:19)." Is it wrong, like some religious farming communities believe, for farmers to use modern machinery to make farming less labor intensive? If not, why should the modern application of Gen. 3:16c be any different? Perhaps framing the modern hermeneutical issue as prescriptive versus descriptive adds more confusion than it does clarity, but at least it highlights the need for disciplined thinking in arriving at modern applications of this ancient text.

Genesis 3:16 and its post-garden application. The question here is did God intend the consequences of Adam and Eve's sin as described in Gen. 3:16-19 to affect their descendants in the same way it affected them?[72] Are these consequences intended as their punishment for their sins and not for the rest of humankind?[73] Are they the effects of their sin that later humankind has been impacted by but has no God-given

---

72   Bilezikian (*Beyond Sex Roles*, 267, n. 13) answers the question this way. "It would seem to me, in view of the total absence of further references to the text [Gen. 3:16] in the Bible, that its original intent concerned the situation of Adam and Eve at the time of the fall, and that universal applications drawn from it are not valid unless they can be corroborated in other biblical teachings."

73   If we include death in the list of consequences of Adam and Eve's sin, the question would apply here as well. Paul explains in Rom. 5:12 that death spread to all men, not as a direct consequence of Adam's sin, but "because all sinned."

obligation to endure unabated? What if Adam and Eve bear
the *guilt* for their sins and the brunt of the *punishment* for
them, but those after them do not bear the *consequences* of
their sins in the same way? This might mean, for example,
that all women are faced with significant pain in childbirth,
but since they are not accountable for Eve's sin, they neither
deserve nor must necessarily endure that pain when they have
the ability to mitigate it through anesthesia. So returning to
Gen. 3:16c, why should women who are guiltless for Eve's sin
share that consequence of her sin when they have the ability
to have a different kind of marriage?

So where did the application of Gen. 3:16c to women after
Eve begin? As we have seen, it is absent in the OT. A few early
extra-biblical Jewish sources concern themselves with Eve's
role in the introduction of sin into the world (Eccles. 25:24
[early second century B.C.], 2 Baruch 48:42 [early second
century A.D.]), but not Adam's rule over her. We found no
clear reference to Gen. 3:16c in the NT. So where did this
idea that Adam's rule of Eve is transferred to all women
thereafter begin? It appears that the earliest clear application
of Gen. 3:16 to women after Eve occurs in Tertullian's early
third century writing, *On the Dress of Women* (1), where he
asserts that women after Eve, specifically Christian women,
share all three of the consequences of Eve's sin in Gen. 3:16.[74]
Later in that century Cyprian will make a similar point in
Treatise II.22 of *On the Dress of Virgins*.[75] This view has

---

74   This is not to say that Tertullian was the first to makes this application, only that he appears to be the earliest extant example. Earl
Lavender ("Tertullian," 331-56), although not specifically referring to
his interpretation of Gen. 3:16, argues that Tertullian's fundamental
views on women in the church came from those before him. The question of when Gen. 3:16 was actually first applied to later women must
for now remain open.

75   In the late fourth century *Apostolic Constitutions* 3.1.9, Gen. 3:16c
is used as part of the justification for prohibiting women from baptizing anyone.

become axiomatic in Christian circles down to the present day, even though there is no biblical evidence for it. So, from a biblical standpoint, in answering the question of Gen. 3:16c, "what *does* it mean"?, we are left with the conclusion that its applicability to women in both NT times and today rests, without supporting evidence, on a foundation of supposition that appears to have had its origin after the NT. None of this *proves* that the traditional interpretation of the scope of the consequences of Adam and Eve's sins is wrong, but it certainly calls it into serious question and shifts the burden of proof.

Conclusions

What has this examination of the NT use of the Genesis creation narrative confirmed about what we found in our exegetical study in chapter four and what has it added to our understanding of the fuller (Christian) meaning of those chapters?

Confirmed

The Genesis Creation Narrative's Focus on a Husband and His Wife. Genesis 1-3 refers almost entirely, if not entirely, to the relationship of a married couple, not women and men in general. In spite of the widely held assumption that Genesis 2 and/or 3 support a hierarchical relationship between men and women in general in the church, in none of the NT uses of these texts in Genesis is there a clear indication of this. The view that the hierarchical relationship between Adam and Eve found in Gen. 3:16c is transferred to men and women in the church is without warrant from an examination of the possibly relevant passages in the NT.[76] There is no passage in the NT that shows that women in general are to be submissive to men in general in the church, unless something other than what we find in Genesis 1-3 is read into it. In fact, there is no clear passage in the entire Bible that puts women in general under men in general.

Jesus on Marriage. Jesus' interpretation of both Gen. 1:27 and 2:24 in Matt. 19:4-5=Mark 10:6-8a confirms the conclusion reached in chapter four of this book that even Genesis 1 refers to the creation of a married couple. Jesus applied these verses to individual men and women in a marriage relationship with each other, not to men and women in general.

New Information

Christ and the Church. Paul's *rāz-pesher* interpretation of Gen. 2:24 in Eph. 5:31-32 as referring to the spiritual union of Christ and the church adds a meaning to Gen. 2:24 that an exegesis of that verse could never have produced.

The Wife as the Glory of the Husband. In I Cor. 11:8-9 Paul alludes to Gen. 2:22-23 and 2:18, 20 respectively. Nothing in his use of these texts calls into question any conclusions reached in the exegesis of Genesis 1-3 in chapter four, nor do they relate to the question of what women may do in the church. However, he adds something to our understanding of the Genesis texts that could not be derived from an exegesis of them alone. These passages in Genesis 2 support his assertion that "the wife is the glory of the husband."

---

76   See, for example, Phil Sanders ("Women Preachers," 17), who writes about Gen. 3:16, "This declaration from the beginning applies to God's order in the home and in the church."

Open Questions

Gen. 3:16 in the NT. Other than the word "childbearing" (*teknogonia*) in I Tim. 2:15, there is no clear reference to Gen. 3:16 in the NT. Where interpreters have speculated that the verse is in the background of a NT passage, Gen. 3:16 seems to be the passage of choice because no other OT text is a more reasonable possibility for a connection. Proposed references to Gen. 3:16 are educated guesses at best. In the absence of such a connection, the suggestion that Gen. 3:16 is the basis of NT teaching about the subordination of the wife to her husband rests on shaky ground. This does not mean that NT writers, in particular Paul, never had Gen. 3:16 in mind or that the verse is not the basis of subsequent wives' subordination to their husbands, but without supporting evidence, the question must remain open.

Gen. 3:16 and Future Women. Although this is a conclusion that breaks with almost the entire interpretive history of this verse, nothing in either Gen. 3:16 or the NT suggests that the consequences of Eve's sin were intended to be experienced by any other woman but her. More work is needed on the question of where and when the application of the verse to future women began, but the source is not the OT or NT.

CHAPTER SIX

Women in the World Of Jesus

*J*esus was born into a world that, for women, was different from our Western world in almost every way imaginable. Jewish women in Palestine and other places in the East were greatly limited in the circles in which they operated. The norm was to get married after they reached majority at age 12 ½. Except for religious observances, like going to the Synagogue or Temple, their activities were almost entirely at home or in support of their duties there. The wife's purpose was to bear and bring up children, thereby enabling her husband to fulfil his obligation to obey God's command to "be fruitful and multiply" (Gen. 1:28). She had little contact with men other than those in her household, and when she went out she was veiled. Concerns about uncleanness brought about by her monthly menstrual cycle (see Lev. 15:19-24) further contributed to her seclusion. Men engaged in the public activities, and although women participated in festivals, they were excluded from some of the ceremonial obligations prescribed in the Law of Moses. Although the provision for a "bill of divorce" (Deut. 24:1-4) gave wives some protection from insensitive husbands who wanted to get rid of them, in actual practice they could be divorced on almost any pretext. While at home, a minor daughter remained under the care and protection—and watchful eye--of her father. That state was merely transferred to her husband when she married. The list could go on and on. Such is the picture drawn in the

Mishnah, our best source for Pharisaic Judaism in Palestine at the time of Jesus.

So the natural question is what signals did Jesus send that the situation for women who would become his disciples would change or be about the same? What would his followers learn from his words and his actions that would signify the direction they should go in these matters? Those questions will be addressed in the next chapter. As background for that discussion, this chapter will survey the state of women in first-century Palestine.[1]

Women in First-Century Palestine

WE ARE FORTUNATE TO HAVE IN THE MISHNAH AN EXCELlent window to view first-century Palestinian Rabbinic (Pharisaic) Judaism. This collection of sayings of rabbis from approximately the late first century B.C. through the second century A.D. reflects the opinions of many Palestinian Jewish scholars on the interpretation and application of the Law of Moses. No other source gives us in one place better insight into the world of the Pharisees with whom Jesus sparred on numerous occasions. The same can also be said for Paul's Palestinian background, because he had rabbinic training under one of the most renowned Palestinian rabbis of the day, Rabban Gamaliel I (Acts 22:3).

The rabbis, like those found in the Mishnah, were the legal experts whose opinions could be used in the courts. Jesus referred to them as "scribes" (e.g., Matt. 23:2), and

---

1   Robinson (*Community Without Barriers*, 27) notes that "one of the best ways that we can see the distinct outline of Jesus' distinctive way of life, is to see how and when he pushes against the typical prejudices and practices of his time. Jesus' interactions with women stand out very distinctly within his culture."

he was highly critical of their legal nitpicking (Matt. 23:4), although he said to follow their teachings (Matt. 23:2-3). In the citations from the Mishnah that follow, we get the flavor of how the Torah was being applied in Palestine in Jesus' day on matters relating to women.[2] Because the rabbis did not always agree with each other and because they represented an elite class, rather than the common people, we cannot take these as hard and fast rules applying to everyone in every situation, but they were common legal opinions on the application of specific passages in the Torah.[3]

The Mishnah contains 63 tractates or chapters, divided into six divisions. The third division (*Nashim*) is called "Women" and contains the following seven tractates: "Sisters-in-law" (*Yebamoth*), "Marriage Deeds" (*Ketuboth*), "Vows" (*Nedarim*), "The Nazirite Vow" (*Nazir*), "The Suspected Adulteress" (*Sotah*), "Bills of Divorce" (*Gittin*), and "Betrothals" (*Kiddushin*). "The Menstruant" (*Niddah*) in the sixth division also deals with women's matters. Many other tractates also

---

2   Since the period reflected in the legal opinions found in the Mishnah goes well beyond the lifetime of Jesus and Paul, for our purposes the tendency where possible to identify the rabbi who is the source of an interpretation enables us to date many of them. This is especially valuable for rabbis who lived before the destruction of Jerusalem in A.D. 70. Nevertheless, even the later texts quite often reflect earlier traditional interpretations, so they are still of great value in understanding the position of women in Palestine in Jesus' day.

3   Randall D. Chesnutt ("Jewish Women," 94) rightly cautions that any depiction of Jesus' world must recognize the tremendous diversity of Palestinian (and Alexandrian) Judaism around the time of the birth of Christianity and take into account the view of women in "such diverse literary sources as the OT Apocrypha and Pseudepigrapha, the works of Philo and Josephus and the Qumran scrolls." He goes on to cite many relevant passages presenting women in more favorable (113-121) and less favorable light (97-107) from these sources, but the general picture of the position of women that emerges is not at all unlike that found in the Mishnah. So we will use the Mishnah here as our primary source, since it best represents the Palestine Jesus encountered in his lifetime, as is abundantly clear from his constant interactions with "the scribes and the Pharisees" in the Gospels.

contain important passages dealing with women.

Quotations from the Mishnah in the following discussion are drawn from *The Mishnah* by Herbert Danby.[4] A few others from non-legal texts by Josephus and Philo, first-century A.D. Jews, are provided to add additional details. In many cases, these Mishnah references are just a sampling of passages that could be cited.

Social Status

WOMEN WERE COMMONLY GROUPED WITH SLAVES AND CHILDREN in the Mishnah.[5] Rabbinic scholar, Herbert Loewe, argues that this grouping of women with slaves and children is because they have in common "restricted freedom of action: they are not independent politically. The exemption of women occurs … only in regard to acts she may or may not have the power of performing."[6] Some of the examples in the Mishnah, however, suggest otherwise. For example, the exclusions of "women or slaves or minors" from being counted to achieve the required three people needed for the common grace in *Berakoth* 7.2 can hardly be explained because they "may or may not have had the power" to be included in the count. These meals were in private, small-group settings. Clearly in the grouping of these three categories of people in the Mishnah something more was going on.[7] Joachim Jeremias sees it differently than Loewe, con-

4 London: Oxford University Press, 1933.

5 For example, *Berakhoth* 3.3 (both), *Pesahim* 8.7 (both), *Rosh ha-Shanah* 1.8 (slaves), *Sukkah* 2.8 (both), *Baba Metzia* 1.5 (both), and *Yebamoth* 16.7 (slaves).

6 *Rabbinic Anthology,* 685, n. 76. Loewe's co-author (Montefiore) expresses a contrary view in the introduction to the same book. In commenting on this frequent collocation of "women, children and slaves" he writes, "Women were, on the whole, regarded as inferior to men in mind, in function and in status." (xviii)

7 Note also that in the immediately preceding section (7.1), whereas women, slaves, and minors were excluded in the count, Samaritans were not, a further indication of the lower status of women even in this informal situation.

cluding that "on the whole, the position of women in religious legislation is best expressed in this constantly repeated" grouping. "Like a non-Jewish slave and a child under age, a woman has over her a man who is her master … and this likewise limits her participation in divine service, which is why from a religious point of view she is inferior to a man."[8]

Submission[9]

NUMEROUS PASSAGES IN THE MISHNAH DEAL WITH THE intricacies of a woman's submission to her father or husband in her home. In general, a woman was under the control of her father until she reached majority at age 12 ½[10] or became married. The father had control over his daughter's betrothal, if she was still a minor. He also had "the right to aught found by her and to the work of her hands, and [the right] to set aside her vows, and he receives her bill of divorce; but he has not the use of her property during her lifetime." (*Ketuboth* 4.4, *Niddah* 5.7) A father could even sell his daughter as a slave (see Ex. 21:7), but only before she reached age 12. (*Ketuboth* 3.8) Then she is under the control of her husband, but if she is a minor when betrothed she is under the control of both her father and future husband until she reaches majority. (*Nedarim* 10.1-5) This section is dealing with the right to revoke a woman's vow in Num. 30:3-15, and both here and elsewhere in the Mishnah (e.g., *Nedarim* 11.10) many technical exceptions are enumerated. What is abundantly clear from the multitude of passages in the Mishnah about a woman's subordination to her father and husband is the absence of opinions placing women in general under the control of men in general. As in the OT, in the Judaism of the time of Jesus reflected in the Mishnah, the subordination of women as women applied only within the family.

8   *Jerusalem*, 375.
9   See the discussion in ibid., 363-64 and *passim*.
10   See Danby, *Mishnah*, 277, notes 4 and 5 and *passim*.

Property

WHEN A MAN MARRIES A WIFE, HE IS SEEN AS GETTING possession of her. (*Ketuboth* 8.1) This, of course, is not the same as saying that a wife was the property of her husband, as some have suggested. It is worthy of note, however, that in *Kiddushin* 1.1-5 the acquisition of a wife is discussed in the context of the acquisition of slaves, cattle, and physical property.[11]

A man may make a prenuptial agreement allowing his wife to have full or partial control over her property, and it is valid. If she dies first, he inherits her property. (*Ketuboth* 9.1) But if she acquires property after she is married, it belongs to her husband. In this case, she is in the same position as a minor son or daughter or a foreign slave but in a lower position than a son or daughter of age or a Hebrew slave. (*Baba Metzia* 1.5) "Aught found by a wife and the work of her hands belong to her husband, and during her lifetime he has the use of her inheritance." (*Ketuboth* 6.1)

A special category dealing with property has to do with family inheritance rights. If a woman inherits something before she is betrothed, she may give it away or sell it. The Schools of Shammai and Hillel are mixed on whether she may do so after she is betrothed, but in any case the transaction is valid. If, however, a woman disposes of inherited property after she is married, the husband may nullify the deal. (*Ketuboth* 8.1) The Mishnah is also quite specific about the inheritance or lack of it for daughters. First of all, while a father had wide ranging authority over his minor unmarried daughter, that did not extend to the use of her inherited property. (*Ketuboth* 4.4) Further, following Num. 27:8, if a man died without a son, his daughter received the inheritance. She passed it on to her offspring, following the general rule "whosoever has precedence in inheritance, his offspring have

---

11   See Stagg, *Women in the World of Jesus*, 49-50.

also precedence." Thus she and her offspring's rights precede those of her father's brothers. However, if there is a son, he gets the inheritance, not the daughter. (*Baba Bathra* 8.2) So how did an unmarried daughter survive after the death of her father? In the case where the inheritance was substantial, the sons provided for their sisters' maintenance. "But if the property was small the daughters receive maintenance and the sons go a-begging." (*Baba Bathra* 9.1) What may seem unusual preferential treatment for the daughter actually makes perfect sense, given the greater ability of a man to support himself in that culture than a woman.

Teaching Children

"AN UNMARRIED MAN MAY NOT BE A TEACHER OF CHILdren, nor may a woman be a teacher of children." (*Kiddushin* 4.13)

Study of the Law

ALTHOUGH THERE IS NO EVIDENCE FROM THE PERIOD THAT rabbis had female disciples, this is not the same thing as saying that no women studied the Law. *Sotah* 3.4 is often used to support the contrary view that men were discouraged to give women, in this case a daughter, a knowledge of the Law. But let us examine this passage. The first part of *Sotah* deals with the meal offering and drinking of the bitter water by a wife suspected of adultery in Num. 5:11ff. *Sotah* 3.4 discusses the fact that a wife's punishment from God is postponed based on her merit—up to three years. One rabbi (Ben Azzai) stated that a man ought to teach his daughter the Law so she would have a sense of her merit, should this happen. R. Eliezer, in a statement often quoted out of context, disagreed: "If any man gives his daughter a knowledge of the Law it is as though he taught her lechery." Obviously in this context R. Eliezer is not opposing teaching a daughter a knowledge of the Law per se, but rather is concerned about being complicit in her sin by teaching her a way to mitigate the punishment for her immoral act.[12]

Nedarim 4.3 provides that a man may teach Scripture to his sons and daughters (though some manuscripts omit "and to his daughters"). This passage illustrates the danger of taking quotations, like that of R. Eliezer above, out of context.[13]

Social Contact outside the Family

JEREMIAS BEGINS HIS CHAPTER ON "THE SOCIAL POSITION OF Women" in Jerusalem at the time of Jesus with these words: "Eastern women take no part in *public life*. This was true of Judaism in the time of Jesus, in all cases where Jewish families faithfully observed the Law."[14] After discussing a number of passages in the Mishnah relating to women, Evelyn and Frank Stagg make the astute observation that "the public life of women in the time of Jesus was more restricted than in Old Testament times."[15] These conclusions are certainly borne out in the Mishnah.

A man could not remain alone with two women (unless his wife was present), but a woman could remain alone with two men. (*Kiddushin* 4.12) Further, "any man whose business is with women may not remain alone with women." (4.14; see also *Bikkurim* 4.2)

"And what (conduct transgresses) Jewish custom? If she goes out with her hair unbound, or spins in the street, or speaks with any man." (*Ketuboth* 7.6) Or again, apparently even in the case of a leper (see Lev. 13:45), a man differs from a woman in that

---

12   See the discussion on p. 46, above and Ross S. Kraemer, *Her Share*, 98.

13   See also the anecdote in the Babylonian Talmud (*Berakoth* 10a) whereby the wife of R. Meir (mid second century A.D.) reasoned with him about the interpretation of a biblical passage and convinced him to change his mind.

14   *Jerusalem*, 359. As the title suggests, the focus of this book is on Jerusalem. Jeremias does note, however, that custom around women in public was more relaxed in the country than in town. (362-63)

15   Stagg, *Woman in the World of Jesus*, 52.

"he may go with hair unbound and his garments rent but she may not go with hair unbound and with garments rent." (*Sotah* 3.8) If a woman did not show proof of her virginity on her marriage bed and she had been seen talking with an unidentified man in the street, R. Joshua said that this alone is enough to presume that she had intercourse with him. (*Ketuboth* 1.8) On the presumption of guilt even in the case of a betrothed couple being alone together, see *Ketuboth* 1.5.

Lest the impression be left that women were secluded in their homes, a number of activities outside the home are mentioned in the Mishnah. Among these are drawing water from a spring (*Ketuboth* 1.10, 7.5), working in the harvest or picking olives (*Yebamoth* 15.2, *Eduyoth* 1.12), operating as a shopkeeper (*Ketuboth* 9.4), "winnow, grind, or sift corn" with a neighbor woman (*Gittin* 5.9), going to a house of mourning or a wedding feast (*Ketuboth* 7.5), and celebrating in festivals in Jerusalem (*Taanith* 4.8).[16] There was also a Court of Women in the Temple where a gallery was constructed "so that the women should behold from above and the men from below and that they should not mingle together." (*Middoth* 2.5)

According to Philo (*Special Laws* III.31 [169-171]), in first century Alexandria, public life was for men only. Women were not to leave the home, over which they were the manager in charge. When they had to leave the home, as to go to worship, they should do so when most people were not out and about. Here is what he wrote.

> Market places and council halls and law courts and gatherings and meetings where a large number of people are assembled, and open-air life with full scope for discussion and action—all these are suitable to men both in war and peace. Women are best suited to the indoor life which never strays from the house, within which the middle door is taken by the maidens as their boundary, and the outer door by

16   Note that on one occasion when Jesus taught in a synagogue his sisters were present (Matt. 13:56=Mark 6:3).

those who have reached full womanhood. Organized communities are of two sorts, the greater which we call cities and the smaller which we call households. Both of these have their governors; the government of the greater is assigned to men under the name of statesmanship, that of the lesser, known as household management, to women. A woman, then, should not be a busybody, meddling with matters outside her household concerns, but should seek a life of seclusion. She should not shew herself off like a vagrant in the streets before the eyes of other men, except when she has to go to the temple, and even then she should take pains to go, not when the market is full, but when most people have gone home, and so like a free-born lady worthy of the name, with everything quiet around her, make her oblations and offer her prayers to avert the evil and gain the good.[17]

However, in the same passage (172-175), in spite of his assertion about what women *ought* not do, he discusses the presumably not uncommon disgraceful conduct of some wives who get into fights in the marketplace to protect their husbands. This passage illustrates the greater freedom to go out in public women had in this Hellenistic city than in Jewish Palestine.

Marriage

MEN WERE TO BE HONORABLE IN ACQUIRING A WIFE FROM one who was authorized to give her away. Because according to the Law woman was inferior to man in every respect, she was to be submissive that she might be directed by the man, to whom God had given all authority. However, this submission should not be used to humiliate her. (Josephus, *Against Apion* II.200-201)

---

17   F. H. Colson, *Philo*, 581, 583. In another passage (*Flaccus* 89) Philo describes the seclusion of women in one household where "their women kept in seclusion, never even approaching the outer doors, and their maidens confined to the inner chambers, who for modesty's sake avoided the sight of men, even their closest relations."

When a man was betrothed to a woman, it was assumed that she would be a virgin on her wedding night. If on the wedding night he learns that she is not a virgin, he can go to court for damages. (*Ketuboth* 1.1) If a girl who is still a minor is seduced, her father (not the girl herself) is due compensation. If her father dies before the fine is paid, her brothers' rights to the money precede her own, presumably because the brothers assume their deceased father's responsibility for her maintenance. (*Ketuboth* 4.1)

Although a woman taken as a captive in war was at the mercy of the man who wanted her as his wife, special protections were, nonetheless, provided for her. (Josephus, *Antiquities* IV.8.25-26) Scattered throughout the Mishnah there are a number of other protections for a wife, such as where a husband may move with his wife without her consent. (*Ketuboth* 13.10-11) However, in the Mishnah, the rights are heavily weighted in favor of the husband.

"How does a man differ from a woman? ... a man may give his daughter in betrothal, but a woman may not give her daughter in betrothal." (*Sotah* 3.8)

"These are the works which the wife must perform for her husband: grinding flour and baking bread and washing clothes and cooking food and giving suck to her child and making ready his bed and working in wool." If she brought one or more female servants to the marriage, she could have them do all these tasks but the last, for, according to R. Eliezer, "Even if she brought him in a hundred bondwomen he [her husband] should compel her to work in wool, for idleness leads to unchastity." (*Ketuboth* 5.5)

"Jose b. Johanan of Jerusalem said: 'Let your house be opened wide and let the needy be members of your household, and do not talk much with women-kind.' They said this of a man's own wife; how much more of his fellow's wife! Hence the Sages have said: 'He that talks much with woman-kind brings evil upon himself and neglects the study of the Law and at the last will inherit Gehenna.'" (*Aboth* 1.5) This often quoted passage, as a number of others in the Mishnah, reflects a concern peculiar to rabbis and their students, namely those who devoted themselves to "the study of the Law."[18] Others deal with the wives of priests as opposed to all other wives. For this reason, we should be careful about generalizing to the population at large concerns like that expressed here in *Aboth* 1.5.

Divorce

WOMEN WERE NOT ALLOWED TO DIVORCE THEIR HUS-bands, but in certain extreme cases they could insist that their husbands divorce them. (*Ketuboth* 7.10; see also *Nedarim* 11.12) The courts would also require that a man put his wife away if he abandoned her (7.1) or denied her her conjugal rights for a specified period (7.2-5). According to Philo (*Special Laws* III.80-82), if a husband is proven to have made a false charge of premarital unchastity against his new wife, he is fined and subjected to corporal punishment and must remain with her if she will have him. But if she wants to leave the marriage, she may do so, and he cannot stop her.

While the School of Rabbi Shammai took the phrase, "some indecency," in Deut. 24:1 to allow a man to put away his wife only for sexual impropriety, the School of Rabbi Hillel broadened the pretexts for divorce to almost anything, including spoiling a dish (*Gittin* 9.10), the wife's barrenness

---

18   See George Foot Moore, *Judaism*, 270. Another example is found in *Ketuboth* 5.6, where a man may vow to refrain from sex with his wife, with her consent, for one or two weeks, but "disciples [of the Sages] may continue absent for thirty days against the will [of their wives] while they occupy themselves in the study of the Law." This sounds similar to Paul's instructions in I Cor. 7:3-5 but with important differences. For Paul, mutual consent was required. Also, these were not a special class of people like rabbinic students, but regular members of the congregation. Finally, the period of abstinence is not specified; the couple agrees on the "season."

(*Gittin* 4.8, *Yebamoth* 6.6), the wife's becoming a deaf-mute (*Yebamoth* 14.1), or if he finds someone else more beautiful (*Gittin* 9.10). Josephus shows his familiarity with the widespread practice of his day of men putting away their wives for many causes (*Antiquities* IV.8.23), as does Philo (*Special Laws* III.5 [30]).

"The man that divorces is not like the woman that is divorced; for a woman is put away with her consent or without it, but a husband can put away his wife only with his own consent." (*Yebamoth* 14.1)

The commandment to "be fruitful and multiply" (Gen. 1:28) required that a man with no children should seek a new wife if his current one bore him no son in ten years of marriage. Thus we read in *Yebamoth* 6.6, "No man may abstain from keeping the law *Be fruitful and multiply*, unless he already has children.... If he married a woman and lived with her ten years and she bare no child, it is not permitted him to abstain" (presumably from being fruitful and multiplying by remarrying).

When a couple marries, the husband pledges a *ketubah* to his wife. It is a specified amount of money she will be paid if he divorces her or dies. This had the effect of making it difficult for a man to divorce his wife, if he had trouble raising the money. However, there was a catch. If the wife transgresses the Law of Moses or Jewish custom he can put her away without paying the *ketubah*. Among the Jewish customs that would disqualify her are "if she goes out with her hair unbound,[19] or spins in the street, or speaks with any man ... or curses his parents in his presence." (*Ketuboth* 7.6) Also, under certain circumstances, if defects were found in the woman her betrothal could be invalidated or if married she could be put away without her *ketubah*. What are these

---

19   The exception to a woman not having her hair bound in public was a virgin in her wedding procession (*Ketuboth* 2.1). See Jeremias, *Jerusalem*, 360.

defects? "All blemishes which disqualify priests disqualify women also." (*Kiddushin* 2.5, *Ketuboth* 7.7)[20]

Women's Testimony

HERE THE EVIDENCE IS MIXED. JOSEPHUS (*ANTIQUITIES* IV.8.15) writes, "From women let no evidence be accepted, because of the levity and temerity of their sex. Neither let slaves bear witness because of the baseness of their soul, since whether from cupidity or fear it is likely that they will not attest to the truth."[21] Presumably women were not allowed to be judges or witnesses in cases involving property, because in a list of 13 types of family members who may not serve in these capacities in litigation of these cases, all are male. Yet the female equivalents of these ("sister" instead of "brother," "mother-in-law" instead of "father-in law," etc.) are conspicuously absent. (*Sanhedrin* 3.4) In considering the types of matters where women were not permitted to give testimony, the general rule was that "any evidence that a woman is not eligible to bring" neither can "a dice-player, a usurer, pigeonfliers, traffickers in Seventh Year produce, and slaves" bring. (*Rosh ha-Shanah* 1.8)

On the other hand, the Mishnah discusses cases where a woman's testimony is heard (e.g., *Sotah* 6.4, 9.8; *Yebamoth* 16.7; *Ketuboth* 2.6, 2.9), although it may be limited in certain instances. (*Sotah* 6.2) In another passage, on the matter of making a guilt offering for refusing to testify on something

---

20   Lev. 21:18-20 lists about 10 defects that prevent a priest from presenting an offering to God. Among others, he could not be blind or lame or be facially disfigured or have an injured hand or foot or be a dwarf. *Bekhoroth* 7.1-6 greatly expands the list, adding minute details. For example, facial disfigurement is specified as "he whose head is wedge-shaped or turnip-shaped or hammer-shaped or whose head is sunk in or is flat at the back." (7.1)

21   H. St. J. Thackeray, *Josephus*, 581. The Staggs (*Woman in the World of* Jesus, 47) note that "Josephus seems to stand alone in explicitly affirming that women were excluded as witnesses in Jewish courts."

that has been witnessed (Lev. 5:1, 5-6), women were exempt (*Shebuoth* 4.1), but the passage does not explicitly forbid their testimony.

If a husband brings an allegation against his wife, such as that she did not have tokens of her virginity on her wedding day, the rabbis were mixed on whether her testimony was to be believed. For example, four such cases are discussed in *Ketuboth* 1.6-9.

Conclusions

THE PEOPLE WITH WHOM JESUS SPARRED THROUGHOUT his ministry and who even early on recognized the threat he presented to them and sought to destroy him (Matt. 12:14=Mark 3:6) had developed a set of traditional applications of the Law of Moses that went well beyond the Law itself. To these men it was "a hedge around the Torah" (*Aboth* 1.1, 3.14) that enabled them to avoid transgressing God's laws. To Jesus it was oppressive and hypocritical legalism that was a burden to the common people (Matt. 23:4, 13; Luke 11:46, 52) and actually *caused* them to transgress God's laws (Matt. 15:3-6, 23:23; Mark 7:8-13; Luke 11:42). The Mishnah preserves the male-centered world view of "the scribes and Pharisees." These views were in continuity with certain elements of the Torah, like the gender of the priests and the requirement for all males to perform certain religious obligations (Ex. 23:17=Deut. 16:16). Additionally, they were also reflected in other OT and intertestamental texts.[22] However, as Jesus pointed out, at least in the case of God's protection for married women, the Pharisees were out of step with the intent or spirit of the Torah (Matt. 19:4-9=Mark 10:5-9).

22　See Chesnutt, "Jewish Women," 97-102, where he discusses passages in Sirach, Letter of Aristeas, Testament of Reuben, Testament of Job, Life of Adam and Eve, Apocalypse of Moses, and II Enoch.

This issue of divorce itself highlights the difference of Jesus' approach from that of his religious antagonists. While Jesus taught that God's original intent was that men should not divorce their wives at all (Matt. 19:8, Mark 10:9), the Mishnah contains a whole tractate dedicated to the intricacies of how the protection for women provided by Deut. 24:1-4 should be applied in everyday situations. (*Gittin*, "Bills of Divorce") This tractate illustrates a characteristic of the entire Mishnah, namely that it is written to aid males in the performance of their religious duties. There are certainly protections for women, but in general they are seen from the point of view of how women can aid their husbands and certainly not hinder them in obeying the Torah. Men, not women, have the obligation to "be fruitful and multiply" (Gen. 1:28). So if after a certain period of marriage no child is produced, he should put her away. (*Yebamoth* 6.6) According to Lev. 15:24, a man can become ceremonially unclean by having sex with his wife while she is menstruating, so a whole tractate of the Mishnah is dedicated to bodily discharges, especially blood during menstruation. (*Niddah*, "The Menstruant") If a wife has sex with her husband during this period of uncleanness, he may put her away without her *ketubah*. (*Ketuboth* 7.6) A man could violate the law by eating food that had not been prepared properly or had not been tithed, so his wife has an obligation to ensure that does not happen, and she can be put away, again without her *ketubah*, if she fails to do so. (ibid.) And the list goes on and on. As we will see on other matters as well, Jesus' approach to women was very different and more in line with positive examples of women found in the OT and intertestamental literature.[23] With this background in place, we will now turn in the next chapter to Jesus' countercultural stance on women as pictured in the Gospels.

---

23   See ibid., 113-118, 121, where he cites examples from Judith, Jubilees, Joseph and Aseneth, Testament of Job, Apocalypse of Moses, Tobit, and IV Maccabees. To these can be added the story of Susanna.

CHAPTER SEVEN

Jesus and Women

As was noted at the beginning of chapter four, we could well have begun with Jesus and in fact felt it important to do so before turning to Paul. The impact of Jesus' attitude toward and treatment of women has received too little attention, and were he usually the starting point, rather than Paul, the history of men and women in the church might have been written very differently. Having laid the groundwork in the preceding chapter for understanding the position of women in Palestine in Jesus' day, we are now ready to examine his refreshing and revolutionary stance on women.

We probably should not consider Jesus' attitude and actions toward women apart from his counter-cultural stance on other marginalized groups of people.[1] The list is a long one and includes sinners, tax collectors, Samaritans, children, poor, aged parents, chronically ill, the unclean, and widows. In connection with most of these categories of often disenfranchised people, Jesus' stance ran counter to that of his contemporaries, both friends and enemies alike.[2] We know that at times Jesus chose not to "make waves," such as when

---

1   On this see Hurley, *Man and Woman*, 83 and Stagg, *Woman in the World of Jesus*, 225.
2   For example, on sinners see Matt. 21:31-32; Luke 7:36-50, 15:1-32; John 8:2-11. On tax collectors see Matt. 9:10-13=Mark 2:15-17=Luke 5-29-32; Matt. 21:31-32; Luke 18:9-14, 19:1-10. On Samaritans see Luke 10:25-37. On children see Matt. 19:13-15=Mark 10:13-16=Luke 18:15-17. On aged parents see Mark 7:9-13. On the chronically ill see Matt. 12:9-14=Mark 3:1-6=Luke 6:6-11; Luke 13:10-17; John 9:1-41. On widows see Mark 12:40=Luke 20:47.

he had Peter pay the Temple tax for the two of them (Matt. 17:27). However, when it came to treating everyone with dignity without regard to his/her social standing, regardless of the consequences, Jesus was inflexibly compassionate and evenhanded.[3] Thus when it came to women, another significantly marginalized group in first-century Palestine, it should not surprise us to find Jesus acting the same way. This chapter is an examination of how women appear in Jesus' teachings, his teachings about women, and finally, his association with women.

Women in Jesus' Teachings

HERE HE IS NOT MUCH DIFFERENT THAN THE RABBIS.[4] Both he and they used women sparingly in stories or parables to illustrate points. In Jesus' case, women appear in four parables: (1) the parable of the woman who hid leaven in meal (Matt. 13:33=Luke 13:20-21), (2) the parable of the ten maidens (Matt. 25:1-13), (3) the parable of the lost coins (Luke 15:8-10), and (4) the parable of the unjust judge (Luke 18:1-8). They also appear in an illustration about a woman in labor (John 16:21) and in a prediction in the Synoptic Apocalypse about two women grinding at the mill (Matt. 24:41=Luke

---

3   Robinson (*Community Without Barriers.* 29) notes that "The tendencies to treat people as stereotypes were everywhere around him— tax collector, sinner, woman of the city, Pharisee, woman caught in adultery, scribe, ambitious mother, Samaritan, zealot, woman in the kitchen, uneducated fisherman, courtier's wife, Gentile centurion, and many others—yet Jesus invariably cut through the stereotypes and looked at each person as a whole and valuable individual."

4   C. E. Carlston ("Proverbs, Maxims," 97) casts the net even broader to the whole Mediterranean world. Here he paints a sordid picture, surveying the overwhelmingly uncomplimentary conventional wisdom in "one liners" about women in Greco-Roman and some Jewish sources and concludes that it is "shocking that so perverse and one-sided a view of half of the human race could be passed along as high wisdom. Jesus' counter-cultural stance on the matter is as refreshing as it is certain."

17:35). Finally, in his dispute with the scribes and Pharisees over their seeking a sign, he made an OT reference to the queen of the South in his critique of them (Matt. 12:42=Luke 11:31). Where Jesus is markedly different from the Palestinian rabbis, however, is in the other two areas, namely, in his teachings *about* women and in his association *with* them. It is to these that we now turn.

Jesus' Teachings about Women

THE GOSPELS RECORD NO SAYINGS WHERE JESUS DISCUSSES the topic of women as a class.[5] As noted above, there are a few incidental references to women, just as there are to numerous other categories of persons. However, there is nothing from which we can construct a theology of women according to Jesus. There are three highly significant areas, though, where women appear in his teachings. These are (1) occasions when he paid a woman a high compliment, (2) divorce and remarriage, and (3) sexual lust against a woman. We will now consider each of these in order.

High Compliments

The Syro-Phoenician Woman (Matt. 15:28). This Gentile woman received one of the highest compliments known to have come off the lips of Jesus: "Oh woman, great is your faith," and it stands in stark contrast with the disciples' "little faith" only two chapters later (Matt. 17:20). The account of this woman's interaction with Jesus appears in Mark 7:24-30 as well, but the acknowledgment of her great faith is found only in Matthew.[6] Earlier in Matthew Jesus had made a

---

5   See Evans, *Woman in the Bible*, 56: "Jesus gives very little teaching on women as such, because he never treats them as a class, all with the same characteristics and tendencies. In a similar way he gives very little teaching for or about males as a class."

6   Elizabeth Malbon ("Fallible Followers," 37) notes that while Mat-

similar comment about another Gentile's faith, a centurion (Matt. 8:10=Luke 7:9). For the story here in Matthew 15 the significant point about this person is that she was a Gentile, not that she was a woman, but it should not be lost that she addressed Jesus by a messianic title ("Son of David") and exhibited extraordinary humility toward him. As he did on so many other occasions, Jesus rewarded her faith with healing.

The Poor Widow at the Temple (Mark 12:41-44=Luke 21:1-4). Both Mark and Luke's accounts of the story of this poor widow come immediately after Jesus' stinging denunciation of the scribes for their open displays of self-importance, coupled with the charge that they "devour widows' houses." This indigent widow was so poor that she had nothing to devour, but that did not prevent her giving everything, "her entire living" (Mark 12:44). Jesus saw this as a teachable moment for his disciples, so he interpreted for them the significance of this woman's beautiful act. That he would even notice such an inconspicuous act in the midst of "large sums" (*polla*) being given by the wealthy speaks volumes about the way he looked compassionately on society's disenfranchised, in this case a destitute widow. From this woman's unselfish act, Jesus gave perhaps his most gripping illustration of what it means to trust God completely.

The Woman Who Anointed Jesus for His Burial (Matt. 26:6-13=Mark 14:3-9). We will return to this story later in the section on Jesus' association with women, but the high

---

thew's account emphasizes the woman's faith, Mark has him responding to her statement (*logos*) in 7:28: "Lord, even the little dogs under the table eat from the children's crumbs." His response was "for this saying (*logos*) you may go on your way; the demon has left your daughter" (v. 29). Hence, the fuller picture we get is that "she achieves her goal… not because of her faith alone or her reasoning alone, but because of her speaking up and speaking out—because of her action." In this she is like the woman with a flow of blood whose faith led her to take drastic action and touch Jesus' garment (Mark 5:27).

compliment Jesus paid this anonymous woman is what is of interest here. The flow of Mark's narrative at this point is instructive. If we remove the Synoptic Apocalypse (Mark 13), the account of the poor widow who gave all her living ends Jesus' Temple ministry during his last week (12:41-44), and this incident in the house of Simon the leper begins the preparation for his death (14:8). Matthew (26:8) identifies those who were indignant at the woman's extravagant gift (roughly worth a common laborer's whole annual wages) as "the disciples." Jesus' rebuke in her defense pointed out that she, not they, had her priorities straight. Little did they know that in two days his body would be laid in a tomb, and she was preparing it for that occurrence. It is at this point that Jesus pays her a compliment unparalleled in all the Gospels and one that transcends both space and time. "Wherever the gospel is preached in the whole world, what she has done will also be spoken in her memory" (Matt. 26:13=Mark 14:9).

Divorce and Remarriage

ANYONE WHO HAS EVER DONE A SERIOUS STUDY OF JESUS' teaching on the matter of divorce and remarriage knows how complex it is. For instance, in contexts in Mark (10:10-12) and Luke (16:18) where he is not discussing the issue with his religious opponents, Jesus is emphatic that divorce is not permitted. Yet, in the Sermon on the Mount he appears to recognize a limited exception that might permit divorce and remarriage (Matt. 5:32). Sorting out all the issues on this difficult subject is beyond the scope of this present study. Here the discussion will be limited to four points Jesus made that, because his position was counter-cultural, give us an indication of his uniquely sympathetic way of viewing women.

No Divorce from the Beginning (Matt. 19:8). The Pharisees who approached Jesus on the subject of divorce in Matthew 19 and Mark 10 believed that a man could divorce his wife, based on Deut. 24:1. The only point of dispute among them was what reasons could legitimize a divorce. One of Jesus' points in response to their question was that Gen. 1:27 and 2:24 trump Deut. 24:1. The latter was a concession by God due to the hardness of their hearts, but God's will since the beginning has been[7] to oppose divorce.

The Current Practice of Multiple Reasons for Divorce Is Wrong (Matt. 5:32, 19:3, 6; Mark 10:9). Although Jesus made it clear that God has always opposed divorce, the Pharisees had a point that the Torah (Deut. 24:1), nevertheless, permitted it. So their question to Jesus in Matthew's account revolved around the possible justifications for a man to divorce his wife. "Is it lawful to divorce one's wife *for any cause*" (*kata pasan aitian*, 19:3)? As pointed out in chapter six in the section on **Divorce** in the Mishnah, the School of Rabbi Hillel differed from the stricter position of the rival School of Rabbi Shammai by allowing many, often frivolous, justifications for divorce. The argument turned on the meaning of "some indecency" in Deut. 24:1. The School of Shammai interpreted the phrase narrowly to refer only to sexual impropriety. The School of Hillel allowed for a wide range of reasons well beyond those sexual in nature. Whether or not Jesus intended to side with the School of Shammai in his response to their original question, his answer certainly had that effect. For him, in the context of Deut. 24:1, the only acceptable cause for a man to divorce his wife was her unchastity (*porneia*, 19:9). It is clear from the Mishnah that common practice in Palestine at the time followed the School of Hillel's view.

What an irony it is that the bill of divorce which God had allowed as a protection for women because of the hardness of men's hearts against their unwanted wives had, itself, in

---

7   Note the wording in Matt. 19:8, "from the beginning it *has* not *been* (*gegonen*) so." The perfect tense here indicates a present state based on a completed past act. God's will at the beginning was not changed by Moses' provision for a bill of divorce. It is still in place.

164 *God's Woman Revisited*

the hands of the rabbis, become a vehicle of further callousness toward essentially defenseless women. The great Jewish rabbinics scholar C. G. Montefiore, in his commentary on Matthew, singles out Jesus' strict stance on divorce as one of three notable areas where he believes Jesus stood out in his attitude toward women.

> The attitude of Jesus towards women is very striking. He breaks through oriental limitations in more directions than one. For (1) he associates with, and is much looked after by, women in a manner which was unusual; (2) he is more strict about divorce; (3) he is also more merciful and compassionate. He is a great champion of womanhood. And in this combination of freedom and pity, as well as in his strict attitude to divorce, he makes a new departure of enormous significance and importance. If he had done no more than this, he might justly be regarded as one of the great teachers of the world.[8]

The Ability to Divorce One's Spouse Is Not Limited to Husbands (Mark 10:12). Here we turn to Mark's version of the dispute with the Pharisees over divorce. Mark is writing for a non-Jewish audience, so he records a follow-up discussion with Jesus' disciples privately "in the house" in which an interpretation of Deut. 24:1 is not under consideration. In fact, in Mark's whole account of the previous dispute with the Pharisees over divorce the question to Jesus was not about acceptable causes for a man to divorce his wife, as in Matthew, but concerned whether divorce itself was allowable—yes or no. "Is it lawful for a man to divorce a wife" (10:2)? Now in the house, Jesus answers his disciples' further inquiries about divorce and makes a leap not possible in the context of Palestinian Judaism. Even though, in line with his interpretation of Gen. 1:27 and 2:24 in the discussion with the Pharisees, he opposes any divorce (Mark 10:6-9), here in the house he

---

8   *Rabbinic Literature*, 47.

teaches his disciples that women and men are on an equal footing in dissolving a marriage relationship, in marked contrast with what we read in the Mishnah.[9] "Whoever divorces his wife and marries another commits adultery against her, and if having divorced her husband she marries another, she commits adultery" (10:11-12).

Adultery Can Be against the Wife, Not Just against the Husband. According to Jesus, the sanctity of the original marriage of a woman whose husband divorces her is so great that for him to marry a second woman is an act of adultery "against her" (*ep' autēn*) (Mark 10:11). This is unheard of among the rabbis, for whom adultery was seen as an offence to the married husband. In fact, the very practice of bigamy or polygamy, which is amply supported and regulated in the Mishnah,[10] indicates that having sex with a second woman (a second wife) did not violate the first wife at all. How different was Jesus' view of marriage for both the man and the woman based on his dedication to God's will "from the beginning."

Sexual Lust against a Woman (Matt. 5:28)

WHEN JESUS SPOKE HERE OF A MAN COMMITTING ADULtery with a woman in his heart, this saying would have resonated well with the rabbis. Montefiore states that "the sayings about adultery [in Matt. 5:27-28] contain nothing new or off the Rabbinic line." He produces ample rabbinic citations to establish this point, as does Moore.[11] In her excellent discus-

---

9   See Ferguson, *Women in the Church*, 70.

10   While Moore (*Judaism*, 122) states that polygamy was not common in Palestine during Jesus' day, the Mishnah provides for it in numerous passages. For example, a man might contract levirate marriages with the wives of four of his deceased brothers at the same time. (*Yebamoth* 4.11) *Ketuboth* 10.1, 2, 6 and *Bekhoroth* 8.4 speak of two wives, *Ketuboth* 10.4 of three wives, *Ketuboth* 10.5 of four wives, and *Kerithoth* 3.7 of five wives, showing that this applied to non-levirate marriages as well.

11   Montefiore, *Rabbinic Literature*, 41 and Moore, *Judaism*, 268-69.

sion of this passage, Evans points out that

> The fundamental dichotomy that existed between Jesus
> and the rabbis on this issue is not on the question of
> lust being sin—they were in complete agreement about
> that—but of lust being inevitable. To the Jews, if the sexes
> were to come into any kind of social contact, lust was
> unavoidable.…. Jesus, in contrast to the rabbis, completely
> dismisses the suggestion that lust is inevitable. He does
> not warn his followers against looking at a woman, but
> against doing so with lust. Women are to be recognized
> as subjects in their own right, as fellow human beings,
> fellow disciples, and not just the objects of men's desire.[12]

It would be hard to overstate the significance of this point.
The rabbis were so concerned about the dangers contact with
women posed to their ability to avoid the sin of sexual lust that
they erected barriers to cut down on that social interaction.
According to Montefiore, "To talk to a woman, to look at a
woman, indeed to have anything to do with a woman, was
regarded as dangerous and objectionable."[13] Jesus rejected the
idea that sexual lust was inevitable. To him it was a choice.[14]
It has been suggested plausibly that Jesus' high standards
about men controlling their lust and about divorce are what
enabled him to associate freely with women and expect his
disciples to intermingle the way they did without endangering
their reputation.[15] Of all the criticisms the Jewish religious
establishment had against Jesus and his disciples, "it must be
admitted that we hear nothing of any criticism of his conduct

---

12   *Woman in the Bible*, 45.
13   *Rabbinic Literature*, 41.
14   See Larry Chouinard, "Women in Matthew's Gospel," 435-36.
In commenting on Matt. 5:28 he states, "rather than demanding the
seclusion of women, Jesus places the responsibility upon the male to
exercise sexual restraint."
15   Evans, *Woman in the Bible*, 47. See also Lightfoot, *Role of Women*,
15.

on this count."[16] The next section expands on this very point, how Jesus interacted with women.

Jesus' Association with Women

His Interactions with Them

PERHAPS THE BEST PLACE TO BEGIN A DISCUSSION OF HOW Jesus interacted with women is to note that it is no different than the way he interacted with men.[17] Men and women were both treated as persons without gender becoming an issue. We find this in Jesus' healing ministry, where there is no discernable difference in the way he treated men and women. Even healing on the Sabbath benefitted both a man (Luke 14:1-6) and a woman (Luke 13:10-17). He healed a widow's son (Luke 7:11-15) and a man's daughter (Matt. 9:18-19, 23-25). His sensitivity and compassion toward women (Luke 7:36-50) and men (Luke 18:9-14) was ever present, including his encouraging sinners to forsake their sinful ways (John 8:11; Luke 19:8-10). Just as with men, Jesus would initiate a conversation with a woman, even one that would lead to his sharing with her some deep spiritual truths (John 4:7). He counted a number of women, not just men, among his closest disciples. In short, in the way Jesus interacted with women we see a stark contrast with the Palestinian rabbis. Because of women's low position, Jesus' treatment of them had the effect of greatly elevating their status. So what are some of the unique features of Jesus' association with women when viewed in the context of his day?

Jesus Interacted Freely with Women. His long conversation with the Samaritan woman at the well (John 4) is probably the

16   Montefiore, *Rabbinic Literature*, 41.
17   Robinson, *Community Without Barriers*, 27-28 and Evans, *Woman in the Bible*, 56-57.

best example, but there are many others. Luke alone records several. On one occasion Jesus joined the funeral procession of a widow's only son, raised him from the dead, and "gave him to his mother" (7:11-15). On another, at a meal in Simon the Pharisee's house, his host was put off by Jesus' interaction with a woman of the city who washed Jesus' feet with her tears and anointed them with the contents of a flask of ointment. He allowed her to touch him, he forgave her sins and told her so, and then announced, "Your faith has saved you; go in peace" (7:36-50).[18] On a preaching tour in Galilee, a group of women disciples traveled with him (8:2-3). He shared a meal with Martha and Mary in their home (10:38-40). On one Sabbath Jesus endured the rebuke of the ruler of a synagogue by touching a woman who had been ill for 18 years and healing her (13:10-17). Finally, and quite significantly, in his most difficult hour as he was being led to the cross Jesus noticed a number of women weeping for him. He turned and spoke to them directly (23:27-31).

Jesus Had Physical Contact with Women, Touching Them and Allowing Them to Touch Him

Touching Women. The Gospels record at least three times that Jesus took a woman by the hand or laid his hands on her when he healed her. The first of these was when Jesus healed Peter's mother-in-law from a fever (Matt. 8:15=Mark 1:31). On another occasion he healed Jairus' twelve-year-old daughter (Matt. 9:25=Mark 5:41-42=Luke 8:54). Note that although she is referred to as a "little girl" (*korasion* – Matt. 9:24-25, Mark 5:41-42) and "little daughter" (*thugatarion* – Mark 5:23), at twelve she was old enough to be betrothed or even married. The third occurrence was when Jesus, in a

---

18   Robinson's (28) summary of Jesus' interaction with this woman is that "he was wholly unembarrassed by the love and extravagant gratitude of a sinful woman who had experienced forgiveness from God, and he insisted that a judgmental Pharisee should learn from her."

synagogue on the Sabbath, healed the woman who had had a spirit of infirmity for eighteen years (Luke 13:13).

Allowing Women to Touch Him. Of the four examples to be mentioned here, three were when Jesus' body was being anointed in a home. They are all indications of his remarkable comfort level with being touched by a woman in a totally asexual way. Two were anointings in Bethany shortly before his death. The first was six days before the Passover presumably in the home of Martha, Mary and their brother Lazarus (John 12:1-3). Here the intimacy of Mary's physical contact with Jesus as she anointed his feet with pure nard and wiped them with her hair is unmistakable. The other was two days before the Passover in the house of Simon the leper where, in preparation for his burial, an unidentified woman anointed Jesus' head with an expensive ointment (Matt. 26:6-13=Mark 14:3-9).

Earlier in his ministry, however, back in Galilee an even more remarkable anointing occurred. A sinner woman of the city, uninvited, interrupted a meal at the home of Simon the Pharisee. She knelt at Jesus' feet, and while she was sobbing washed his feet clean with her tears, dried them with her hair, and only then anointed them with ointment she had brought (Luke 7:36-38, 44-50). Simon's reaction was instant and harsh in judgment against both the woman and Jesus. In what for any other rabbi would certainly have been an embarrassing and compromising situation, Jesus displayed no discomfort with her actions at all, calling particular attention to the intimacy of her physical contact with him. "You did not give me a kiss, but from the time I came in she has not stopped kissing my feet" (7:45). The contrast with the attitude and practice of the rabbis could not be greater. Finally, the example of women touching Jesus that did not involve an anointing was when the two Marys at the tomb were greeted by Jesus, and "they coming up took hold of his feet and worshiped him" (Matt. 28:9).

Closely related to Jesus' touching and being touched by women is the matter of ceremonial uncleanliness brought on by physical contact. The rabbis were obsessed with ritual uncleanness. For them contact with women, including their own wives, was one of the primary ways they could contract it. By contrast, Jesus put ministering to people ahead of maintaining ceremonial cleanliness. We see this repeatedly in his contact with women. The interaction with the woman with a flow of blood is a case in point (Matt. 9:20-22=Mark 5:25-34=Luke 8:43-48). According to Lev. 15:25-30 she was unclean, and coming into contact with certain things she had touched could render another person unclean for at least the rest of the day. As noted in chapter six, the Mishnah devoted a whole tractate (*Niddah*) to such situations. Jesus, however, instead of expressing concern that he had been violated by being rendered unclean by her touching him, tenderly responded to her: "Daughter, your faith has rescued you. Go in peace, and be healed of your disease" (Mark 5:34). The raising of the son of the widow from Nain is another example. In the course of performing that miracle for this poor woman, Jesus touched the son's funeral bier (Luke 7:14), an action that would have rendered him ceremonially unclean.[19]

The final example involves the Samaritan woman at the well (John 4). According to *Niddah* 4.1, from birth a Samaritan woman was as unclean as a Jewish woman who was menstruating. They were, therefore, always unclean. Touching a vessel that had been used by an unclean person also rendered one unclean (*Kelim* 1.1ff.). Thus Jesus was associating with a woman considered ritually unclean and was asking to use a vessel she had touched. The significance of this action was not lost on the woman. "How is it that you, being a Jew, ask to drink from me, since I am Samaritan woman" (4:9). The older English translations uniformly render the

---

19   See, for example, in the Mishnah, *Oholoth* 1.2-3.

verb (*sugchraomai*) in her next statement as "have dealings with" or "associate with." Some more recent translations have followed David Daube's convincing suggestion that in this context the better translation is "use something together with another person."[20] Her statement, then, would be rendered, "For Jews do not share the use of objects with Samaritans." Thus, by quoting the Samaritan woman here, the author of the Gospel of John is highlighting the point that Jesus was going against convention by asking for use of a vessel touched by a Samaritan. Again, where women were concerned, and from other examples where men were involved as well, Jesus did not allow the possibility of being rendered ritually unclean to prevent him from ministering fully to their needs.

Jesus Had a Committed Group of Female Disciples. If a rabbi ever had a female disciple, he would have been in the extreme minority. Jesus had many (*pollai*) of them (Luke 8:3; Matt. 27:55=Mark 15:41). The introductory summary statement in Luke 8:1-3 about one of his evangelistic tours through Galilee is quite instructive. Note, first of all, that other than the twelve, the only disciples Luke mentions in this traveling entourage is a group of many women. The prominence or importance of at least some of them is further seen in the fact that they are mentioned by name.[21] They were women of

---

20   "Samaritan Woman," 137-47. See also Stagg, *Woman in the World of Jesus*, 116. Bauer (*Greek-English Lexicon*, 3rd edition, 953-54) gives both meanings, but it identifies "make use of" as the first meaning. Among the more modern translations that follow the meaning Daube assigns to *sugchraomai* are the Good News Translation, Expanded Bible, Holman Christian Standard Bible, and New English Translation. Notably the New RSV now reads "Jews do not share things in common with Samaritans" in place of the original RSV's rendering, "for Jews have no dealings with Samaritans."

21   Mary Magdalene reappears in all four Gospels in Jerusalem during Jesus' final days. She is present at Jesus' crucifixion (Matt. 27:56=Mark 15:40; John 19:25), at Jesus' tomb on the day of the crucifixion (Matt. 27:61=Mark 15:47), at Jesus' tomb on the morning of his resurrection (Matt. 28:1=Mark 16:1; John 20:1), and with Peter and other disciples

some means and so were able to provide support (*diakoneō*) for Jesus' traveling band. Later we find a large group of female Galilean disciples witnessing Jesus' crucifixion from a distance, and again their financial assistance to him is mentioned (Matt. 27:55-56=Mark 15:40-41). Mark provides a detail of great importance in showing that these Galilean women at the cross were actually disciples in a formal sense. He makes it clear that they followed (*akoloutheō*) him *when* he was in Galilee (15:41), not simply that they followed him (i.e., followed along with him) *from* Galilee when he came to Jerusalem, as Matthew (27:55) and Luke (23:49) record. Mark uses the word "follow" (*akoloutheō*) here in the way it is employed repeatedly in the Gospels to mean "become a disciple" or "be a disciple."[22] Thus when Jesus called someone to discipleship, he said, "follow me" (*akolouthei moi*).[23] When they answered the call to discipleship they are said to have followed (*akoloutheō*).[24] Following (*akoloutheō*) Jesus is the comprehensive description of what it means to be Jesus' disciple.[25] When Peter described the depth of his and his companions' commitment to Jesus as his disciples, he said, "We

to whom she reported the empty tomb (John 20:2) and that Jesus was alive (John 20:18; Matt. 28:8=Luke 24:9-10). Joanna, the wife of Chuza, Herod's steward, reappears at Jesus' tomb on resurrection morning and, along with Mary Magdalene and Mary the mother of James, tells the apostles that Jesus is alive (Luke 24:10). Susanna appears only here in the Gospels.

22   *Akoloutheō* in this sense is defined by Bauer (*Greek-EnglishLexicon*, 3rd edition, 36) as "to follow someone as a disciple, be a disciple, follow." Gerhard Kittel ("ἀκολουθέω," 213) describes this as "the special use" of the word and says that it "is strictly limited to discipleship of Christ." He continues that all other occurrences of the word in the NT "speak of a following which has no religious significance" (n. 28).

23   See for example, Matt. 9:9=Mark 2:14=Luke 5:27; John 1:43, where Matthew and Philip heeded the call and Matt. 19:21=Mark 10:21=Luke 18:22, where the rich young ruler sadly did not.

24   For example, Peter, Andrew, James and John (Matt. 4:20, 22=Mark 1:18).

25   See Matt. 10:38, 16:24=Mark 8:34=Luke 9:23.

have left everything and followed (*akoloutheō*) you" (Matt. 19:27=Mark 10:28). Thus Mark's description of these women's commitment to Jesus back in Galilee as "following" him is an indication that they were his disciples, not just hangers on. Note finally how Mary Magdalene addressed Jesus at the tomb as "Rabboni" (John 20:16).[26]

Jesus Taught Women. One thing a rabbi or teacher does to his disciples is teach them. The Gospels make it clear that Jesus taught his female disciples just as he did his male followers. Most studies on this topic emphasize the fact that, in the manner of a student with his rabbi,[27] Mary, the sister of Martha and Lazarus, sat at the feet of Jesus while he was teaching (Luke 10:39). While this is true, more weight is often placed on this text than this simple statement ("sitting at the Lord's feet, she listened to his word") can bear. There is not enough evidence to conclude that she had the more formal status of a rabbi's student, nor that this happened on any other occasion. Yet it should not be lost that here she was, soaking up Jesus' teachings with whomever else he was instructing, not a common activity for a woman.

Two other passages, however, offer a better glimpse of the content of Jesus' teaching to some of his female disciples. The first is John 11:25-27. Mary may have been the recipient of Jesus' teaching in Luke 10, but her sister Martha was on this occasion. There are two parts to this encounter. First, Jesus revealed to her on the spot a message found nowhere else in the Gospels. "I am the resurrection and the life. The one who

---

26   Bauer (*Greek-English Lexicon*, 3rd edition, 902) defines this as "my lord, my master." According to Gustaf Dalman (*Words of Jesus*, 340) Rabboni "cannot have been materially distinguished from" Rabbi as a form of address. So here Mary is addressing Jesus as her rabbi.

27   See Mishnah, *Aboth* 1.4: "Let thy house be a meeting-house for the Sages and sit amid the dust of their feet and drink in their words with thirst." Paul describes his instruction by his former rabbi as "sitting at the feet of Gamaliel" (Acts 22:3).

believes in me, though he die, will live" (11:25). But this was
not the first time he had taught her a profound truth, as is
evidenced by her response to his question about whether she
believed him. "Yes, Lord. I have come to believe that you are
the Christ, the Son of God who is coming into the world"
(11:27). Where but from Jesus would she have been taught
this? Here she betrays a remarkable and accurate understanding of Jesus' true identity, which clearly indicates that she was
the recipient of some of Jesus' most intimate teaching.

The second example is found in Luke 24:6-7. At the empty
tomb, at least three of Jesus' Galilean female disciples encountered two men. They reminded the women of something Jesus
had taught them back in Galilee. "The Son of man must be
handed over into the hands of sinful men, and be crucified,
and on the third day rise." This message was so private and
sensitive that Jesus did not even consider his closest disciples
ready for it until their retreat in the region of Caesarea Philippi
(Matt. 16:21=Mark 8:31), and even then Peter was not ready
for it (Matt. 16:22=Mark 8:32). Yet in time, Jesus taught the
same message to some of his women disciples.

As the encounter with the Samaritan woman at the well
in John 4 shows, Jesus did not limit his teaching of women to
his Jewish disciples. The record of this interchange is notable
for both the manner and content of Jesus' teaching. Robinson writes about the similarity in the manner in which Jesus
approached teaching this woman and Nicodemus shortly
before this (John 3): "He showed the same degree of seriousness, the same concern to lead both to deeper insights, and the
same perception as to where they each were in their own spiritual development."[28] Yet the contrast between the two figures
could hardly have been greater. Nicodemus was the ultimate
insider: a Pharisee (3:1); a ruler of the Jews, which probably

---

28   *Community Without Barriers*, 7. Robinson's whole discussion of
Jesus' meeting with this woman is excellent and worthy of reading.

means that he was a member of the national Sanhedrin (3:1
and see 7:50); and some kind of a religious teacher (3:10).[29]

From Jesus and any other Jew's perspective, this woman
was anything but an insider: a woman, a Samaritan, and
having a questionable marriage history (4:18). Yet here Jesus
was with her, sharing three or four spiritual truths found here
either for the first time on record or the only time in the Bible.
The first dealt with living or running water (4:10, 13-14). Jesus
will return to this theme in John 7:37-39, where he connected
it with the Spirit. Jesus also linked water with the Spirit in
his conversation with Nicodemus (3:5-8). The second is the
spiritual character of God: "God is spirit," a revelation not
found explicitly stated elsewhere in the Bible (4:24).[30] Closely
associated with this is the third—the spiritual nature of true
worship: "the true worshippers will worship the Father in
spirit and truth.... those who worship Him must worship
in spirit and truth" (4:23-24). Only here in the Gospels did
Jesus disclose this to anyone, and remarkably it is to a woman
and an outsider. Finally, here for the first time in the Gospels
Jesus revealed to this woman that he was the Messiah (4:25-
26), although John the Baptist had already implied as much

---

29   Jesus referred to him as "*the* teacher (*didaskalos*) of Israel" (3:10).
Given the fact that John has already told his readers that *didaskalos* is
the Greek translation of the Aramaic word *rabbi* (1:38), he could have
been a rabbi himself. However, the use of the definite article "the" with
"teacher" in 3:10 makes it unlikely. More probable is the notion that
Jesus' meaning is that "*You* are supposed to be the teacher here, not me,
so why don't you know this"? Nevertheless, regardless of whether or not
Nicodemus was actually a rabbi in a formal relationship with his own
students, Jesus identified him as a teacher of some sort.

30   Two other characteristics are attributed to God in similar statements in a Johannine writing: "God is light" (I John 1:5) and "God is
love" (I John 4:8). In the case in John 4:24, the word "spirit" (*pneuma*)
appears first in the clause, presumably because of the central role of
pneuma in Jesus' new definition of worship. Leon Morris (*Gospel according to John*, 271) writes about this that "since He is essentially spirit
it follows that the worship brought to Him must be essentially of a
spiritual kind."

to his disciples (3:28). The uniqueness of what Jesus had just done in engaging a woman here was not lost on his disciples, who upon returning from their shopping trip, "marveled that he was speaking with a woman" (4:27). F. F. Bruce rightly comments on their surprise that "for a religious teacher to do this was at best a waste of time and at worst a spiritual danger."[31] From these few examples we learn that Jesus was not inhibited by custom when it came to teaching women.

Jesus Defended Women. The Gospels record a few instances where Jesus came to the defense of women. Well known is his defense of Mary to her sister, Martha, for making a better choice when he visited their home (Luke 10:38-42). However, more to the point are those times when he defended a woman against hostile men. The greatest hostility came when a group of scribes and Pharisees at the Temple brought forward an adulteress and defiantly asked Jesus to pass judgment on whether she should be stoned or not (John 8:2-11). Jesus avoided their trap calculated to bring charges against him. Rather than arguing the interpretation of Lev. 20:10 and Deut. 22:22-24 with them or asking them to produce her adulterous partner whom the Law said should also be executed, he skillfully confronted them with their own sinfulness. To the woman he offered no condemnation but rather a plea to reform her life. In another case, where Jesus healed a woman who had been chronically ill for 18 years, the hostility was directed toward Jesus rather than the woman (Luke 13:10-17). However, his response to the ruler of the synagogue concerned his hypocrisy in not recognizing the worth of this daughter of Abraham.

The other three examples involve women who anointed Jesus in different homes. First, at a meal at Simon the Pharisee's house, Jesus strongly defended the actions of a woman of the city who was a sinner (Luke 7:36-50). In his answer to

---

31   *Mind for What Matters*, 261.

Simon's judgmental thoughts, Jesus challenged Simon with a parable about two creditors and followed up by highlighting three ways the woman showed him greater respect and hospitality than he. Jesus then capped his praise for her with the comment, "I tell you, her many sins are forgiven because she loved much. But the one who is forgiven little, loves little" (7:47). The second occurrence also involved anointing Jesus' feet, this time by his friend Mary, the sister of Martha and Lazarus (John 12:1-8). On this occasion it was Judas Iscariot who criticized her act as wasteful, since the ointment could have been sold for a large sum and the money given to the poor. In Mary's defense, Jesus told Judas to "Leave her alone that she may keep it for the day of my burial" (12:7). The final instance occurred only a few days later, shortly before Jesus' crucifixion, in the home of Simon the leper (Matt. 26:6-13=Mark 14:3-9). This time an unnamed woman anointed Jesus' head with expensive ointment, and it was the disciples who became indignant at the waste, using the same excuse Judas had (Matt. 26:8-9). Jesus' response to this criticism was as beautiful as this woman's act.

> Why do you trouble the woman, for she has done a beautiful thing for me? For you always have the poor with you, but you do not always have me. For in pouring this ointment on my body, she has prepared me for burial. Truly I tell you, wherever this gospel is preached in the whole world, what she has done will also be spoken of in her memory (Matt. 26:10-13).

Their Interactions with Him

IN ORDER TO COME TO AN ADEQUATE UNDERSTANDING OF Jesus' relationship with women, especially his female disciples, we need to consider both sides of the equation. The preceding pages have dealt with the Jesus side—his association with women. Now we need to examine the relationship from these women's point of view. We have already seen some of this. He had a committed group of "many" female disciples in Galilee who chose to travel with and support him in his evangelistic work (Luke 8:1-3). Martha and Mary were Judean disciples who invited Jesus into the intimacy of their home on at least three occasions (Luke 10:38; John 11:1ff., 12:1-3). However, what is more telling are the actions of a loyal group of women we encounter at the cross and the tomb.

One has to look long and hard to find any positive element in the male disciples' actions surrounding these events. There is the case of Jesus' secret disciples, Joseph of Arimathea (Matt. 27:57-59=Mark 15:43-46=Luke23:50-53; John 19:38-42) and Nicodemus, (John 19:39) taking charge of Jesus' body and burying it. About the only encouraging feature of the apostles' response to these events was the excitement exhibited by Peter and the disciple whom Jesus loved in their foot race to the empty tomb and the latter's belief[32] when he saw the state of the inside of the tomb (John 20:2-9), but that is about all. Anyone who has read the Passion Narratives carefully has probably been struck by the fear, doubt, and downright cowardice of the male disciples, especially the twelve, during this time. Peter's denial[33] (Matt. 26:69-75=Mark 14:66-72=Luke 22:56-62) and Thomas' refusal to accept the disciples' testimony that Jesus was alive (John 20:24-25) are always noted in this regard, but it went deeper than that. The Gospels place only one male disciple anywhere near the cross (John 19:26-27),[34] but many (*pollai*) of Jesus' female disciples from Galilee were there watching from a distance (Matt. 27:55-56=Mark 15:40-41=Luke 23:49). In addition,

---

32   For a helpful discussion of what the author meant by "he believed," see Morris, *Gospel according to John*, 833-34.

33   As much as Peter was culpable for denying Jesus, at least he was present at the high priest's residence to deny him, having earlier fled with the rest of his companions (Matt. 26:56=Mark 14:50).

34   At best they were included among the non-specific "all his acquaintances" who observed the crucifixion "from a distance" (Luke 23:49).

four women, including Jesus' mother, stood by the cross to the very end (John 19:25-30). When several women reported to the apostles that Jesus had arisen, as he had told them he would do, they refused to believe them, regarding them with disrespect (Luke 24:8-11).[35] Even after the apostles had gone to Galilee where he had told them to meet him (Matt. 28:7, 10; Mark 16:7), "some doubted" upon seeing him alive (Matt. 28:17). The story of the women at the cross and the women at the tomb, then, deserve a closer look.

The Women at the Cross. The conduct of women during Jesus' last hours of life was in stark contrast to the wild mob who shouted, "crucify him." Pilate's wife interceded on Jesus' behalf (Matt. 27:19), while her husband took the coward's way out (Matt. 27:24; John 18:38b, 19:12-16). On the way to the cross Jesus had a remarkable interaction with women in the crowd who were "lamenting and weeping for him" (Luke 23:27). Here, in his darkest hour, he turned and acknowledged this act of compassion and spoke to them (23:28-31). This is just another example of how he was ever aware of the women in his presence. While Jesus was still alive on the cross four women, including his mother and Mary Magdalene, stood "by the cross" close enough to converse with him (John 19:25-27). In fact, a number of Jesus' female disciples who had followed him to Jerusalem from Galilee observed both what happened at the cross and some of them at least where his body was laid (Matt. 27:55-56=Mark 15:40-41=Luke 23:49, 55). Coupling this with the fact that a few women, including Mary Magdalene, were the first to visit Jesus' tomb on resurrection Sunday, it appears that women were the last at the cross and the first at the empty tomb![36]

---

35   Bauer (*Greek-English Lexicon*, 3rd edition, 594) defines the totally dismissive word usually translated "idle tale" or "nonsense" (*lēros*) in 24:11 as "that which is totally devoid of anything worthwhile, *idle talk, nonsense, humbug.*"

36   See Silena Holman's gripping description of the scene ("Peculiar

The Women at the Tomb. The Gospels are uniform in recording that certain women were the first and only people at the tomb at the beginning of resurrection morn. The central figure was Mary Magdalene. The testimony of the Gospel of John to her participation in the events of that day tells a remarkable story. She was the first at the tomb (20:1), the first to proclaim the empty tomb (20:2), the first to see and converse with the resurrected Jesus (20:14-17), and the first to bear witness to the resurrected Jesus (20:18), having been commissioned by Jesus himself to deliver the news to the disciples (20:17). On this latter point, some modern writers argue too much. Certainly Jesus would have entrusted the message of his resurrection to whoever was there, men or women. But, in point of fact, men were not there. This speaks volumes, especially in light of the fact that Jesus had told his closest disciples that he would rise from the dead. Further, Jesus could have delivered the message to the apostles and other disciples himself, but he didn't. He entrusted the announcement of what would become the most fundamental tenet of the Christian faith—Jesus has been raised from the dead--to Mary.[37] Many years ago Alexander Campbell captured the significance of this in a way that still resonates today.

> The highest and most attractive encomium pronounced in Christian history upon woman is not that she bathed the feet of Jesus in her tears and that she wiped them with the tresses of her hair; it is not that she was last at the cross, in solemn contemplation of the fearful agonies of his death; but that she was first at the sepulcher in the early dawn

People," 12): "Men reviled and persecuted him, and crucified him, but no woman was found among his enemies. The wife of Pilate pleaded for his life. A mad crowd of Jews surged around the Roman Tribunal, howling like wild beasts for his blood and the cry ascended to heaven again and again, crucify him! crucify him! But 'a great company of women,' followed him to the place of crucifixion weeping and lamenting him."

37   See Stagg, *Woman in the World of Jesus*, 144.

of the first day of the week, making her way through the Roman guard, with full intent to embalm his lacerated body; in honor of which most affectionate and grateful devotion he presented himself to her in that same body, as the triumphant conqueror of death and of the grave, and commissioned her, as his prime-minister, to announce the gospel of his resurrection to her mourning and disconsolate companions.[38]

Conclusions

WHAT ARE WE TO MAKE OF ALL THIS? AS FAR AS JESUS' references to women and activities of their lives in his teachings is concerned, there is little to distinguish him from the Palestinian rabbis whose teachings are found in the Mishnah. However, in his teachings *about* women and his association *with* them and they with him he broke the mold. It is not an exaggeration to say that here Jesus comes across as decidedly counter-cultural.[39] In Mark, Jesus' observation about the sacrificial gift of the poor widow at the Temple follows immediately his denunciation of the scribes for devouring widows' houses. His stance on divorce and remarriage differs from that of the rabbis in the Mishnah on at least four counts: (1) from the beginning God intended that there be no divorce; (2) the practice of allowing multiple reasons for a man to divorce his wife is wrong; (3) the ability to divorce one's spouse is not limited to husbands; and (4) adultery can be against the wife, not just against the husband. Here Jesus sets the stage for Paul's likewise strong stance against Christians initiating a divorce against their Christian spouses, attribut-

---

38   "Woman and Her Mission," 225. This is from an address delivered to the Henry Female Seminary in Newcastle, KY on May 30, 1856.
39   See Ferguson, *Women in the Church*, 70; Robinson, *Community Without Barriers*, 27; Stagg, *Woman in the World of Jesus*, 255; and Montefiore, *Rabbinic Literature*, 217-18.

ing this teaching to Jesus himself (I Cor. 7:10-11). Finally, in his teaching on male sexual lust he differed sharply from the rabbis in his insistence that a man can control his lust. With this high standard in sexual matters and by his own example in dealing with women even in close relationships, Jesus made it possible to create a band of men and women disciples who could associate freely with one another without raising the suspicion of immorality. This paved the way for similar close relations between men and women in the church.

Even more than his teachings about women, Jesus' own association with women opened up the possibilities well beyond male-female interactions customary in the Palestine of his day. Jesus entered into conversations with women both publically and in private. He had close women friends and even accepted meal invitations from them in their homes. Many of his women disciples traveled with and supported him and the twelve as he toured Galilee preaching and evangelizing. He showed no revulsion or embarrassment when being lovingly touched by even a sinner woman. Nor did he express concern that he had been rendered unclean by a sick woman's touch. Unlike his rabbinic counterparts, he had a committed band of female disciples, and he shared with them certain of his most important teachings, some of them for the first or only time in the biblical record. Among them are

- His gift of living water that wells up into eternal life (John 4:14).

- The spiritual character of God: "God is spirit" (John 4:24).

- The spiritual nature of true worship: "the true worshippers will worship the Father in spirit and truth…. those who worship Him must worship in spirit and truth" (John 4:23-24).

- That he was "the Christ, the Son of God who is coming into the world" (John 11:27). See also his revelation to the Samaritan woman at the well that he was the Messiah (John 4:25-26).

- "I am the resurrection and the life. The one who believes in me, though he die, will live" (John 11:25).

- "The Son of man must be handed over into the hands of sinful men, and be crucified, and on the third day be raised" (Luke 24:7).

Additionally, on more than one occasion Jesus defended a woman against hostile men, even his own disciples. Finally, he interacted and conversed with women on the way to the cross, while on the cross, and shortly after his resurrection. He could not have been more different than his opponents among the scribes and Pharisees.

So what are we to make of these significant changes in the position of women that could affect the future church? First, as has been pointed out above, they are in line with Jesus' general compassionate approach to other marginalized groups in his day. If, after his death, his disciples are to follow in the trajectory set by Jesus, the lives of many downtrodden or ostracized people, not just women, will change dramatically for the better. Secondly, there is no discernable difference in the way Jesus treated or regarded men or women. This plays out especially in the fact that Jesus called both male and female disciples and seems to have made no distinction in teaching them. The significance of this for the church is obvious. Finally, the account in all four Gospels of the conduct of Jesus' closest male and female disciples around the events of his passion gives us a window into the status of women in the first-century church. Here, decades after the establishment of the church, the four Evangelists portray women in the most positive light, particularly when contrasted with their male counterparts. Jesus set the stage for this new view of women, and we see his vision carried out in the church in the first few decades after his departure. That story begins in the next chapter.

Postscript

BEFORE LEAVING JESUS, TWO OTHER MATTERS REQUIRE our attention. Neither of them relates to the topic of Jesus and women, but they, nevertheless, have some bearing on discussions of Paul's limitations on women in the assembly.

1. **Jesus' Appointment of Only Men among the Twelve**. A number of writers have made the suggestion that the fact that all the Twelve were men is evidence for the limiting of women's participation in the assembly and in the church at large. The weakness of this view was discussed at the end of chapter three, including C. R. Nichol's difficulties with it. Jesus simply did not tell us why he chose those whom he chose. We are left to figure that out on our own, realizing that any suggestion is at best an educated guess. Must we conclude that Jesus chose only men to be in the Twelve because it has always been God's intent that men lead and women follow, so Jesus was not at liberty to choose a woman if he was to be faithful to his Father's will? Might there be other possible explanations?

    Robinson in his fine discussion in *A Community Without Barriers* proposes three (15-19). His points are worth restating here, although one of them is not completely in sync with some of the conclusions reached in this chapter. First he notes, as many others have done, that in addition to being men "they were all Jewish as well, perhaps all from Galilee, and certainly all from Palestine" (16). Not included were Gentiles or Samaritans, although many of them lived in Palestine. If women were later to be excluded from service in the church based on who made up the Twelve, why would this not apply to Gentiles and Samaritans as well? There must have been something else at work here. Robinson's three suggestions follow.

The Twelve correspond to the twelve tribes of Israel.
According to Jesus, the number, twelve, for this group
relates to the twelve tribes of Israel. "When the Son of
man sits on his glorious throne, you also will sit on twelve
thrones judging the twelve tribes of Israel" (Matt. 19:28).
Thus, according to Robinson, "in the twelve men whom he
named his twelve apostles, Jesus symbolically reconstituted
the twelve patriarchs / tribes of Israel" (16). This is a role
that naturally needed to be filled by men. This number,
twelve, had to be maintained, as we see after the death of
Judas when the eleven apostles (Acts 1:26) were brought
back up to strength with Matthias being named Judas'
replacement.

The Twelve were official witnesses. "Jesus intended for
the twelve to serve as witnesses of the resurrection to the
outside world (Acts 1:8, 15-26; 2:14, 32; 3:15; 5:32)"
(17). Robinson observes that in first-century Palestine, the
testimony of women could be suspect and its acceptance
limited. This sad state of affairs prevailed outside of
Palestine as well and has continued to persist widely into
modern times. While women could certainly bear witness
to what they had seen, as did Mary Magdalene and two
others on resurrection morn, the skeptical reaction of even
the apostles was, unfortunately, typical (Luke 24:10-11).

The Twelve were expected to travel with Jesus. Robinson
noted that although women traveled with Jesus' entourage
some of the time, the Twelve would be expected to go
anywhere with him or where he sent them. This could have
been very difficult at times for women, whose freedom of
movement was more restricted than men's. Although not
mentioned by Robinson, this situation would have become
much more of an issue in subsequent years as the Twelve

were commissioned to "go and make disciples of all the nations" (Matt. 28:19).

Robinson concluded his study by stating that "Jesus himself never linked his choice of twelve Jewish men to any limitation on the ministry of others—Jewish or Gentile, male or female, slave or free" (19). For us to do so goes beyond what is written.

2. **Jesus' Approach to Leadership**. Much of the literature on what women may or may not do in the assembly is littered with the "rulers of the Gentiles'" approach to leadership. After Jesus left Galilee for the last time, he was teaching in the Jordan valley of Judea before going up to Jerusalem for the final time. On one occasion the sons of Zebedee, along with their mother, tried to get Jesus to promise them positions of prominence in his kingdom. This did not sit well with the other disciples, so Jesus brought them down to earth with one of his most shocking declarations (Matt. 20:25-28=Mark 10:42-45).[40] He defined greatness or leadership in terms of service. "You know that the rulers of the Gentiles lord it over (*katakurieuō*) them and their great ones (*megas*) exercise authority over (*katexousiazō*) them. It shall not be so among you, but whoever wants to be great (*megas*) among you will be your servant (*diakonos*), and whoever wants to be first among you will be your slave (*doulos*)." Here Jesus defines leadership among his disciples

---

40   Luke's description of a similar incident takes place at the Last Supper (22:24-27). There, to address a dispute about which of the apostles was to be regarded as the greatest (*meizōn*), Jesus provided a similar definition of servant leadership. In this case the word "leader" (*hēgeomai*) actually occurs: "Let the greatest among you become as the youngest and the leader as one who serves (*diakoneō*)" (22:26). Given that Jesus ended this teaching with the declaration that "I am in your midst as one who serves (*diakoneō*)" (22:27b), it is not difficult to imagine that this is the point during the evening when he girded himself with a towel and washed their feet (John 13:3ff.).

as *servant* leadership, rejecting the exercise of authority as an acceptable approach.

Yet, if the literature on the subject is typical, the prevailing view of leadership among many who support the traditional limitations on women in the church is one of authority. This is in stark contrast with Jesus' model of servant leadership.[41] How could praying out loud in the presence of others be construed as an act of assuming authority over them? Such an extreme view is not only mind boggling, but it flies in the face of Jesus' teaching about servant leadership. To presume that when someone "leads" a prayer in the assembly he is in an authoritarian position is to interject into Christian ministry what Jesus sought to remove. Note also that Jesus' model of leadership applies to men as well. In the assembly, when men pray and speak and read Scripture and pass communion plates, they are *serving* the congregation, not doing it in a way that lords it over or tries to exert authority over the church. As long as our primary model for male leaders is that they are authority figures, rather than servants, we show that the world, rather than Jesus, has shaped our understanding of leadership and public ministry.

---

41   Two examples should suffice. Roy Deaver ("Women and Prayer," 15) in discussing the issues of prayer and teaching in I Tim. 2, states this: "Being the *leader* in teaching and/or in praying *does* involve the authority of dominion which is forbidden to women." Dave Miller ("Permit Not a Woman," 27) makes an even broader application to today. He argues that "based on 1 Timothy 2, women in our day should not read Scripture to the congregation, lead in prayer in mixed groups, or 'wait' on the Lord's Table since in each of these activities, the participants are functioning as worship leaders. They are standing before the assembly in an authoritative capacity in order to direct the worshipers in a specific worship activity." In both of these cases the operative definition of leadership is that of the rulers of the Gentiles, rather than the servant leadership required by Jesus.

CHAPTER EIGHT

Galatians 3:28 and Ephesians 5:21-33

A ny serious consideration of Paul's contribution to the matter of women in the church, especially what they may or may not do in the assembly, must necessarily examine in depth the three Pauline passages where he treats women in the assembly: I Corinthians 11 and 14 and I Timothy 2. Unfortunately, that is where most studies on the topic begin and not a few of them end.[1] However, there are other texts in his writings, as well as in Acts, that provide significant information to paint a fuller picture. This chapter will deal with two of them: Gal. 3:28 and Eph. 5:21-33.

Paul and Jesus

PAUL WAS A SERIOUS STUDENT OF RABBAN GAMALIEL I the Elder of Jerusalem (Acts 22:3).[2] His approach to the Law

---

1   Thomas Robinson's excellent chapter on Women in the Ministry of Jesus at the beginning of his book (*Community Without Barriers*) is a refreshing exception.

2   Gamaliel was the grandson of Rabbi Hillel. As the head of the school of Hillel, he was the leading rabbi of his day and is notably the first to have the title "Rabban" applied to him. He was also a leading member of the national Sanhedrin in Jerusalem and in the early days of the church Gamaliel is the one who convinced the Sanhedrin to release the apostles with merely a warning and a beating (Acts 5:33-40) after their arrest at the Temple. In a nostalgic passage in the Mishnah (*Sotah* 9.15) it is said of Gamaliel that when he died, "the glory of the Law

and its traditional interpretation would have been more heavily influenced by that of his own rabbi than of any other one.[3] When he became a Christian he transferred his allegiance to another teacher or rabbi—Jesus Christ. It makes sense, then, that his approach to matters relating to women would be more influenced by what he learned from and about Jesus than what he had earlier learned from Gamaliel. So, do we find characteristics of his attitude toward and association with women in his ministry that are more consistent with those of Jesus than with the Palestinian Rabbis of his day? An examination of the evidence leads us to a strong affirmative answer.

In the content of Paul's teaching, he treats the matter of marriage and divorce among Christians much like Jesus' overall approach. In marriage, the husband and wife are on equal footing (I Cor. 7:2-5), unlike the norm in either Jesus's world or in Paul's Greco-Roman world. As far as Christians divorcing each other is concerned, they are simply not to do

---

ceased and purity and abstinence died." See Travers Herford, *Ethics of the Talmud*, 35.

3   Although there is some information on Gamaliel in the Mishnah and the Babylonian Talmud, Jacob Neusner and Bruce D. Chilton ("Paul and Gamaliel," 114) have observed that "we have only episodic and anecdotal data, bits and pieces of this and that, which scarcely cohere to form a recognizable whole." They did, however, find one discernable similarity between Paul and Gamaliel in their use of logic and method of argumentation (149, 156). The few teachings of Gamaliel found in the Mishnah deal with diverse topics: movement on the Sabbath (*Rosh ha-Shanah* 2.5), what does or does not make dough forbidden (*Orlah* 2:11-12), the Shekel Temple offering (*Shekalim* 3.3), and a fourteenth location for prostration at the Temple (*Shekalim* 6.1). More to the point of this study, in three passages Gamaliel deals in one way or another with women. In one he rules that a man may not annul a bill of divorce without his wife's knowledge (*Gittin* 4.2). The next section records his provision for a widow to receive her *ketubah* upon making a vow to the orphans (*Gittin* 4.3). Finally, and perhaps most significantly, he went against the Sages of the Land of Israel in allowing a woman to marry again on the testimony of her husband's demise by only one witness (*Yebamoth* 16.7). This became the standard, though not universal, practice.

it, and this directive comes from the Lord (Jesus) himself (7:10-11).

It is in Paul's *relationship* with women, however, that we find the strongest echoes of Jesus' example. Just as with Jesus, Paul had close female friends and he interacted freely with them. He was quite inclusive of women as evangelistic co-workers whom he treated on a par with himself and any others (Rom. 16:3, 6, 12; Phil. 4:3). Not only was it expected that women be taught (I Cor. 14:31, 35; I Tim. 2:11, 5:4), as with Jesus' female disciples, they were also to be teachers (Tit. 2:3-5; cf. Acts 18:26). He paid high compliments to various women, including one who was his benefactor (Rom. 16:2), another who had risked her neck for him (16:4), and one who had shared prison with him (16:7). He referred to women in the warmest and most affectionate terms: "outstanding" (*episēmos* – Rom. 16:7), "beloved" (*agapētē* – 16:12), and "my (surrogate) mother" (16:13). Just as Jesus had done, he favored asexual physical contact among all the disciples. Note that at the end of his long list of greetings of both men and women, he urged the Romans to "greet one another with a holy kiss" (16:16).

These sisters in Christ were integral to the spread of the Gospel and service to the church, just as the male disciples were. The path Paul laid out for the church in both his attitude and actions toward women looks remarkably similar to and just as counter-cultural as that of Jesus. Had Paul's interpreters through the ages begun at this point, rather than focusing on the two passages where he places limitations on women in the assembly, the story of women in the church might have been written much differently. It is such a tragedy that those two passages, which go against the flow of everything else in the NT about women as disciples of Jesus, should be regarded as the norm, rather than as anomalies that demand an explanation for their strangeness.

Galatians 3:28

There is neither Jew nor Greek; there is neither slave nor free; there is neither male and female, for you are all one in Christ Jesus.

ON THE MATTER OF WOMEN IN THE CHURCH, PROBABLY more ink has been spilled on Gal. 3:28 than on any other passage in the NT than perhaps I Cor. 14:34. Sadly, interpretations of these two verses are frequently more influenced by conclusions the reader brings to the text than by the actual contexts. In other words, too often these verses are treated in proof-text fashion. Those favoring a wider role for women in the church find respite in their interpretation of Gal. 3:28, while those who support more traditional limitations on women rely on their understanding of I Cor. 14:34. Neither gives adequate weight to the contexts in which Paul made these two statements.

For many, Gal. 3:28 is the single most important passage in the NT dealing with the position of women. To them it expresses Paul's social agenda to eliminate, or at the very least, minimize male-female distinctions in the church and home. A few examples will suffice. With reference to the verse, Gilbert Bilezikian asserts: "Sex distinctions are irrelevant in the church. Therefore, the practice of sex discrimination in the church is sinful."[4] The passage has been described as "the Magna Carta of Christian liberty"[5] and "the Magna Carta of Humanity."[6] Both F. F. Bruce[7] and W. Ward Gasque[8]

---

4   *Beyond Sex Roles*, 128.
5   Donald G. Bloesch, *Is the Bible Sexist?*, 32.
6   Paul K. Jewett, *Male and Female*, 142.
7   Bruce, *Galatians*, 190.
8   Gasque, "Response to Galatians 3:28," 189. Gasque even goes so far as to assert that "In Galatians 3:28, Paul opens wide the door for women, as well as for Gentiles and slaves, to exercise spiritual leader-

assert that Gal. 3:28 is Paul's primary text on women, and
other Pauline statements must be interpreted in light of it.
For Mary Hayter, Gal. 3:28 is "the *locus classicus* of biblical
texts for those who believe that, ultimately, Scripture does
not discriminate between male and female."[9] Rebecca M.
Groothuis states that "of all the texts that support biblical
equality, Galatians 3:26-28 is probably the most important."
She continues, "the spirit and intent of Galatians 3:26-28 is
that differences of race, social class, and gender should no
longer determine differences of status and privilege within
the religious community."[10] Perhaps no one's statement is
stronger and more direct that that of David M. Scholer: "I
understand Galatians 3:28 to be the fundamental Pauline
theological basis for the inclusion of women and men as equal
and mutual partners in all of the ministries of the Church."[11]
But can any of this be substantiated by a careful examination
of what the verse actually says (the first question, what does
it say?) and what it meant *in its context* (the second question,
what did it mean?)?

   Most interpreters agree that the verse has an explicit
meaning that relates to the vertical relationship with Christ.
As can be seen from the paragraph above, what is disputed
is whether Paul also implied a secondary horizontal or social
meaning. Here we will begin with Paul's primary meaning.
His argument in Galatians, particularly in chapter 3, is well
laid out by Jan Faver Hailey[12] and Carroll Osburn.[13] Paul is
trying to counter Judaizing teachers who are attempting to
force Jewish practices on new Gentile Christians as require-

ship in the church." (192) To this can also be added David M. Scholer's ("Galatians 3:28," 8) contention that Gal. 3:28 is "a 'window' text
through which to assess and adjudicate other Pauline texts."
9   Mary Hayter, *New Eve in Christ,* 134.
10   *Good News for Women,* 25, 28.
11   ."Galatians 3:28," 8.
12   "Neither Male and Female," 148-61.
13   *Reclaiming the Ideal,* 134-37.

ments of their new faith. Galatians 3 has an extended counter argument centered on Abraham. It culminates in 3:26 with the statement, "for you are all sons of God through faith in Christ Jesus." Rather than observance of the Jewish law as the vehicle to be in a relationship as a child of God, faith in Christ is the key. It is through baptism that this union with Christ has occurred and the result was clothing oneself with Christ (v. 27) or, put another way, being one with/in Christ Jesus (v. 28). Hence, the three pairs in the first part of v. 28 have to do with becoming one with Christ through faith and baptism.

Before turning to the proposed secondary or social interpretation of the verse, what two or three modern interpreters have written about Paul's primary meaning are worthy of mention. Thomas Robinson explains that Paul's inclusion of the slave-free and male-female pairs into his discussion of Gentiles is that he is making a point about inheritance.

> In his illustration to show that believers inherit the promise of Abraham, he reflected the common practices of inheritance. Slaves inherited nothing, daughters inherited little if anything, sons were the almost universal heirs of their family property with first-born sons having the greatest rights. His point of illustration was that believers are not slaves but that all believers (male and female, slave and free, Jew and Gentile) become "sons of God" and thus full heirs.[14]

Roy H. Lanier, Jr. provides one of the best explanations of the verse both for the point it makes and its succinctness.

> The language here is about salvation not social conduct. This passage is not about how salvation affects social and sexual distinctions; rather, it is about whether social and sexual distinctions will keep one from becoming an heir

---

14   *Community Without Barriers*, 83. Note how the "inheritance" word group appears five times in this part of Galatians: *klēronomia*, "inheritance" – 3:18; *klēronomeō*, "to inherit" – 4:30; *klēronomos*, "heir" – 3:29, 4:1, 7.

of salvation, promised through Abraham and perfected in Christ Jesus.[15]

Certainly Paul's explicit point is clear, but does he also imply something else? An implication is just that. It is something that the reader believes the author meant, but did not state. As such, an implication is subjective. It may be right; it may be wrong, but it comes from the interpreter, not the writer. An implication bypasses the first question (what does it say?) and goes straight to the second (what did it mean?). Klyne R. Snodgrass has called Gal. 3:28 "the most socially explosive statement in the New Testament."[16] That might very well be the case if the social implication that is often applied to the verse were accurate. Snodgrass continues by addressing the way Gal. 3:28 has been viewed by many of those who find the key meaning in what Paul did not say.

> The attempt to explain the setting and role of Galatians 3:28 have left a trail that is not particularly flattering to biblical and theological studies. Any attempt at biblical studies involves some reading between the lines, but too often our studies have focused more attention on the material between the lines than on the lines themselves. This text, like some others, has become a hermeneutical skeleton key by which we may go through any door we choose. More often than not, Galatians 3:28 has become a piece of plastic that people have molded to their preconceived ideas.[17]

Sadly, disconnected from its context, an implied second-

---

15   "Galatians 3:28," 20. His father's earlier summary ("Woman's Liberty," 9) is also worth repeating: "The teaching of this verse is that there is no distinction between Jew and Greek, between master and slave, between male and female with reference to justification by faith in Christ." See also Wayne Walden's grammatical analysis of the verse and his conclusion that it has nothing to do with "gender roles" ("Galatians 3:28," 45, 48, 50).

16   Klyne R. Snodgrass, "Galatians 3:28," 161.

17   Ibid.

ary meaning has often been attached to Gal. 3:28 and in proof-text fashion has been promoted as the central Pauline teaching on women in the church and the family. Not only is this methodologically suspect from an exegetical standpoint, but it has created unnecessary difficulties for those interpreters. They find it necessary to explain how Paul could be so strong on women's liberty in Gal. 3:28, but backtrack in such passages as I Cor. 11:2-16, 14:34-35; Eph. 5:22-24, 33; Col. 3:18, and I Tim. 2:8-15. Their explanations run the gamut from (1) a denial of Pauline authorship for some of these passages[18] to (2) the belief that the realities of the church's position in the Greco-Roman world caused Paul to be more cautious[19] to (3) problems within Pauline churches, including pushing Christian liberty too far[20] to (4) the assertion that Paul was simply inconsistent[21] to (5) the view that whatever these other Pauline passages mean, they must be interpreted in light of their interpretation of Gal. 3:28.[22] Remove what

---

18   This is generally the position of non-evangelical scholars, but even the well-known evangelical NT specialist, Gordon D. Fee, (*First Epistle to the Corinthians*, 697) questions the Pauline authorship of I Cor. 14:34-35. Snodgrass ("Galatians 3:28," 166) summarizes six different approaches, including this one, that have been used to explain the presumed tension between Gal. 3:28 and other Pauline texts.

19   See Clarence Boomsma, *Male and Female,* 40; Snodgrass, "Galatians 3:28," 179; Gasque, "Response to Galatians 3:28," 191; Stagg, *Woman in the World of Jesus,* 191; and Paul Jewett, "No Male and Female," 26. This point actually has some merit even apart from the social interpretation of Gal. 3:28, as will be seen later in discussions of some other Pauline passages.

20   See Scholer, "Galatians 3:28," 9; Boomsma, *Male and Female*, 39-40; Gasque, "Response to Galatians 3:28," 191; Stagg, *Woman in the World of Jesus,* 188-89; and Bobbie Lee Holley, "God's Design, Part III," 13-14.

21   See Snodgrass' ("Galatians 3:28," 166) characterization of this as Jewett's position in *Male and Female,* 112.

22   In addition to the Bruce (*Galatians*, 190) and Gasque's ("Response to Galatians 3:28," 189) citations in notes 7 and 8 above, see Scholer's reference to Gal. 3:28 as "a 'window' text through which to assess and adjudicate other Pauline texts." ("Galatians 3:28," 8).

is obviously an unwarranted interpretation that has been imposed on the verse, and the presumed conflict vanishes.

This is not to say that being one with Christ Jesus as God's heirs is without implications for the saved community. There certainly are implications. Paul specifies elsewhere what they are for each of the three pairs. The point is that we simply should not use Gal. 3:28 as a proof text, or as Snodgrass would say, as a skeleton key to unlock any implication we fancy. We need to look to Paul's explicit statements elsewhere, not to what we subjectively find implicit in this verse. We now turn to one of those passages relating to men and women where Paul is explicit—Ephesians 5:21-33.

Ephesians 5:21-33

HAVING ATTEMPTED TO REMOVE THE CLOUD SOME INTER-pretations of Gal. 3:28 have unnecessarily cast over Eph. 5:21-33, we are now free to examine Paul's beautifully clear exposition here. Before doing that, however, the meanings of two words used in this passage and other places in Paul need to be examined. The words, *hupotassō*, "to submit" (5:21, 24), and *kephalē*, "head" (5:23), have been at the center of a firestorm on the matter of women in the church. Therefore, before considering their specific meaning in Eph. 5, each will be examined in its own excursus.

Excursus 7: **Hupotassō** *("to submit") in the New Testament.* The Greek word in Eph. 5:21 that is usually translated in English as "to submit" or "be subject" (*hupotassō*) is used 37 times in the NT (38 if the textual variant in Eph. 5:22 is authentic). It occurs three times in the Gospels, all in Luke, where it refers to Jesus' submission to his parents (2:51) and twice to the submission of the demons/spirits to the Seventy (10:17, 20). In the epistles outside of Paul it appears 12 times.[23] All the rest (22 instances) appear in Paul. Of those in Paul, ten have God or Christ as the subject or agent of the action of the verb.[24] In the active voice (the act of subjecting someone or something), God or Christ is always the subject of the verb, both in Paul and in the rest of the NT.[25] Fourteen times in the NT epistles God is either the subject or agent of the action of *hupotassō*. All but three instances (God's subjecting the creation to futility in Rom. 8:20 [twice] and Christ's future submitting himself to God in I Cor. 15:28) refer to God's subjecting all things to Christ, and in all but two of these there is an explicit reference to Psalm 8:7(6).[26]

In the NT, where humans are the subject or agents of the action of *hupotassō*, the voice of this Greek verb is always middle or passive.[27] If it is middle it would be rendered something like "submit yourself," and if passive, "be submissive." Ten times Paul uses the word of submitting oneself to other people,[28] and five additional times it is used this way in I

---

23   Heb. 2:5, 8 (3 times), 12:9; Jas. 4:7; and I Pet. 2:13, 18, 3:1, 5, 22, 5:5.

24   Rom. 8:20 (twice); I Cor. 15:27 (three times), 28 (three times); Eph. 1:22; and Phil. 3:21.

25   According to Gerhard Delling ("ὑποτάσσω," 39), in pagan authors at that time, the active voice meant a. "to place under" or b. "to subordinate." Referring to these cases where God is the subject or agent of the action of *hupotassō*, Marcus Barth (*Ephesians*, 709) writes, "In all of these cases the act of subjugation and the fate of the submission reveal the existence of a hierarchy, or establish the proper order of right and might. The weaker is put 'in its place'; he has to obey and serve; law and order are thus established."

26   The other two—Phil. 3:21 and I Pet. 3:22—though not explicit references to Psalm 8:7, may be verbal allusions.

27   In Greek the passive voice is the same as it is in English. There is, however, an additional voice referred to as middle. It pertains to the subject of the verb acting on or in some way related to itself.

28   Rom. 13:1, 5; I Cor. 14:34, 16:16; Eph. 5:21, 24; Col. 3:18; and Tit. 2:5, 9, 3:1.

Peter (2:13, 18, 3:1, 5, 5:5). Unfortunately, all of Paul's ten occurrences are in the present tense, meaning that we cannot distinguish between the middle and passive voices, because in the present tense the middle and passive forms of the verb are the same. The middle translation, "submit yourself," is probably to be preferred to the passive, because the verb is talking about something a person actually does.

The exact meaning of *hupotassō* in a given NT passage is determined both by its lexical definition and the specific way it is used in the passage at hand.[29] Thus, although the matters of subordination to authority or obedience or inferiority may be present in some contexts where *hupotassō* is used, none of these is inherent in the verb itself. For example, subordination to authority can hardly be involved in I Cor. 16:16, where Paul directs the Corinthians to submit to several people in the congregation, none of whom is indicated as having any kind of authority. The beginning of the household code in Eph. 5:21-6:9 has all of the six types of individuals submitting to one another (5:21);[30] yet clearly children are not in a position of authority over their fathers (6:1), nor slaves over their masters (6:5).[31] The same can be said about obedience. While the idea of obedience may be present in some contexts

---

29   See Delling, "ὑποτάσσω," 45. "In exhortation the middle embraces a whole series of meanings from subjection to authority on the one side to the considerate submission to others on the other. As regards the detailed meaning this can finally be decided only from the material context."

30   See Ferguson, *Women in the Church* 58 and Joyce Hardin, "Women's Role," 14.

31   To submit oneself to others out of reverence for Christ (Eph. 5:21) has nothing to do with the authority of one person over another. For a father to submit to his children or a master to his slaves, relationships covered in this household code, authority does not come into the equation at all. It could mean such things as submitting to another's wishes or to what is best for him/her or something else similar. Submitting oneself to another does not need to involve the authority of one person over another.

where *hupotassō* is used, that nuance cannot be derived from the verb itself.[32] On the matter of inferiority, George Kraus correctly observes that "subjection is not the equivalent of inferior. The Lord Jesus washed the feet of His disciples; does that make Him their inferior?"[33]

Returning to the point that consideration of the context is essential to determine the meaning of *hupotassō* in a particular passage, not only is the respect in which the submission is to be exhibited at issue, but sometimes to whom or what submission is due is not immediately apparent. Thus in I Cor. 14:34 the women who are asked to "submit themselves" are not told to whom/what that submission should be directed—their husbands,[34] the leaders of the congregation, other members of the congregation, the need of the congregation for order (see 14:40),[35] or what? Unfortunately, the reference to "the law" is so general that it is of no help. Then again, the cognate noun, *hupotagē*, "submissiveness," is applied to certain wives in I Tim. 2:11. Is Paul indicating these wives' submission to the message being taught,[36] to their husbands, to the men in the congregation,[37] to the leaders of the congregation,[38] to

---

32   Gerhard Delling ("ὑποτάσσω." 40) defines *hupotassō* in the middle as "to subject oneself" or "to submit voluntarily." He states further that "in the NT the verb does not immediately carry with it the thought of obedience." (41)

33   "Subjection," 21. Also see Barth's (*Ephesians*, 714) discussion of *hupotassō*, where he argues forcefully that the verb does not imply any kind of rank or hierarchy.

34   So Coffman, *1 and 2 Corinthians*, 241 and McGarvey, *Commentary*, 142.

35   So Osburn ("Interpretation of 1 Cor. 14:34-35," 237 and *Refocusing the Discussion*, 108).

36   Witherington III, *Women in the Earliest Churches*, 263, n. 208.

37   So Frank Bellizzi, "Principle of Submission," 32.

38   See Matt Soper, "I Timothy 2:8-15," 5. "Paul is probably thinking here primarily of the marriage relationships with reference also to submission to the leaders of the church." According to Manfred T. Brauch (*Hard Sayings of Paul*, 256), "the 'submission' enjoined on them is most likely a submission to the elders in the church, who are guardians of the

the designated teachers of the congregation[39] (cf. Rom. 12:7, Eph. 4:11), or to whom? The context must be our guide here.

The absence in the NT of any instances of *hupotassō* referring to one person subjecting another highlights another aspect of the universal use of the middle ("submit yourself") and passive ("be submissive") voices. The submission is voluntary. It comes from within the person submitting, rather than being forced on him/her by another person. Although this point should be self-evident, many interpreters have felt it useful to underscore it.[40] For instance, Osburn observes that in the NT *hupotassō* never suggests "the propriety of a human being forcefully subjugating another for any reason.... As middle [*hupotassō*] invariably involves willing submission."[41]

Of special interest for our study of women in the NT are the four times *hupotassō* is directed toward women and the two where the context implies the application of the verb to them. Of these six, five refer to wives' voluntary submission to their husbands. In Eph. 5:22, Tit. 2:5, and I Pet. 3:1, it is "to their own husbands" (*tois idiois andrasin*). In Eph. 5:24 and Col. 3:18 it is simply "to the/their husbands" (*tois andrasin*). Eph. 5:22 and 24 stand out. Here the verb is not actually used of these wives. In the former case it is implied from the immediate context (5:21). In the latter it is picked up from the use of the verb of the church's submitting itself to Christ in the same verse (5:24). The sixth instance is I Cor. 14:34, where the context ("their own husbands," *tous idious andras*, v. 35) clearly indicates that wives, not women in general, are in view. As noted above, to whom/what this submission is to be directed is unclear.

***Excursus 8:* Kephalē (*"head"*) *in Paul's Writings.* In**

---

truth and ordered worship."

39   So Padgett, "Wealthy Women at Ephesus," 24.

40   For example, Evans, *Woman in the Bible*, 68; Barth, *Ephesians*, 710; and Delling, "ὑποτάσσω," 42.

41   "Interpretation of 1 Cor. 14:34-35," 238.

serious discussions of what the NT says about women in the family and the church, two Greek words with disputed meanings have occupied center stage. The first is *authenteō*, which is commonly translated "have authority over" or "exercise authority over" and in the NT occurs only in I Tim. 2:12. It will be dealt with in the chapter on that passage. The other is *kephalē*, the Greek word for "head." Paul uses it 18 times, including twice in Eph. 5:23. This excursus will examine *kephalē* in the broader context of Paul's writings as a foundation for some of the discussion of Eph. 5:21-33 and its depiction of the husband-wife relationship.

While Paul employs *kephalē* a few times in its literal sense as an anatomical head (e.g., I Cor. 11:4, 5, and 7), it is his figurative or metaphorical uses of the word that are so widely disputed by those on both sides of the matter of women in the family and the church. Joesph Fitzmyer frames the issue succinctly with the question, "does it mean 'head,' like the head of a department, or does it mean 'source,' like the source of a river?"[42] Those who support a more traditional view of women in the church typically chose the former; whereas, those who seek a wider role for women in the church usually affirm the latter. In the debate in the literature that has arisen in the last few decades, many on both sides have taken extreme positions[43] and on examples of *kephalē* that could be interpreted either way, uniformly define the word to fit the conclusions they have already reached on women in the church. It is not a pretty picture. What is needed is a dispassionate treatment of the topic by someone who is not committed to either one of the sides in the battle over women in the church. Fortu-

---

42   "*Kephalē*," 52.
43   For example, on the one side Berkeley and Alvera Mickelsen ("*Kephalē*," 110) assert that *kephalē* with the meaning "superior rank" "does not appear in secular Greek of New Testament times." See for another example Richard S. Cervin, "Κεφαλή," 112. On the other hand, Wayne Grudem ("*Kephalē*," 80) contends that "'source, origin' is nowhere clearly attested as a legitimate meaning for *kephalē*."

nately, Kenneth V. Neller's excellent article in volume one of *Essays on Women in Earliest Christianity*[44] is just such a study.

Neller begins by surveying briefly the claims on both sides of the question. He suggests that the divide between the two is so great that it might cause one "to despair over ever understanding the statement, 'the husband is the head of the wife.'" However, he proposes that a careful look at the evidence for *kephalē's* usage and Eph. 5:23's context can produce "a fairly clear picture." Following Heinrich Schlier,[45] he notes that in extra-biblical Greek writings, *kephalē* "refers primarily to what is first or supreme, or to an extremity, end, or point." It could also signify what was prominent, outstanding or determinative. In the Septuagint, *kephalē* usually translates *ro'sh*, the normal Hebrew word for "head." When the Septuagint translates *ro'sh* metaphorically to mean leader, chief, or ruler, it usually uses other Greek words.[46] However, there are some clear examples of where the translators chose *kephalē* to render *ro'sh* with this meaning.[47] In the NT period, Philo and Josephus, first century AD Jews, use *kephalē* of one who leads.[48] All this demonstrates the existence of this meaning of *kephalē* at the time of the NT and before. Neller next observes that examples of *kephalē* meaning "source" in

---

44   "Submission," 251-58.

45   "κεφαλή," 673-4.

46   According to the Mickelsens' ("*Kephalē*," 102-04) count, 14 different Greek words render *ro'sh* in the "about 180 times" it means "the leader or authority figure of a group." *Archōn*, "ruler," is by far the most frequent translation, rendering *ro'sh* 104 times in eleven OT books. Over half the occurrences (58) appear in I Chronicles. None of the other 13 words occurs more than ten times each. Edwin Hatch and Henry A. Redpath, *Concordance to the Septuagint*, 166-69.

47   Deut. 28:13, 44; Judg. 10:18, 11:8, 9, 11; II Sam 22:44 (II Kings 22:44 in Septuagint); Ps. 18:43 (17:44 in Septuagint); Isa. 7:9; Jer. 31:7 (38:7 in Septuagint), and Lam. 1:5.

48   Perhaps the best examples are in Philo. In *Op. Mund.* 119 he refers to the *kephalē* as the part of the body most fit to rule (superlative of *hēgemonikon*). See also *Spec. Leg.* III.184 for a similar meaning.

pre-Christian writings do exist as well, but they are "scant, if not more scant, than for the meaning 'leader.'" Thus, it is an overstatement "that a Greek Christian who read Paul's 'head' metaphor would have understood it naturally to mean 'source' or 'source of life.'"[49] So, since *kephalē* in Paul's day was ambiguous, capable of multiple meanings, we are left to defining the word in context on a case-by-case basis.[50]

With this foundation from Neller, we can now proceed to determine whether in any of his 18 examples of *kephalē* Paul uses the word with either the meaning "source"[51] or "leader."[52] Here is a breakdown of Paul's use of *kephalē*.

Physical, Anatomical Head. This is clearly the meaning of *kephalē* in Rom. 12:20 (quotation of Prov. 25:22), I Cor. 11:4 (first instance), 5 (first instance), 7, 10, and 12:21. It is unclear whether in the second instances of the word in I Cor. 11:4 and 5 the reference is to the man and the woman's physical head or to their head identified in 11:3. This question will be addressed more fully later in the chapter on I Cor. 11:2-16.

Christ as Head

Indicating "ruler." This is the clear meaning in Eph. 1:22 and Col. 2:10. The context in Eph. 1 underscores the force of

49   "Submission," 255.

50   Thus, Scholer ("Headship," 43) correctly observes that "the determinative evidence for the meaning of *kephale* is its use and function in particular contexts."

51   Those who support this meaning often connect it with additional nuances, such as "first," "beginning of," "point of departure," "origin," "source of life," "derivation," or "originator and completer." See Catherine C. Kroeger, "Head," 376; Mickelsen, "*Kephalē*," 105-108; and Stephen Bedale, "*kephale*," 213.

52   Those who support this meaning often connect it with additional nuances, such as "authority over," "ruler," "person in authority, " or "person of superior authority or rank." See Curry, "Male and Female," 184; Fitzmyer, "*Kephalē*," 54-55; and Grudem, "*Kephalē*," 45-80. It is difficult to escape the impression that at least some of these additional meanings found here and in the preceding footnote represent the taking of many liberties in defining this word.

the supreme power of the "head" here. God set Christ at his right hand in the heavenly places in fulfilment of Ps. 110:1 (1:20). His position is *above* all rule (*archē*) and authority (*exousia*) and power and dominion" (1:21), terms used in Ephesians and Colossians especially for the spiritual opponents amassed against Christ in the spiritual world.[53] God "has placed all things under his feet," a direct quote from Ps. 8:7 (1:22). Only after all of this description of Christ's overwhelming might does Paul finally assert that God has made him "head (*kephalē*) *over* all things for the church" (1:22). It could hardly be clearer, to use Fitzmyer's earlier alluded to terminology, that *kephalē* here means "head," like the head of a department, not "source," like the source of a river. The same can also be said of *kephalē* in Col. 2:10. Here he is "head" (*kephalē*) of all rule (*archē*) and authority (*exousia*), the same spiritual opponents found in Eph. 1:21 and disarmed by God when he raised Christ from the dead (Col. 2:15). The picture we get of Christ's headship in Eph. 1:22 and Col. 2:10, then, is one of a powerful ruler.

This meaning for Paul's use of *kephalē* in the Christ hymn in Col. 1:18 probably also fits better than any other. Some try to connect the statement, "he himself is the head (*kephalē*) of the body, the church" with the word "beginning" (*archē*) later in 1:18 as support for defining *kephalē* as "source."[54] The problem with this is that *kephalē* in 1:18 is in the first strophe or verse of the hymn, but *archē* in 1:18 is in the second. What is in the first strophe, however, are words relating to power and rule as created by Christ: "whether thrones or dominions or rulers (*archē*) or authorities (*exousia*)" (1:16). Note the two uses of *archē* in these verses, a perfect example of two very different meanings of the word, "beginning" and "ruler." The

---

53   See Eph. 3:10, 6:12; Col. 1:16, 2:10, 15; I Cor. 15:24. Note also the cognate noun, *archōn*, "ruler," used with "authority" (*exousia*) in Eph. 2:2.
54   Kroeger, "Head," 376.

one connected with *kephalē* here (1:16) is "ruler." Thus, the one who is "the head of the body, the church," is over all those other powerful forces, a strong indication of the meaning Paul intended for *kephalē* in 1:18.

Indicating provider or source of growth. Eph. 4:15 and Col. 2:19 talk of the growth of the body coming from Christ. In both cases Christ is seen as the "head" (*kephalē*). He is the one who enables the body to "build itself up in love" (Eph. 4:16) and "grow with a growth from God" (Col. 2:19). Technically, in both passages the provider here is Christ, not *kephalē*, because the antecedent of the pronoun "whom" ("from whom") is masculine, not feminine, as it would have to be for *kephalē* to be the antecedent. Nevertheless, in context it seems legitimate to associate *kephalē* with the word "source" in the sense of "source of growth."[55]

Head in I Cor. 11:3. In this verse, Christ, man/husband, and God are all called "head" (*kephalē*). Because it is seen by many as critical to a proper understanding of women in the church and home in Paul, the precise meaning of *kephalē* here is by far the most disputed of all Paul's 18 uses of the word. Those on both sides of the "women" question argue either for a meaning of "authority over"[56] or "source."[57] Not surprisingly, the stronger their particular stand about women in the church, the more predictable is their opinion on the meaning of "head" here. Because this dispute is much more complex than can be dealt with adequately in an excursus of this modest length, this matter will be deferred to the chapter on I Cor. 11:2-16.

Head in Eph. 5:23. The final two occurrences of *kephalē* in

---

55   See Jay Guin, *Buried Talents*, 78.
56   For example, Curry, "Male and Female," 183; Fitzmyer, "*Kephalē*," 55-57; Dave Miller, "Role of Women," 21; and Allen Black, "Paul's Use of Genesis," 301.
57   For example, Kroeger, "Classical Concept of *Head*," 277; and Mickelsen, "*Kephalē*," 106-08.

Paul's writings occur in Eph. 5:23. Paul writes, "The husband is head (*kephalē*) of the wife as Christ also is head (*kephalē*) of the church." If the choice for the meaning of "head" here is between "leader" or "source," the context provides strong evidence for the former. First, there is "head" as it relates to Christ. The way the church responds to Christ's headship is by submitting itself to him (5:24). Here Christ is unambiguously seen as the leader of the church. Since the pattern of the church's submitting itself to Christ is the basis for the wife's submitting herself to her husband's headship, the way Paul is using "head" is as a leader. The question, then, is not whether Paul regards the husband as his wife's leader, but what that leadership looks like. For example, is it autocratic, as in a Roman household or as is Christ's headship of the spiritual forces in the heavenly places (Eph. 1:22, Col. 1:18, 2:10)? Paul answers that question in the next several verses with an emphatic negative, as he makes crystal clear the aspect of Christ's headship of the church that serves as the model for the husband's headship of his wife. To that passage we now turn.

Ephesians 5:21-33 (Continued)

Literary, Social, and Biblical Contexts

AT THE OUTSET WE NEED TO RECOGNIZE THAT THIS PASsage is a part of a larger one continuing through 6:9. To understand it properly we need to set it in its literary, social, and biblical contexts.

Literary Context. Eph. 5:22-6:9 is a household code. This is a common literary type in Greco-Roman literature of the time. These codes, which are often referred to in the literature by their German name, *Haustafeln*, cover the various relationships that are present in Roman households. In the NT there are two other household codes: Col. 3:18-4:1 and I Pet. 2:18-3:7. They deal with the husband-wife, father-children, and master-slave relationships. The passages in Ephesians and Colossians deal with all six, whereas I Peter addresses only the husband-wife and servant roles.

Social Context. While these three relationships are found in Roman homes, they go back ultimately to Aristotle in his *Politics*. Russ Dudrey's excellent treatment of these household relationships in the ancient Mediterranean world is worth summarizing here.[58] He begins by providing some key quotations from Aristotle.

> The male is by nature superior, and the female inferior; and the one rules, and the other is ruled; this principle of necessity extends to all mankind.[59]

> Of household management we have seen that there are three parts—one is the rule of a master over slaves... another of a father, and the third of a husband. A husband and father rules over wife and children.... For although there may be exceptions in the order of nature, the male is by nature fitter for command than the female, just as the older and full-grown is superior to the younger and more immature. (1259a 37-39, b 1-4)

> The freeman rules over the slave after another manner from that in which the male rules over the female, or the man over the child.... For the slave has no deliberative faculty at all; the woman has, but it is without authority, and the child has, but it is immature.... The courage of a man is shown in commanding, of a woman in obeying.... All classes must be deemed to have their special attributes;

---

58   "'Submit Yourselves," 27-44, esp. 27-31.
59   1254b 12-14. All the citations from Aristotle's *Politics* are from the translation of Richard McKeon, *Basic Works of Aristotle*.

as the poet says of women, 'Silence is a woman's glory.'"
(1260a 9-30)

Having given these examples of Aristotle's words on
the subject, Dudrey next points out that Aristotle's analysis
formed the basis of the threefold relationships addressed in
ancient Greco-Roman household codes. *Ruling* or *commanding* is what the man does, and the duty of the three subordinate roles (wives, children, slaves) is *obedience*. This is true in
all the cultures with which the NT church interacted. Further,
whether legally or not, functionally throughout the culture
women, children, and slaves were all treated as property of
the father or husband. This family patriarch in the Roman
world was known as *paterfamilias*.

Biblical Context. Ephesians and Colossians are sister epistles
written at essentially the same time to the same general area
(Western Asia Minor). They are two sides of one coin with
over 60 points of contact between them. Colossians has the
most highly developed Christology in the NT with Ecclesi-
ology (the doctrine of the church) as the secondary theme.
Ephesians is just the opposite. In the first three chapters of
Ephesians, Paul develops the thought that what Christ has
done in bringing salvation to both Jews and Gentiles in one
body was God's secret (*mysterion*) plan hidden from the ages.
The recipients of the letter were members of the household
of God (2:19), and chapters 4-6 tell them how to live as that
household. The current passage, 5:22-6:9, instructs them how
to conduct themselves in their own households.

When we compare this household code in Ephesians with
the one in Colossians 3 and I Pet. 2-3, we see several similarities. However, the best way to understand the significance of
a passage is to consider the differences, not the similarities. In
this case, the big difference is the eight verses Paul devotes to
husbands in Ephesians 5, as opposed to one each in Colossians
3 and I Peter 3. This is where Paul puts the emphasis, and this
is where we should look to find his major point.

Exposition

Submitting yourselves to one another out of reverence for Christ. (5:21)

Submit to One Another. Verse 21 is connected with both what goes before and what follows.[60] In 5:18 Paul says to "be filled with the Spirit." This is followed by five participles: "speaking," "singing," "making melody," "giving thanks," and "submitting yourselves" (*hupotassō*). This last participle (5:21) serves as a transition and the heading for the household code that follows in 5:22-6:9. The connection to what follows is seen in the implied repetition of *hupotassō* in verse 22, where it is necessary to complete the thought,[61] and its actual use in verse 24. The generic nature of *hupotassō* in the statement, "submitting yourselves to one another out of reverence for Christ" (verse 21), just as that of the preceding four participles, shows that this call for mutual submission controls all the six relationships discussed immediately in the household code in 5:22-6:9.[62] In each case, what wives, husbands, children, fathers, slaves, and masters are asked to do is an expression of what Paul means by "submitting yourselves to one another

---

60   On this see Hurley's (*Man and Woman*, 139-40) discussion and Osburn, *Reclaiming the Ideal*, 168.

61   This is not obvious in most English translations, where the translator supplies some form of "submit yourselves" for the sake of the sense. The New American Standard Bible alerts the reader by putting "*be subject*" in italics. Although there is a textual variant in 5:22 that supplies *hupotassō*, most critical editions of the Greek NT reject the word as a later interpolation.

62   Scholer ("Headship," 44) calls 5:21 "*the* theme of the passage" and Grant Osborne ("Women in the Church," 349) "the 'title' verse for the marriage passage." In his commentary on the passage (*Ephesians*, 609), Barth wrote, "The single imperative of vs. 21 ('subordinate yourselves to one another') anticipates all that Paul is about to say not only to wives, children, and slaves, but also to husbands, fathers, and masters."

out of reverence for Christ."[63]

As any of the three weaker parties in the household code would have read how they were to behave, they would have found nothing new. What was new, however, was the motivation. Just as the motivation for all the parties to submit to one another was "out of reverence for Christ" (5:21), so some aspect of their relationship with Christ was the motivation for their specific behavior, and that was totally new. Wives are to submit themselves to their husbands "as to the Lord" (5:22) and "as the church submits itself to Christ" (5:24). Children are to be obedient to their parents "in the Lord, for this is right" (6:1). Slaves are to be obedient to their masters "as to Christ" (6:5), "as servants of Christ doing the will of God from the heart" (6:6), "as to the Lord and not to men" (6:7), and "knowing that whatever good each one does he will receive back from the Lord" (6:8).

In the case of the stronger parties (husbands, fathers, and masters), both the behavior and motivation for it were new. The motivation for husbands to love their wives is "as Christ loved the church and gave himself up for her" (5:25). Further, husbands are to nourish and cherish their wives "as Christ also does the church, because we are members of his body" (5:29-30). Fathers are not to make their children angry, but rather to "bring them up in the discipline and instruction of the Lord" (6:4). Masters are to realize that their conduct toward their slaves should reflect the fact that their "master is in heaven and there is no partiality with him" (6:9). Christ has changed everything!

---

63   As Neller ("Submission," 259) put it, "The heading found in Eph. 5:21 'Submit yourselves to one another in reverence to Christ' controls and influences everything Paul says in the following *Haustafel* (5:22-6:9)." See also, Ferguson (*Women in the Church*, 58), "The passage is part of a whole section that spells out how mutual submission (5:21) expresses itself in various household relationships (continuing through 6:9)." The excellent discussion in *Life Links to God* (105-06) is also worth reading.

> *Wives to your own husbands as to the Lord. For the husband is head of the wife as Christ is head of the church, being himself Savior of the body. But as the church submits itself to Christ, so the wives also to their husbands in everything.... And the wife that she should respect her husband. (5:22-24, 33b)*

Wives. Several points stand out as we look at what wives are asked to do and why. First, they are to submit themselves to their husbands. As Dudrey pointed out,[64] in any culture at the time this was understood. Note, however, that this is a voluntary act on the wives' part, just as the act of submission by all parties in 5:21 is voluntary. Nothing in either Paul's instructions to the wives or the husbands gives the husband the right to demand or enforce the wife's submission.[65] It is something she freely gives, "out of reverence for Christ." Second, as concluded in the excursus on "***Kephalē* ('head') in Paul's Writings**" above, the word "head" in 5:23 in the statement "the husband is head of the wife" refers to his function as leader. Again, there is nothing new here. Third, wives are not told to obey their husbands, as children are their parents (6:1) and slaves are their masters (6:5), but rather to submit themselves to them.[66]

Something entirely different than autocratic rule is going on in Paul's view of marriage here. This leads to the fourth point, namely that the nature of the husband's headship that Paul develops beginning in verse 25 is already indicated by what Paul says about Christ's headship of the church in verse 23. Rather than emphasizing Christ's authority over the church, Paul characterizes Christ's headship as what he

---

64   See above in the section, **Social Context**.

65   See Ferguson, *Women in the Church*, 58 and Osborne, "Women in the Church," 349.

66   This is noted by Ferguson, *Women in the Church*, 58. and Neller, "Submission," 248-49.

lovingly did for the church in becoming its savior. In a similar way Paul will show in the following verses what it means for the husband to emulate Christ in his loving care for the church. Finally, the motivation for the wife's submitting herself to her husband brings in what is totally new—"as to the Lord" (verse 22).

> *Husbands, love your wives as Christ also loved the church and gave himself up for her, that he might consecrate her by cleansing her in the washing of water by the word, that he might present the church to himself resplendent, not having spot or wrinkle or any of such things, but that she may be holy and unblemished. In this way husbands also ought to love their own wives as their own bodies. He who loves his own wife loves himself. For no one has ever hated his own body, but he nourishes and cherishes it, as Christ also does the church, because we are members of his body.... Let each one of you individually in this way love his own wife as himself. (5:25-30, 33a)*

Husbands. What does it mean for the husband to be his wife's head? Fortunately, Paul does not leave us in the dark here. What he asks of husbands was revolutionary against any backdrop—Jewish, Roman or Greek. It is not the exercise of authority over his wife. Rather than treating a wife as a personal possession or as one who is to be ruled or commanded, Paul says she is to be loved, and he is very explicit about what that means. It involves an entirely different kind of headship, one defined by Christ's love for his church.[67] But Paul does not

---

67   See Ron Highfield's ("Man and Woman in Christ," 141-42) rich theological discussion of this point: "A husband acts as a 'head' when he leads in following the way of Christ. He disregards his own safety, comfort, and preferences to 'save' and 'nurture' his wife. Surely, this is almost a complete reversal of the pagan meaning. Christ was strong but made himself weak, rich but took on poverty. He was the master who

leave it there. He identifies the characteristics of Christ's love for the church that the husband is to emulate in his headship and turns them into what Christ expects of the husband in turn. Love for one's wife is to go as far as to give his life for her (5:25), to be as intense as for his own body or self (5:28, 33), and to be serving ("nourish and cherish," 5:29)—all based on the way Christ expressed his love for the church. This kind of love leaves no room for abuse or divorce or selfishness. This is the way a Christian husband lives out the words, "submitting yourselves to one another out of reverence for Christ" (5:21).[68]

In light of all of this, Marcus Barth's assessment of Eph. 5:22-33 is worthy of a resounding "Amen":

> If ever there was a joyful affirmation of marriage, without any shadow and misgiving, then it is found in Eph 5. It is, therefore, altogether unlikely that either by defining the husband's headship or by demanding the wife's subordination Paul aimed at anything other than helping the couples in the congregation to live in joy and peace. A greater, wiser, and more positive description of marriage has not yet been found in Christian literature.[69]

Galatians 3:28 and Ephesians 5:21-33 Taken Together

THE DISCUSSION OF GAL. 3:28 AND EPH. 5:21-33 BELONGS together because of their interpretive history. That interpretive history involves a blurring of the line between the first two questions (what does it say? and what did it mean?), the

---

made himself a servant, the dignitary who accepted indignities for our sakes. The Christian husband is the head; he must take the lead in following Christ, the powerful servant."

68   A discussion of Paul's use and application of Gen. 2:24 in this passage will not be repeated here. For that see under the section, **Direct Quotations,** in chapter five of this book.

69   *Ephesians*, 715.

exegetical questions, and the third question (what does it mean?), the hermeneutical question.[70] Some of those who argue for a wider role for women in the church than the traditional one, in the way they often proof text Gal. 3:28, make an application of their questionable interpretation of the verse that Paul himself does not make. In viewing Gal. 3:28 as teaching the equality of men and women in Christ, they see the verse as signaling a reversal of the consequence of Adam and Eve's sin. This has the effect of wiping out a "hierarchical" relationship between men and women.[71]

This does not mean that Paul does not have something liberating to say about the relationship of married Christians. This is where Eph. 5:21-33 comes into play. It, not Gal. 3:28, is where he develops the effect of the gospel on gender relations within marriage. Paul's treatment of the marriage relationship here has the effect of "baptizing" it into Jesus Christ. Rather than negating the so-called hierarchical relationship between Christian husbands and wives, he shows how Christ's sacrifice has totally redirected the relationship, as well as those between fathers and children and between masters and slaves. For Paul, wives are still to submit themselves to their husbands (5:22-24, 33b), but the foundation for that submission has changed. It is now based on Christ's sacrificial act. Paul goes even farther with Christian husbands. The depth of love for one's wife that Paul demands in 5:25-30, 33a is unprecedented. Their love for their wives transcends mere feeling into action that is based on the model of Christ's sacrificial giving for the church, his beloved bride.

What Paul does here, rather than applying the gospel to

---

70   See the section, **Say, Meant, Mean**, in chapter three of this book.
71   More appropriately in dealing with the Genesis creation texts exegetically, we should be talking about the relationship between husbands and wives, not men and women. The Genesis creation narrative about Adam and Eve has nothing to do with men and women in general, as the context in Genesis makes abundantly clear.

wipe out any hierarchical relationship that may be a remnant of the creation story, is to so elevate the status of the wife in a Christian marriage as effectively to wipe out any advantage or imbalance in the relationship held by the husband. There is no trace of ruling or any other form of domination by the husband in the marriage relationship in this passage. In its place is serving ones wife in unprecedented ways based on an unprecedented foundation—Christ's love for his bride as demonstrated by what he has *done* for her.

This is far more powerful than the supposed removal of hierarchy by a questionable interpretation of Gal. 3:28. It puts the responsibility for the relationship on both parties and provides the motivation to make it work. If the submission of wives to their husbands is the point[72] in the two passages where Paul elsewhere directs wives to reform their conduct in the assembly (I Cor. 14:34, I Tim. 2:11), his correction of these wives' actions makes perfect sense. Their behavior in light of what was appropriate at that time and in that place was inconsistent with their newly redefined responsibilities to their husbands in Christ.

But in going back to Gal. 3:28, what about the third question (what *does* it mean?) Is it possible, as some have suggested,[73] that the NT does not give the last word on the three relationships in the verse—Jew-Greek, slave-free, male-female? In order for us today to answer the third question, are there applications in our modern world that, while consistent with what we learn from an exegesis of the verse by answering the first two questions, could hardly have been imagined by Paul? For the Jew-Greek relationship the answer seems

---

72   See above in the excursus, **Hupotassō** *("to submit") in the New Testament*, where multiple possibilities of to whom or what these wives are being asked to submit themselves are suggested.

73   See, for example, Jewett, "No Male and Female," 25: "In the question of Jew and Greek, Paul went all the way; in the question of slave and free, part of the way; in the matter of women's equality, he made only a beginning."

simpler, because in the NT the particulars of breaking down those natural barriers are well defined. Also, we seem to have no trouble applying the NT here to other ethnic and racial barriers in our world.

The matter of slavery is more complex. Few Christians today would argue that it is acceptable to take away other people's freedom by personally owning them. Yet the NT does not condemn this practice; rather it "baptized" it into Christ. Slave owners and slaves alike had new responsibilities imposed on them by what Christ had done for them.[74] Nevertheless, it has been the influence of Christianity both in the Roman world and in most of our own that has brought an end to slavery in the Western world. The most widely held view today, and the one that seems most likely, on why Paul and others in the NT did not oppose slavery directly is that it was just too much a part of the social fabric.[75] Christians were a fragile, infant movement that had to pick its battles carefully, just as Jesus did when he chose not to give offense when he paid taxes he did not owe (Matt. 17:27). Their own safety and the survival of the movement were at stake.[76] But probably more importantly, their ability to reach an already suspicious populous with the gospel message was a major

---

74   See Eph. 6:5-9; Col. 3:22-4:1; I Tim. 6:1-2; and Tit. 2:9-10.

75   S. Scott Bartchy ("Slave, Slavery," 1098) notes that "as many of one-third of the population of the empire were enslaved, and an additional large percentage had been slaves earlier in their lives." In another dictionary entry ("Slavery: New Testament," 69) he wrote about the economic dependence on slavery, "Greco-Roman society had come to depend on persons in slavery as the basic labor force, as essential components of the imperial economy, and a normal part of the daily life of most families. This exhaustive use of slave labor produced much wealth and the leisure that permitted the development of Greco-Roman culture."

76   Of Paul's approach to slavery Hans Dieter Betz wrote in his commentary on Gal. 3:28 (*Galatians*, 195), "Paul shied away from the alternative of social rebellion which no doubt would have been suppressed violently."

concern.[77] Hints of the final destination were already there in NT passages that changed the way Christians were to act toward their slaves and in Philemon, where Paul went about as far as he could without telling Philemon to free Onesimus.[78] But it was left to Christians in more stable and favorable times to take on this battle.

So now we ask the third question (what *does* it mean?) in the matter of husband-wife relations. Is it possible that for the relationship between Christian husbands and wives the last chapter had not been written in Paul's day for similar reasons than were true of slavery? Are there hints in the NT that point to a more egalitarian relationship in marriage, to use a modern term? Gal. 3:28 and I Cor. 11:11-12 are certainly possible candidates, as is the lack of any clear reference in Paul to Gen. 3:16 as the source of his teaching on wives' subordination to their husbands. This is a complex question, and it is potentially affected by one's interpretation of the meaning of I Tim. 2:13, among other passages.

The most that can be said here is that although the

---

77   Paul's concern about the effect Christians' behavior has on outsiders is especially prevalent in the Pastoral Epistles. The bishop is to be "well thought of by outsiders" (I Tim. 3:7). The bad behavior of some younger widows had the potential of leading the enemy to have "an occasion to revile us" (I Tim. 5:13-14). Slaves were so to conduct themselves toward their masters "that the name of God and the teaching may not be defamed" (I Tim. 6:1). The behavior of young women, including submitting themselves to their own husbands, is "in order that the word of God not be defamed" (Tit. 2:5). Similarly, the conduct of young men should be such that "an opponent may be put to shame, having nothing bad to say about us" (2:8). To these may be added Paul's concern for the effect of Christians' behavior and speech on outsiders (Col. 4:5-6), his point that conduct be becoming to outsiders (I Thess. 4:12), and Peter's similar thoughts (I Pet. 2:12, 3:1, 16). See Bobbie Lee Holley, "God's Design, Part III," 14. Referring to Paul's teachings on women, she wrote, "He did not want outsiders scandalized and hindered in their response to the Gospel." Snodgrass ("Galatians 3:28," 179) and Anthoine van den Doel ("Submission," 124) make similar points.

78   See Jewett, "No Male and Female," 25.

answer must begin by being faithful to the findings from the first two questions, it is really a matter of addressing the third. Certainly, just as it was in the case of slavery discussed above, for many it may be worth their effort to pursue the question of what *does* it mean in our modern world. My two caveats are these. First, this present book is concerned primarily with what the biblical text says and meant in Paul's day. For Paul, the author of Gal. 3:28, for whatever his reasons, wives were still to be submissive to their husbands (Eph. 5:22-24). Secondly, for me the above analysis of Paul's teaching about husband's responsibilities to their wives renders the effort to mitigate the effect of wives' submission to their husbands unnecessary, even counterproductive for wives. Speaking as a Christian husband, when I read Ephesians 5 and ask the third question—what *does* it mean for me and my behavior toward my wife?—it elevates her needs and wellbeing above my own. From my perspective, that is a different kind of hierarchy, but one that is much more weighty on me than on her.

CHAPTER NINE

I Corinthians 11:2-16

We are now ready to examine the first of the three NT passages that have had the most influence on the role of women in the church down to our day. All three are in Paul (I Cor. 11:2-16, 14:34-35, and I Tim. 2:8-15. It is no exaggeration to say that were it not for these three passages the history of women in the church would have been written very differently. If you remove these passages from the mix, there is nothing in the NT that would cause one to suspect there are any restrictions on what women may do in Christian assemblies. In fact, these three passages, especially the latter two, move against the flow of NT teaching about the status and role of women in congregational life. Other passages in Paul evidence a much wider role for women in congregational, missionary and evangelistic activities than has traditionally been recognized,[1] due to the overshadowing effect of the "big three" passages. Further, when we consider Jesus' example and teachings discussed in chapter seven of this book, we are again struck by how foreign these three Pauline texts sound.

For some, the traditional interpretation of these three passages flows from a long history, both before and since Paul, of subjecting women to male dominance. While there has certainly been enough of that, it does not adequately explain the differences in interpretation of these texts. They are difficult and filled with many ambiguities caused by our ignorance of elements of the setting against which they were

---

1   See the section in chapter eight on "Paul and Jesus."

written. Good, well-trained, dedicated and sincere Christians can be found on all sides of the issue. It is not good enough or helpful to question the motives of those with whom we disagree. Although some find it difficult to separate their own understanding from what the Bible actually *says* and *meant* (the first two questions), it is possible to hold the Bible in high regard as our final authority in matters of faith and disagree on particulars in these passages.

Introduction

I COR. 11:2-16 PRESENTS THE MODERN READER WITH almost insurmountable interpretive difficulties.[2] Not only are we in the dark at every turn on statements that are inexplicable without the aid of knowledge of the historical, linguist and cultural background, but the matters discussed find parallels in almost no other Pauline, not to mention biblical, passages.[3] When we look at the textual evidence for this passage, the striking fact is that there are almost no variant readings in the Greek manuscript tradition.[4] So, while there are many unanswered questions about individual elements of these

---

2   Craig Blomberg in his commentary on I Corinthians (*1 Corinthians,* 214) writes, "This passage is probably the most complex, controversial, and opaque of any text of comparable length in the New Testament." I am tempted to add, tongue in cheek, from my own struggle with it that this is an understatement. See also Carl Holladay, *Corinthians,* 139: "The meaning of these verses appears to be hopelessly unclear, in spite of many ingenious, but ill-fated attempts to explain them."

3   These include, but are not limited to, the threefold headship (11:3), head coverings for women and the lack of them for men (11:4-6, 13), man/husband alone being the image of God (11:7), woman/wife being the glory of man/husband (11:7), and customs about hair styles for women and men (11:14-15).

4   The only variant reading of any consequence is the substitution of *kalumma* ("head covering," "veil") or equivalent for *exousia* ("authority," "right") in a few church fathers and early translations, but not in any Greek manuscripts.

verses, fortunately these are not further complicated by variant readings in the Greek text.

With so many puzzling and tantalizing features of this passage, it is tempting to get bogged down in matters that are peripheral at best to our focus on women in the church, in this case what they may or may not do in the assembly. Were we doing a full exegesis of 11:2-16, all of these would necessarily be examined. However, for our purpose it boils down to answering five questions: (1) what is the setting being addressed, (2) who are the man and woman in 11:3b, (3) what is their relationship, (4) what activities in that setting are being addressed and what restrictions are place on them, and (5) how wide spread was the application of those restrictions among sister congregations.

The Key Questions

The Setting

11:2 BEGINS A LONG, MULTI-CHAPTER SECTION THAT DEALS with the regular Corinthian assemblies. There is even some discussion of the Lord's table (mixing pagan and Christian elements in the context of the Lord's table) prior to this (10:14-22). The overall section concerns three problem areas in the assembly: (1) head coverings while engaging in praying and prophesying (11:2-16), (2) abuses of fellow Christians in the observance of the Lord's Supper (11:17-34), and (3) disorderly conduct in the exercise of spiritual gifts in the assembly (chapter 14). Even the discussion of spiritual gifts addressed in chapters 12 and 13 prepares the reader for Paul's treatment of how they are to be exercised when the church comes together for worship (chapter 14). Seven times in this four-chapter section Paul refers to the church coming together (*sunerchomai*) (11:17, 18, 20, 33, 34, 14:23, 26), in two of which (11:18 and 14:23) he specifically mentions the assembly (*ekklēsia*). The specific connection of the discussion of head covering in 11:2-16 and the Lord's Supper in 11:17-34 is evident from the introductory words of each section ("I commend," 11:2 and "I do not commend," 11:17). All of this strongly suggests that what Paul is dealing with in 11:2-16 is the regular Corinthian assembly.[5]

The Man and Woman in 11:3b

... and the head of a woman/wife is the man/husband (11:3b)

PAUL BEGINS THIS SECTION ON HEAD COVERINGS IN THE assembly with a statement unlike any other in the Bible. "Now I want you to know that the head of every man is Christ, and the head of a woman/wife is the man/husband, and the head of Christ is God" (11:3). Immediately here we encounter one of the major interpretive difficulties of this passage. The word for the female person in 11:3b, *gunē*, is ambiguous. It can mean either a woman in general or a wife specifically.[6] The same is true for the word for the male person, *anēr*, which

---

5   See Nichol, *God's Woman*, 124. This conclusion is not limited to those who support a wider role for women in the assembly. Even many who hold to more traditional views on women on the subject see this as the regular Corinthian assembly. Among these are Yeakley, Jr. (*Why They Left*, 191); Dave Miller ("Role of Women," 21) and "Permit Not a Woman," 26); Neil R. Lightfoot ("Headdress, Long Hair," 137-38, 141-42), ("Women in Religious Services," 130), and (*Role of Women*, 21, 27, 34); Guy N. Woods ("Exposition," 6, 14) and ("Principle or Custom?," 7); John T. Lewis ("Death in the Pot," 12); David Lipscomb (*First Corinthians*, 163); and J. W. McGarvey (Commentary, 108).

6   Albrecht Oepke ("γυνή," 776) defines the word from Homer forward with two basic meanings: "a. the 'female' as distinct from the male" and "b. the 'wife.'" With respect to the NT and early Christian literature, *gunē* is defined in Bauer, *Greek-English Lexicon*, 3rd edition, 208-09 as "1 an adult female person, *woman*," "2 a married woman, *wife*," and "3 a newly married woman, *bride*."

can mean either a man in general or a husband specifically.[7] While it is true that Paul almost always uses *anēr* with the meaning "husband," this fact alone is not enough to tip the scale in favor of that meaning in disputed passages, because in all of those undisputed usages the topic under discussion is marriage.[8] The situation is nearly the same with *gunē*, for which only four times in undisputed passages in Paul does the word not refer to a wife.[9] Since Wycliffe's translation, most English translators have rendered *gunē* as "woman" and *anēr* as "man," but in more modern times a few translations have interpreted the passage as referring to married people.[10]

---

7   Oepke ("ἀνήρ," 360-61) lists five distinct meanings in pre Christian authors: (1) "the human species," (2) "man as opposed to woman," (3) "the husband," (4) "an adult man as distinct from a boy," and (5) "full manhood." Paul uses the word with all of the meanings but (1), the human species: (2) -- "man as opposed to woman" (I Tim. 2:8); (3) – the husband (at least 38 times); (4) – an adult man as distinct from a boy (I Cor. 13:11); and (5) – full manhood (Eph. 4:13). This does not include the eleven instances in I Corinthians 11 and I Timothy 2 where the precise nuance is not as evident from the context and is disputed among interpreters. In Bauer (*Greek-English Lexicon*, 3rd edition, 79), the basic meaning in the NT is defined as "an adult human male, *man, husband*."

8   38 of Paul's 56 usages of *anēr* are in contexts where marriage is under consideration. To these can be added the five in I Cor. 11:7c-9, where the reference is to Adam and Eve, the first married couple. Only twice in undisputed passages does Paul use *anēr* of someone other than a husband (I Cor. 13:11 and Eph. 4:13). While this fact alone is not enough for a decisive determination of the meaning in the I Corinthians 11 and I Timothy 2, it certainly has some weight.

9   Paul uses *gunē* 64 times. Of these, 44 clearly refer to married women. Twice *gunē* refers to a mother (I Cor. 11:12 and Eph. 4:4) and twice to an unmarried woman in a context where marriage is being discussed (I Cor. 7:1, 34). In the other 16 uses the meaning is not directly specified. Ten of them are in I Corinthians 11, one in I Corinthians 14, and five are in I Timothy 2-3, passages where the meaning is disputed by writers on women in the church. Everett Ferguson's observation (*Church of Christ*, 339) is instructive here: "*Gune* would be expected to mean 'wife' when used in context with men without other specification."

10   Wife-husband – ESV, NRSV, Goodnews; woman-husband –

The question is larger than simply Paul's meaning in 11:3, because *gunē* occurs 15 additional times in 11:2-16, more than in any other passage of comparable length in Paul. Much of the literature on this matter is divided among three possibilities. Either (1) *gunē* usually or always means "woman" in 11:2-16[11] or (2) it usually or always means "wife" or (3) sometimes it refers to a married woman and sometimes not. Certainly its use to refer to a mother in 11:12 ("through the woman") eliminates the possibility that *gunē always* means either "woman" or "wife" in this section. In connection with the third alternative, the issue is not whether in an individual instance of *gunē* Paul had "woman" or "wife" in mind, but whether the passage as a whole, beginning with 11:3, is best seen as referring to married women or not.

The best way to address that question is to begin with Paul's point in 11:2-16—the covering of the head by men and women in the Corinthian assembly. Everything in the passage serves as Paul's support for this major point, from the three-fold head relationships (11:3) to the matter of dishonoring one's head (11:4-7) to what is shameful (11:6) to the reference to the creation narrative (11:8-9) to the angels (11:10) to what is fitting (11:13) to nature (11:14). Looking at the passage as a whole, as well as its individual parts, there are at least six reasons to conclude that Paul has husbands and wives in mind.[12]

RSV, Weymouth, Young. Note also the translations of 11:3 by Ferguson (*Women in the Church*, 57): "the husband is the head of his wife" and Russ Dudrey ("Unveiled Woman," 9): "the head of [every] woman is her husband."

11   See, for example, Oster (*1 Corinthians*, 249): "Not only is it poor translation technique, but it also confuses the historical issues at Corinth to vacillate between man-woman and husband-wife in this section." It is clear that Oster prefers the former.

12   A few interpreters, like Neil R. Lightfoot (*Role of Women*, 22, 35), find it difficult to decide between "wife" and "woman." Others prefer "woman," but the prevailing view, for good reasons, is that Paul intends the meaning "wife" in 11:3 and/or in the passage as a whole. Here

First, there is Ferguson's conclusion from his extensive review of the matter of head coverings in antiquity that concern for head covering in the assembly points to husbands and wives as Paul's objects of concern.[13]

Second, up to this point in I Corinthians, *anēr* had always meant husband; *gunē* had meant wife in all but two of its occurrences.[14] Thus, the natural way for Paul's audience to have interpreted these words in 11:3-15, in the absence of some indication to the contrary by Paul, is as referring to husbands and wives.

Third, the only other passage in Paul where *anēr* is said to be head (*kephalē*) of *gunē* is Eph. 5:23, which is specifically discussing husbands and wives. Though it is not absolutely necessary for the two passages to be talking about the same thing, for Eph. 5:23 and I Cor. 11:3 to be consistent with

---

is a sampling of interpreters on both sides of the question of women in the church who believe husband and wife is Paul's meaning here. Ferguson, "Of Veils and Virgins" (2014), 241 and "Of Veils and Virgins," (1985), 2-3, 15; Reese, *Bound and Determined*, 42; Christopher R. Hutson, *Transforming Word*, 927; Dudrey, "Unveiled Women," 5, 9; Howard, "Women's Role," 2-3; Coffman, *1 and 2 Corinthians*, 168; Roberts, "Veils," 185-6, 197; Gobbel, "Principle or Custom," 7, 14; and McGarvey, *Commentary*, 109-11.

13   "Of Veils and Virgins," (1985). He writes, "the primary significance of the veil for the woman was to indicate that she was a married woman.... A central meaning of the unveiled woman was that she was available for marriage; for the veiled woman, that she was unavailable." (2-3) "Paul had a specific situation in mind. He addressed married women." (15) In his later expansion of this article ("Of Veils and Virgins" [2014], 243) Ferguson seems less certain but clearly sees the weight of the evidence as supporting the veil as an indication of a married woman. "Jewish sources confirm my initial hypothesis by treating the veil as a sign of a married woman.... Whether the veil distinguished married women from unmarried or pertained to all females of marriageable age is debated and remains unresolved." See also David Parrish, "Submission," 18 and J. W. Roberts, *Letters to Timothy*, 24. Roberts writes, "the veil signified woman's subjection to her husband and where taking it off was brazen."

14   I Cor. 7:1, 34. Even here the context deals with marriage.

one another, 11:3 would have to be talking about husbands and wives.[15]

Fourth, Paul describes the three relationships in 11:3 in individual, rather than group terms. Of course the relationship between Christ and God is by its very nature one on one. However, that is not necessarily the case with the other two relationships. Note how Christ is not the head of men in general, but *of every man*. There is a one-on-one relationship between Christ and every man. The same is true of the man and woman in the verse. Paul refers to *gunē* and *anēr* in the singular, not in the plural as men and women. Thus, just as with the other two relationships in 11:3, Paul envisions the relationship between the man and the woman as individual and person to person. The place where this type of relationship exists is in marriage with one's own wife, not with other men's wives. This is reinforced in 11:4-5, where the conduct of *every* man and *every* woman (not *men* and *women*) might dishonor their head. Even the reference to "head" (*kephalē*) is not collective but individual (*his* head and *her* head; see 11:3).

Fifth, 11:8-9 draws on the creation narrative and refers to a married couple, the first one, and their specific relationship with each other.[16] Nothing in these two verses could refer to a generic relationship between men and women.

Finally, and perhaps most important, to the extent that 11:3 affirms a hierarchal relationship between the three pairs, this would point decisively toward husband and wife, not man and woman generically. Nothing in Paul or in any of the rest of the Bible, including the Genesis creation account, puts men in general in a hierarchal relationship with women

---

15   On this see Howard, "Women's Role," 3.

16   See chapter five above, "*I Corinthians 11:8, 9*," and note 27. William F. Orr and James A. Walther (*I Corinthians*, 263) argue that the Eden story "is directed toward the married state, so it is probable that this relationship underlies this whole passage."

in general.[17] Where there is a hierarchy, it is only in the family (husband-wife,[18] father-daughter[19]). If 11:3b were referring to men and women in general, rather than to a husband and his wife, it would run counter to rest of the Bible, including the creation account. For all of these reasons, the overwhelming probability is that Paul has husbands and wives in view in 11:3 and the passage overall. Consequently, this passage is misused when it is taken to refer to men and women generically in the church.

The Relationship between the Man and the Woman

Every wife praying or prophesying with her head uncovered dishonors her head …. The wife is the glory of the husband…. Neither is the wife without the husband, nor the husband without the wife in the Lord. (11:5a, 7c, 11)

THE NATURE OF THE RELATIONSHIP BETWEEN THE MAN and the woman (the husband and the wife) is influenced by the meaning of the word "head" (*kephalē*) in 11:3b and is both applied and further developed in 11:5, 7c, and 11. From the wife's side of the equation, whether or not she covered her head while praying or prophesying in the assembly directly affected her husband, "her head" (11:5). She dishonored him if she did not cover her head. Though many interpreters

---

17   See Howard, "Women's Role," 3: "Nowhere, however, in the New Testament are women generically said to be in submission to men generically." Robert H. Rowland (*I Permit Not a Woman*, 65) goes even farther. With reference to I Cor. 11:3 he writes, "I cannot find any other passage in the Old or New Testament which even suggests that men are the heads of women, generally…. Nowhere in the Bible does God teach that someone else's woman is subject to me or any other man or that my wife is subject to other husbands or other men."

18   E.g., Gen. 3:16?; Num. 30:6-8, 10-15; Eph. 5:22-24; Col. 3:18.

19   Num. 30:3-5.

read subordination into the passage, that is not Paul's point at all.[20] The reason for her to cover her head while praying or prophesying is not that she should submit herself to him (*hupotassō* appears nowhere in the passage) but rather the positive thought that she is his glory (11:7c). Then in 11:11 Paul says that nevertheless "in the Lord" there is a beautiful mutuality in their relationship. "Neither is the wife without the husband, nor the husband without the wife."

But what is the meaning of *kephalē* in 11:3, and what impact does that have on Paul's core argument about head covering? There is not enough in the context for certainty about whether Paul intended *kephalē* with a meaning more like "source" or more like "leader," so his other uses of the word provide the best help for a definition here. Since the only place Paul employs the word with the meaning "source" ("source of growth") is the somewhat parallel passages of Eph. 4:15 and Col. 2:19,[21] but he uses it with the meaning "leader" multiple times, both of Christ[22] and of a husband,[23] "leader" is the more probable meaning here in 11:3. However, for Paul's application of the husband's headship of his wife to his major point in the passage about head covering, the meaning of *kephalē* in 11:3 does not make a difference. Whatever the precise meaning of *kephalē* in 11:3 is, all that is needed to make sense of 11:5 is that there is a relationship—source

---

20   See Oster, *1 Corinthians*, 249 and Thomas C. Geer, Jr. ("Situation," 6). Miller ("Role of Women," 21) acknowledges that Paul does not state "the subordination principle" until chapter 14.
21   See the earlier discussion in chapter eight in the section "**Indicating provider or source of growth**."
22   Eph. 1:22, 5:23; Col. 1:18, 2:10. See the discussion in chapter eight in the sections "**Indicating 'ruler'**" and "**Head in Eph. 5:23**."
23   Eph. 5:23. See the discussion in chapter eight in the section "**Head in Eph. 5:23**."

or hierarchy, it does not matter—between the husband and wife that is to be applied by her refraining from dishonoring "her head" (husband) by covering her head when she prays or prophesies. "Every wife praying or prophesying with uncovered head dishonors her head" (11:5).

Activities and Restrictions on Them

Every husband praying or prophesying having his head covered dishonors his head. But every wife praying or prophesying with her head uncovered dishonors her head…. For a husband ought not to cover his head, since he is the image and glory of God…. Is it fitting for a wife to pray to God uncovered? (11:4-5a, 7a-b, 13)

THE INTERPRETIVE HISTORY OF THIS PASSAGE IS A PERFECT example of the need to address properly the first two questions: what does the text actually say (and not say) and what did it mean originally? That type of endeavor reveals that only two activities for both men and women are under consideration: praying and prophesying (11:4-5, 13) and only one restriction: that on head covering or lack of it for both women and men (11:4-7, 13). This seems quite straightforward, but the text permits us to be a bit more specific. Hence, we will look a little deeper into these activities and Paul's restrictions on them.

Activities. We should not allow the massive amount of smoke [24] that has been generated around these verses to obscure the

---

24   Various ways of expressing women's subordination that are frequently introduced into this discussion include "the subordination principle," "a sign of subordination," "submission," "subjection," "symbol of subordination," or "symbol of wifely submission." The inappropriateness of inserting this element in to this passage is dealt with above in the section on "**The Relationship between the Man and the Woman**" and in note 20. Other extraneous elements that are sometimes brought

one simple teaching here. Both men and women prayed and prophesied in Christian meetings in Corinth, and the only distinction between the two was their head covering. This is what the passage says. So much of what has been written beyond this has been what interpreters have brought to the text, not what Paul actually left there. Thus, some suggest that the women's prayer was silent, with others leading. Other than the fact that the passage says no such thing, why do these interpreters not make the same claim about the men's prayers? Paul makes no distinction between what the women and men did. Further, women not only prayed, but they prophesied. Prophecy, by its very nature is spoken out loud to others. If women did that in the assemblies, why should they be forbidden to pray out loud? What men did women did. Paul makes no distinction between what women and men did (*what* they did, *how* they did it, *where* they did it, etc.) other than the matter of head covering. The conclusion is inescapable. Women prayed and prophesied aloud in the Corinthian assemblies!

Restrictions on Them. Veil or hair, that is the question. Although a few modern students of this passage see the head covering in 11:4-7, 13 to be the man or woman's hair,[25] by far the majority of interpreters, for good reason, believe that Paul has in mind a covering over the hair or head.[26] For an expla-

---

into the discussions include the matter of *leading* prayer, praying or prophesying as exercising authority over those in the assembly, women being the only ones present when women were praying or prophesying, women removing their head covering being a sign of their rebellion, and whether or not Paul was actually approving women's praying and prophesying in Christian assemblies.

25   For example, Coffman, *1 and 2 Corinthians*, 171. Lipscomb ("Covered Heads," 114-15) concludes that Paul actually intended both hair and a separate head covering.

26   Ferguson ("Of Veils and Virgins" [1985], 2) observes that this was "the uniform understanding of the passage by the ancient church." See also his later article, "Of Veils and Virgins" (2014), 241-42. Here is a sampling of others who believe that Paul has an actual head covering

nation of what that head covering was, we turn to Richard Oster's ground breaking article on this passage.[27] Thanks to Oster's research, to a greater extent than before, interpreters of 11:2-16 have been made aware of Paul's concern for head covering of *both* the woman and the man in Corinth. Oster argues that at the time Paul wrote I Corinthians Corinth was, and had been for some time, a Roman colony. In fact, using archaeological, inscriptional, and numismatic (coinage) evidence, he is able to establish that in certain respects Corinth was more Roman than Greek at the time.[28] One of these is in liturgical settings, where Romans covered their heads during such acts as prayer, sacrifice, and prophecy. The clue that this is what Paul was talking about in 11:4 is found in the literal translation of the phrase "with his head covered": "having on the head" (*kata kephalēs echōn*). (486) According to Oster, the gesture of covering the head during a worship activity "consisted of pulling part of one's garment or toga over the back of the head and then forward until it approached or covered the ears." (496)[29] The same was true of both men and women. The head, including the hair, was completely covered.[30]

For this reason the wife ought to have authority on her head, because of the angels. (11:10)

---

other than hair in mind here: Ken Cukrowski, "Uncovered Prophets," 141; Mark Black, "1 Cor. 11:2-16," 200-01; Lightfoot, "Headdress, Long Hair," 140-41; Roberts, "Veils," 192, 197-98; and Guy N. Woods, "Exposition," 6.

27   "When Men Wore Veils," 481-505.

28   He writes, "Although the population and culture of this colony were surely heterogeneous, Corinth was nevertheless 'in a way, a copy' of Rome, and correspondingly, it possessed all the appropriate Roman laws, magistrates and officials." (490)

29   On this see also Hutson, *Transforming Word*, 927: "Roman men and women pulled their togas up over their heads when offering sacrifices" and Ferguson, "Of Veils and Virgins," (2014), 231-32.

30   See Ferguson, "Of Veils and Virgins," (2014), 231-32.

The final matter needing attention relating to any potential restrictions on women in the assembly arises in 11:10. Here Paul writes, "For this reason the wife ought to have authority on her head, because of the angels." This verse has baffled readers for centuries, especially the reference to angels. Interpretations have been all over the place, but for our purpose here it is not the angels, but the words, "have authority on her head," that require our attention. The fact that Paul uses the word "authority" (*exousia*), instead of the normal word for "veil" (*kalumma*), seems to have caused a few church fathers and early translations to substitute the word for "veil" for *exousia* in this verse. However, the Greek manuscript tradition is uniform in the use of *exousia*, "authority," here.[31] So what does Paul mean when he uses the word "authority" in this context?

Does *exousia* mean authority that a woman has or the authority of another that she is under? An examination of Paul's 26 uses of *exousia* provides strong evidence for the former, namely, the authority a woman has. Paul uses the word 14 times of those who are in positions of authority, clearly not relevant to his use here in 11:10.[32] All of the other eleven occurrences, excluding the one here in 11:10, have to do with one's right or authority over something or to do something.[33] Thus, if as is so widely asserted, *exousia* here in

---

31   See note 4 above. Note that in modern times the RSV rendered the word "veil," although the NRSV later changed this to "symbol of authority," bringing it in line with most modern English translations.

32   Five times *exousia* refers to ruling or governing authorities (Rom. 13:1 [twice], 2, 3; Tit. 3:1). In the other nine occurrences it refers to the authorities that are Christ's opponents in the spiritual world (I Cor. 15:24; Eph. 1:21, 2:2, 3:10, 6:12: Col. 1:13, 16, 2:10, 15).

33   Four of these refer to the authority of a potter over clay (Rom. 9:21), a man's rights relative to his fiancée (I Cor. 7:37), Paul and his co-workers' right to build up the Corinthians (II Cor. 10:8), and Paul and his co-workers' right to financial support (II Thess. 3:9). Of particular interest are the seven times in I Corinthians where he asserts his own right or authority to do something: eat foods sacrificed to idols

11:10 means authority which a woman is under, Paul would be employing the word in an entirely different way than anywhere else in his writings.[34] The meaning here is clear. The authority resting on a woman's head is her authority or right to do something. How, then, does this fit in with the context in 11:2-16? Here is a suggestion as to how. While in that cultural setting, unlike our own, it could be shameful (*aischron*) for a wife to speak in a religious assembly (14:35), her right to do so in the form of praying or prophesying was signified by what was on her head (11:10). She did not have the right to be disruptive to the assembly (14:34-35), just as was the case with tongue speakers (14:27-28) and prophets (14:29-33), but her head covering gave her the right to pray and prophesy. In the final analysis, according to Paul in 11:2-16 the only restriction on a wife in the assembly was that she cover her head when she prayed and prophesied.

How Widespread the Restrictions Were Applied

We do not have such a custom,
nor do the churches of God. (11:16)

THE KEY TO ANSWERING THIS QUESTION IS PAUL'S STATE-ment "we do not have such (*toiautē*) a custom (*synētheia*)" in 11:16. The use of *toiautē* ("such"), rather than *allē* ("other") or *hetera* ("other" or "different"), suggests that the practice he is

---

(8:9, 9:4), travel with a wife (9:5), and be supported financially (9:6, 12 (twice), 18).

34   More than a century ago, William M. Ramsey (*Cities of St. Paul*, 203), the distinguished archaeologist of Asia Minor and NT scholar, referred to the view that *exousia* in 11:10 means "the authority to which she is subject" as "preposterous" and laughable to any Greek scholar but a NT Greek scholar. Others who see *exousia* here as authority that the woman has include Robinson, *Community Without Barriers*, 60; Scholer, "Headship," 43; Bruce, *A Mind for What Matters*, 262; Harris, "Eve's Deception," 344; Witherington III, *Women in the Earliest Churches*, 87; Hurley, *Man and Woman*, 176; and Colin Brown, "Head," 161.

urging on the Corinthians (men with no head covering and women with head covering) is one that fits their particular cultural setting, rather than a uniform practice in the other churches. He is stating that the practice he is proposing for Corinth was not the same as his own[35] or that of "the churches of God," i.e., the general practice elsewhere.[36]

Why would Paul issue such a disclaimer when he has expended so much effort to urge such particular directions on head coverings?[37] This must be the reason so many English translations mistranslate the word *toiautē* ("such").[38] This approach jumps over the first question (what does it say?) and moves directly to the second (what did it mean?). I propose that there is a way to take seriously what Paul actually *says* and make sense of it in the context. A reasonable explanation is that he wanted the Corinthians' practice to be sensitive to their cultural setting. If you want to be contentious (*philonei-*

---

35 Presumably the "we" (*hēmeis... echomen*) is he and Sosthenes (1:1).

36 Note the use of the pronoun "we" (*hēmeis*) to strengthen the "we" inherent in the verb "to have" and its emphatic position at the beginning of the clause. This strongly suggests that Paul is not proposing that the Corinthians follow *his* customary practice about head covering but rather one that is culturally appropriate specifically in Corinth.

37 Lightfoot (*Role of Women,* 23) senses this difficulty when he writes that "Paul would not go into prolonged reasoning for the veiling of women and then drop the subject with one remark." However in an earlier article ("Women in Religious Services," 131) his solution fails to grapple with the fact that Paul uses the word "such." Lightfoot prefers to follow the RSV's translation, "no other practice," which, of course, is not what Paul wrote.

38 Hutson (*Transforming Word,* 928) argues that "there is no one rule for all Christians, since 'we have no such custom, neither the churches of God' (11:16). The NIV gives the opposite sense, *we have no other practice* (11:16, also RSV, NAS), which is a blatant mistranslation." Among the other translations that render the word "other" are the RSV, NCV, NET Bible, and GNT. The NASB, CSB, and HCSB, while translating the word, "other," put "such" in the footnote. Among the translations that correctly render *toiautē* as "such" are the ASV, CEB, ESV, KJV, MEV, NAC(RE), NKJV, NRSV, WEB, YLT, Wycliffe, and Geneva Bible.

kos) about it (11:16), you don't have to do it the way he was proposing. If, however, you were to be imitators of him as he was of Christ (11:1), you would forgo your freedom to do as you please. You can use the slogan, "all things are lawful," but realize that not all things are helpful (*symphero*) or build up (*oikodomeo*) (10:23). Paul's own practice relative to eating food sacrificed to idols and other matters was to forgo his freedom so as not to give offense (*aproskopos*) to others and to bring the many to salvation (10:32-33; cf. 9:1-6, 12). It is at this point in the letter that he writes, "Become imitators of me just as I am also of Christ" (11:1).

This overall interpretation of the meaning of 11:16 is further supported by two additional considerations. First, it is widely believed by interpreters today, and rightly so, that Paul was not laying down a rule about head covering for every congregation for all time.[39] This practice was culture bound. It was a convention that made sense in the unique cultural setting in Roman Corinth. Thus, few interpreters today would use Paul's reference to "the churches of God" (11:16) to support the adoption of what the Corinthians were being asked to do about head covering as universally applicable today. We will return to this point later when we consider whether "all the churches of the saints" in 14:33b is being used properly when it is employed to support the view that the silencing of some women in the Corinthian assembly was for every assembly in every place for all time. For the moment, however, the point is simply that the phrase, "the churches of God," does not indicate that Paul was here nailing down a rule for all congregations for all time.

---

39   Here is just a sampling of the voluminous literature making this point. Sanders, "Are Women Limited," 34; Ferguson, "Of Veils and Virgins" (2014), 243 and *Women in the Church*, 24-25; Coffman, *1 and 2 Corinthians*, 165-67; Lightfoot, "Women in Religious Services," 135; Roy H. Lanier, Sr., "Long-Hair Question," 9; Gobbel, "Principle or Custom," 14; and McGarvey, *Commentary*, 110.

Secondly, Corinth is the only place we encounter instructions about head coverings in the assembly. This is more than simply an argument from silence. There is evidence for a different practice in Ephesus. Ferguson, in his previously mentioned article on women's head-coverings in antiquity, observes that "the instructions about hairstyles in 1 Tim. 2:9 and 1 Pet. 3:3 imply women's heads were uncovered."[40] The logic behind this conclusion is that if the women in Ephesus were covering their heads, what their hair looked like would have been obscured by that covering. Yet Paul writes against braided hair (*en plegmasin*) in I Tim. 2:9. This suggests that the women in Ephesus did not cover their heads (hair) in the assembly. If Ferguson and this logic are correct, as seems reasonable, then Paul could hardly have meant in I Cor. 11:16 that his instructions about head covering for women in that passage reflect the uniform practice of "the churches of God." Note further that he was in Ephesus when he wrote I Corinthians (I Cor. 16:8), so he would have been well acquainted with their custom.

Conclusions

IN SPITE OF THE LARGE NUMBER OF ELEMENTS OF THIS passage that present the modern reader with such difficulties, a few points come through rather clearly.

First, Paul's key concern is to convince the Corinthian men to keep their heads uncovered when they prayed or prophesied in the assembly and the women to cover theirs when they prayed or prophesied in the same setting. The reason was so as not to be so out of step with local custom that they would dishonor Christ or their husbands respectively.

Second, the context within the letter supports the conclusion that the activities described took place in the regular

---

40   "Of Veils and Virgins" (2014), 242.

Corinthian assemblies. There is no basis in the text for assuming that Paul viewed men as performing these acts in one type of Christian meeting and the women in another. Nor is there any indication that men and women were not in the meetings together.

Third, in 11:3 and in the passage as a whole, Paul primarily has husbands and wives in mind, not men and women generically. Nothing, either in this passage, in Paul generally, or anywhere else in the Bible supports the view that God has placed men in general over women in general in any setting. In other words, there is no situation where God has placed me over any other man's wife simply because I am a man and she is a woman.

Fourth, the way Paul describes covering the head when he is talking about the man suggests that the covering he has in mind for both men and women is the toga pulled up completely over the head.

Fifth, what men and women were permitted to do in the assembly was exactly the same. They both prayed and prophesied out loud in these Christian meetings. The only difference was in their head covering or lack of it.

Sixth, it would seem that Paul's instructions for head covering for men and women reflected the unique cultural situation in Roman Corinth at the time. They were not the universal practice of the churches with which Paul was acquainted, nor were they intended to be the universal practice for every congregation for all time.

CHAPTER TEN

I Corinthians 14:34-35

We now turn to the short passage that contains the most widely used proof text in support of traditional limitations on what women may do in the assembly. In the extensive literature on these two verses, it is far too common for writers to introduce multiple elements into the text that do not belong there and for them to fail to give proper weight to those that are there. Consequently, differences of opinion on these matters are enormous.[1] Unlike I Cor. 11:2-16, this passage does not present us with questions at every turn that expose our ignorance of the background against which Paul wrote his instructions. Here the context is clear, as is the place of 14:34-35 in it. What follows is an examination of the key features of the passage that relate to the question of what women may or may not do in the Christian assembly.

The Text

UNLIKE I COR. 11:2-16, THIS PASSAGE CONTAINS A FEW textual variants, two of which require consideration here. The most significant of these is the placement of 14:34-35 in chapter 14 itself. The other is the punctuation of 14:33.

---

1 See the section, **Lack of Consensus** and **Excursus 2: Diversity in the Interpretation of the Three Key Pauline Passages**, both in chapter two.

Placement of 14:34-35

A FEW INTERPRETERS[2] QUESTION THE AUTHENTICITY OF these two verses based on the fact that, although none of the manuscript tradition leaves them out entirely, a small number of Western manuscripts put 14:34-35 after 14:40. Most notable of these interpreters is Gordon Fee in his highly regarded commentary on I Corinthians.[3] Fee begins by trying to explain how these two verses could have appeared in the manuscript tradition in two different places. He opts for there being a non-Pauline marginal gloss (note) added very early in the copying of I Corinthians with the result that all the early manuscript evidence would place the verses where they appear in our modern translations. He then buttresses his argument that Paul did not write them by developing three points. First, the two verses do not fit well in the context and intrude on the flow of Paul's argument. Second, they contradict I Cor. 11:2-16, "where it is assumed without reproof that women pray and prophesy in the assembly."[4] Finally, some of the wording in the verses seems quite foreign to Paul. Fee's second point will be dealt with in *Excursus 9* at the end of this chapter, and the third is quite subjective, as any who have spent much time pondering Paul's use of language can attest. Fee's first argument, however, requires a closer look.

Given the extremely weak manuscript evidence for placing these two verses after 14:40, taking the next step by denying their Pauline authorship is quite a stretch. Arguing that the two verses do not fit the context of chapter 14 is somewhat

---

2   For example, *Woman in the World of Jesus*, 178-79 and Hans Conzelmann, *1 Corinthians*. 246.

3   *First Epistle to the Corinthians*, 699-705.

4   Allen Black ("1 Corinthians 14:34-35," 179) writes, "Most scholars acknowledge the presence of similar difficulties in other Pauline texts without resorting to interpolation theories. Paul has a well-known tendency toward diversions and occasionally makes statements that raise harmonization questions."

dependent on how one reads that context. Certainly, if the reader focuses on tongue speaking and prophesying as Paul's primary interest in this chapter, then the two verses seem out of place with no easy explanation for them at all. However, when one recognizes that edification and order during the assembly were Paul's concern and that tongue speaking and prophesying were his cases in point, especially the former, then the placement of these two verses where the vast majority of the manuscript evidence puts them makes perfect sense.

From the beginning of the chapter through verse 26 Paul centers his argument on the need for edification in the assembly.[5] Then in 14:27, still talking about tongue speakers, he introduces the idea of order ("in turn").[6] This is followed immediately with the same concern for prophets ("one by one," 14:31). Next, in 14:33, immediately before the verses in question, Paul denounces disorder or confusion (*akatastasia*). That this continues to be his point after the discussion of these women's behavior is seen as he concludes his argument in the entire chapter. "All things should take place decently (*euschēmonōs*) and in order (*taxis*)" (14:40).

Clearly these women's repeatedly questioning speakers during the assembly (see 14:35, *eperōtaō*, "to question") was an affront to order in the assembly, and that is why Paul discusses their conduct at this point in the chapter. There are at least two other points of contact with the immediately preceding

---

5   The verb, *oikodomeō*, is used in 14:4 (twice) and 17. The noun, *oikodomē*, occurs in 14:3, 5, 12, and 26. A similar thought is also expressed in 14:19, where Paul uses the verb, *katēcheō* ("to inform" or "teach").

6   Oster (*1 Corinthians*, 340) notes this shift and comments about its relevance to Paul's discussing these women's behavior at this point: "Since Paul's strategy toward the end of ch. 14 has shifted from demanding intelligibility to demanding an orderly demeanor, his critique of certain women on this basis is not so out of step with the surrounding context."

context in the words "to be silent" (*sigaō*) in 14:28, 30,[7] and 34 and "learn" (*manthanō*) in14:31 and 35. Thus, in view of the weight of the manuscript evidence and compatibility with the context, these two verses should be regarded both as correctly placed at 14:34-35 and genuinely Pauline.[8]

Punctuation of 14:33

SINCE ANCIENT GREEK MANUSCRIPTS OF THE NT DO NOT contain punctuation, these markings are based on the best judgment of the editors of the critical Greek editions and modern translations. Even chapter and verse divisions were added hundreds of years after the NT was written. Consequently, scholars are not always in agreement on when one thought ends and another begins. I Cor. 14:33 is one of those passages. It presents the interpreter with the difficulty of determining whether Paul intended 14:33b, "as in all the churches of the saints," to go with what preceded or what followed. The verse division in our modern Bibles connects it with what goes before, but that is meaningless for discovering Paul's original intent. Most critical editions of the Greek text end the sentence at 14:33a, thereby connecting 14:33b with the discussion of women that follows.[9] English translations are fairly evenly divided,[10] just adding to the confusion for

---

7   See Everett Ferguson, "Assembly Part 2," 11.

8   This is the view of the vast majority of interpreters. Here are a few examples. Ferguson, *Women in the Church*,13 and *Church of Christ*, 341-42; Blomberg, *1 Corinthians*, 279; Keener, *Paul, Women & Wives*, 74-75; Gary Workman, "I Corinthians 14:34-35," 35-36; and Lightfoot, *The Role of Women*, 28, 33 and "Women in Religious Services," 131-32.

9   The Westcott-Hort edition is a notable exception. It treats 14:32-33a as parenthetical, presumably regarding 14:33b as referring to 14:31, not 14:33a. At any rate, it does not connect 14:33b with the woman's section that follows. Another more recent exception is *Greek New Testament: SBL Edition*.

10   Those English translations that punctuate 14:33 to connect 14:33b to what goes before include the NLT, NAS 1977, NASB, KJV, NKJV,

the modern reader. Factors within the biblical text itself, then, must be considered to make an informed judgment.

The difficulty in coming to a firm decision is perhaps best illustrated by David Lipscomb's vacillating between the two, even in the same document.[11] Most interpreters are willing to admit that it could go either way, although they prefer one to the other. On both sides of the question usually there are simple statements of preference without accompanying evidence or reasoning.

Goes with What Follows. Some who see the phrase as going with the following section on women have difficulty seeing what 14:33b would mean if it completed the thought in 14:33a.[12] This is rather subjective, and others have no trouble at all in reading it that way. However, there may be another more substantial justification for connecting it with 14:34-35. 14:36, immediately after the women's section, reads, "Or did the word of God go out from you, or did it reach you only"? Although this may not be Paul's point, it does make sense as a reference to "*all* the churches" in 14:33b, as opposed to "you *only*" in 14:36.[13] This would mean that 14:33b and 14:36 would frame 14:34-35, making it a self-contained unit. On the other hand, there is good reason instead to take 14:36 with the next verse, where the reference to prophet (*prophētēs*) and

---

ERV, MEV, Douey-Rheims, Darby, Weymouth, Phillips, Young's Literal, Geneva Bible, and Wycliffe. The English translations that punctuate the verse to connect 11:33b with the following women's section include the ESV, ISV, ASV, CSB, CEB, CEV, GNT, NCV, RSV, NRSV, WEB, and NET. The first edition of the NIV connected 11:33b with what follows; the current edition with what goes before.

11   In his *First Corinthians*, 215) he connected 14:33b with what follows. However, in an article in the *Gospel Advocate* ("Woman's Work in the Church," 7) he does not include it in his discussion of 14:34. In "Should Women Preach Publicly," 486 he first connects 14:33b with 14:33a but then seems to see it as a part of Paul's women discussion.

12   For example, John MacArthur, *1 Corinthians*, 392 and Orr and Walther, *1 Corinthians*, 311.

13   See F. W. Grosheide, *First Corinthians*, 343.

spiritually gifted (*pneumatikos*) points back to all of chapter 14, and "a command of the Lord" may be a critique of the presumptiveness expressed in 14:36.[14]

Goes with What Precedes. There are at least three good reasons to take 14:33b as completing the thought in 14:33a. First, the women's section as reflected in the Western manuscripts and versions that place it after 14:40 (see discussion above) does not include "as in all the churches of the saints." It begins with 14:34. Other early evidence for the exclusion of 14:33b from the woman's passage is Chrysostom's (ca. 347-407) *Homily 36 on First Corinthians*.[15] Thus, the earliest known evidence on this question supports the conclusion that 14:33b does not go with what follows. Second, if 14:33b ("as in all the *churches* of the saints)" and 14:34a ("let the women be silent in the *churches*") made up the same sentence, an awkward, though not impossible, redundancy would be created with the repetition of the word "churches" (*ekklēsia*).[16] Finally, in all three of the other places in I Corinthians where Paul makes a similar statement (4:17, 7:17, and 11:16), the words conclude the previous thought rather than begin the following one.[17] This is particularly noteworthy in 11:16, because it too is in a passage that deals with women in the assembly. For these reasons it seems more likely that 14:33b should not be taken as a part of the woman's passage in 14:34-35, though certainty is impossible.

---

14   See Oster, *1 Corinthians*, 344 and Alford, *Greek Testament*, 600-01.

15   Fee (*First Epistle to the Corinthians*, 697, n. 49) claims more than the evidence he provides supports when he says that "the idea that v. 33b goes with v. 34 seems to be a modern phenomenon altogether," but it is worthy of note that Calvin (*I Corinthians*) connects 14:33b with 14:33a.

16   See Matt Soper, "I Corinthians 14," 6; Fee, *First Epistle to the Corinthians*, 698; and F. F. Bruce, *1 and 2 Corinthians*, 135.

17   See Fee, *First Epistle to the Corinthians*, 697, n. 49; Alford, *Greek Testament*, 600; and Robertson and Plummer, *Corinthians*, 324.

On one final note, whether or not 14:33b goes with the following section on women's behavior makes no difference to the question of its universal applicability to the matter of women in the church. Paul's teaching about women in the assembly in 14:34-35 would apply anywhere else the conditions that prevailed in Corinth at that time also exist, but they should not be removed from their context and interpreted as if they stood alone. Further, as was noted in chapter nine of this book, the similar statement at the end of 11:16 did not mean that the matter of head coverings for men and women in that passage applied to all churches everywhere for all time. Nor should "as in all the churches of the saints" in 14:33b necessarily be read that way.

Exposition

Let the women/wives be silent in the assemblies/ churches (14:34a)

OTHER THAN GAL. 3:28, NO PASSAGE RELATING TO WOMEN in the church has been detached from its context and treated as a proof text more frequently than this statement: "let the women be silent in the churches." The justification for this has often been that the statement seems to be absolute,[18] but this assumes what one sets out to prove. Is it any more absolute than "do not forbid the speaking in tongues" (14:39); yet, in how many congregations today is this Pauline injunction

---

18   See, for example, Ferguson, *Women in the Church*, 15-16. Lipscomb ("Woman's Work," 7) makes the point this way: "This seems to be, given as it is, an absolute and universal rule. We can find nothing in the context or occasion that would modify it by temporary or local surroundings. The reason given is one of universal application." The problem with this, however, is that there *is* something relevant in the context here that should prevent us from treating this statement as a proof text for every congregation in every place for all time.

followed?

The context is clear. As discussed earlier in this chapter, the context is the need for order in the assembly (14:27, 31, 40) or, expressed another way, the lack of disorder (14:33a).[19] The same corrective for disorder created by some of the tongue speakers and prophets—silence (*sigao*)—is prescribed for certain women who were interrupting the flow of the assembly with their persistent questions when they had a better alternative for getting them answered. In context, the silence required of these tongue speakers and prophets pertains to the point of order under consideration. Who would argue that they were also forbidden to speak in other respects in the assembly simply because of this requirement for silence?[20] Why should it have been any different for these women?[21]

Just as some of the tongue speakers and prophets were bringing about disorder in the assembly, so were some of the women. But who were these women? Paul leaves no doubt that they were certain married women.[22] Most English translations

---

19   See above in the section, **Placement of 14:34-35**.

20   See Workman, "I Corinthians 14:34-35," 39. Of the tongue speaker he writes, "This injunction did not prohibit that man from leading or participating in the assembly in some other capacity.... The prohibition had only to do with publicly speaking in tongues to the congregation." He made the same point about the silenced prophets: "The prohibition did not mean that the first man had to remain silent through the rest of the assembly as far as other activities are concerned."

21   Wayne Jackson's comment on this ("Women Translators," 25) is instructive. First he writes, "The term 'silence' of verse 34 is not employed absolutely, but relatively; i.e., it is qualified by the *context*." He then discusses how this applied to the requirement of silence for tongue speakers and prophets and finally writes, "Similarly, the woman's requirement to keep silence was not absolute. There was only a *certain sense* in which she was not to 'speak.'"

22   See chapter nine in the section, **The Man and Woman in 11:3b**, for a discussion of the dual meaning of the word for woman in this passage (*gunē*, "woman" or "wife") and man (*anēr*, "man" or "husband"). Here is a sampling of a large number of interpreters on all sides of the question of women in the church who see these women as wives of Christian men, rather than as women in general. Paul Watson, "Some

muddy the water by translating *gunē* here and in the next verse generically as "women" and "woman," but the words "their own" (*tous idious*) in 14:35 leaves them no choice but to translate *anēr* more precisely as "husbands."[23] That the women (wives) who have "their own husbands" in 14:35 are the same as the women who are to be silent 14:34 could not be clearer. Note the unmistakable grammatical connection. "Let the women/wives (*gunē*) be silent in the assemblies/churches, for it is not permitted for *them* (*autais*) to speak, but let *them* submit themselves, just as the law says. But if *they* want to learn something, let *them* ask *their own* husbands at home, for it is shameful for a woman/wife to speak in the assembly."[24] Thus, there is no justification for reading "women" (*gunē*) in 14:34 or "woman" (*gunē*) in 14:35 generically as women, rather than as wives.

Why did Paul single out these wives for the same restriction he put on tongue speakers and prophets? Unfortunately we do not know enough about the particular disruption they

Pastoral Implications," 164, n. 1; Guy N. Woods, "Open Forum*,*" 3 and *Questions and Answers*,(1976), 106; Roy Deaver, "First Corinthians 14:26-40," 11; Luther Martin, "Orderliness," 180-81; Howard, "Women's Role," 6-7; Coffman, *1 and 2 Corinthians*, 241, 244-45; and J. W. Chism, "Woman's Work," 451.

23   Of 30 English translations consulted, including all of the most popular ones, only Weymouth ("married women") and the WEB ("wives") do not translate *gunē* in 14:34 as "women." In 14:35 Weymouth ("married woman") was the only exception. All 30 translations render *anēr* in 14:35 as "husbands." The inconsistency of these translations, especially in 14:35, where wives are clearly under discussion, is mind blowing. At least there *gunē* should be rendered "wife," but apparently the power of the traditional interpretation of these two verses is so strong that translators have found it difficult to break with tradition. We all grew up reading these translations, and they have had an enormous influence on our views of women in the church. How different it might have been had these versions translated *gunē* consistently with its context.

24   Workman ("I Corinthians 14:34-35," 42) makes the same point: "It is as clear as it can be that the words 'they' and 'them' of verse 35 refer to the 'women' of verse 34."

were causing to be certain, but there are at least two possible explanations. First, they were the only ones disrupting the order in the assembly in this way. Had anyone else, even some of the men, been guilty of what they were doing, Paul would have included them in this corrective, because his overriding concerns in this chapter were edification and order in the assembly. It just happens that these wives were the only ones who needed to be corrected for this particular conduct.

Second, these wives had the advantage over other women in that they had a better alternative than interrupting the flow of the assembly to get their questions answered. They had Christian husbands who were capable of answering questions about what went on in the assembly on a given day. The other women did not.[25] In the case of these particular women, the solution was simple—ask your husbands at home rather than disrupting the assembly. This is a simple solution to a simple problem involving only a specific group of women.

For it is not permitted for them to speak, but let them submit themselves, just as the law also says (14:34b)

Speaking. We now turn from these wives being silent in the assembly, like the tongue speakers and prophets, to their speaking. Paul uses the common Greek word for speaking, *laleō*, twice in these two verses. A few writers find in this word a suggestion of the type or manner of their speaking,[26] but *laleō* is used in both Paul and the NT as a whole in such a wide range of situations that such precision in its meaning

---

25   Other women in the congregation—unmarried, widows, or wives whose husbands were not Christians or not mature enough in their knowledge to answer their questions or were not present in the assembly on a given day--did not have the advantage these wives had, so Paul does not silence them.

26   For example, Owen D. Olbright, "Speak in the Assembly," 37 (making a public speech) and Woods, "Open Forum," 3 (uttering any sound, not just words).

here is impossible.[27] What *is* relevant to the meaning of this infinitive is its tense. In Greek, infinitives in the aorist tense signify that action simply has occurred without specifying anything about its duration or repetition. An infinitive in the present tense, the one Paul uses here, refers to the action as occurring repeatedly.[28] Thus Paul is not talking about these wives speaking up or asking their questions every once in a while. This was something they were repeatedly doing, and herein lay at least a part of the problem. In the context of order in the assembly (14:27, 31, 33, 40) that surrounds these two verses, such recurrent questioning of the speakers would have been disruptive to that order, so Paul asks that they stop doing it. To generalize this prohibition to all speaking in the assembly does not take adequate account of either the context or the force of this present infinitive for "speak."

Submitting Themselves. The meaning of *hupotassō* , "submit themselves," in this verse has already been addressed in *Excursus 7:* **Hypotassō *('to submit') in the New Testament** in chapter eight of this book. Three general features of the way Paul uses *hupotassō* are worth repeating here.

First, when Paul is referring to submitting to other people, he always uses the word in the present tense, which does not distinguish between the middle voice ("submit yourself") and the passive voice ("be submissive"). Although the difference in English is quite subtle, the middle translation, "submit yourself," is probably to be preferred to the passive, because the verb is talking about something a person actually does.

---

27   Paul uses *laleō* 63 times, more than a third of which (24) occur in I Cor. 14 alone. In that chapter over two thirds of the time (18) *laleō* refers to speaking in tongues. Bauer (*Greek-English Lexicon*, 582) defines the word, when a person is the subject, as "to utter words, *talk, speak*." Ferguson (*Women in the Church*, 14) is correct when he writes, "The word is an ordinary word in Greek for any kind of speaking or other vocal sounds."

28   See Carroll Osburn, *Reclaiming the Ideal*, 199 and "Interpretation of 1 Cor. 14:34-35," 234.

Second, although the matters of subordination to authority or obedience or inferiority may be present in some contexts where *hupotassō* is used, none of these ideas is inherent in the verb itself. For example, subordination to authority can hardly be involved in 1 Cor. 16:16, where Paul directs the Corinthians to submit to several people in the congregation, none of whom is indicated as having any kind of authority. The beginning of the household code in Eph. 5:21-6:9 has all of the six types of individuals submitting to one another (5:21); yet fathers are not under the authority of their children (6:4), nor are masters under their slaves (6:9).

Third, an examination of Paul's uses of *hupotassō* reveals that this submission is voluntary. It comes from within the person submitting, rather than being forced on him/her by another. Thus when a prophet silences or submits his urge to prophecy (14:32), it is something under his control that he does of his own volition.

A key consideration, however, in Paul's use of *hupotassō* of these wives in 14:34 is to whom they are to submit. Unfortunately, in this passage he does not indicate to what or whom that submission should be directed—their husbands (see 14:35), the leaders of the congregation, other members of the congregation, the need of the congregation for order (see 14:27, 31, 33, 40), or what. Further, as will be seen shortly, the reference to "the law" is so general that it is of no help. The most that can be said here is that Paul is asking these wives to submit themselves to another/others by modifying their behavior in the assembly.

The Law (*ho nomos*). Paul's justification for asking these wives to submit themselves is "just as the law also says." Many have noted that nothing in "the law," assuming that "the law" refers to something in the OT,[29] fits Paul's specific point

---

29   The use of "the law" here is unusual as a reference to something specific in the OT. Fee (*First Epistle to the Corinthians*, 707) observes

here,[30] and he does not provide any further information to help the modern reader determine the meaning. This vacuum has not prevented modern interpreters from filling it with their own speculative suggestions. By far the most common one is Gen. 3:16, a passage that refers to a husband ruling over his wife.[31] Other passages in the OT that have been proposed include Gen. 1:26ff.,[32] Gen. 2:21ff.,[33] and Num. 30:3-16.[34] Because of the difficulty in finding an OT passage that fits, some have even suggested that "the law" refers to a

---

that "when Paul elsewhere appeals to 'the Law' he always cites the text (e.g., 9:8; 14:21), usually to support a point he himself is making. Nowhere else does he appeal to the Law in this absolute way as binding on Christian behavior." If this is a reference to something in the OT, it need not be limited to the Pentateuch, as is clear earlier in the chapter in 14:21 where Paul introduces a quotation of Isa. 28:11-12 by the words, "it stands written in the law." As can be seen from the discussion below, most interpreters take "the law" in 14:34 to refer to something in the OT.

30   Ferguson (*Women in the Church*, 19) notes that "in the case of 1 Corinthians 14:34... there is no explicit statement corresponding exactly to Paul's affirmation." See also Yeakley, *Why They Left*, 189; Hutson, *Transforming Word*, 932; Robinson, *Community Without Barriers*, 78; and Olbright, "Speak in the Assembly," 38.

31   Serious questions about this view are raised in chapter five of this book in **Excursus 6: The Meaning of Genesis 3:16 for the Matter of Women in the Church**. Since Gen. 3:16 refers to the relationship of a husband and a wife, not men and women, if Paul is referring to Gen. 3:16 to support his point about these women submitting themselves, it can only apply to married women submitting to their husbands. This point seems to have escaped some interpreters who suggest that Gen. 3:16 may be Paul's reference here. For example, Highers ("Keep Silence," 26) writes, "The law did... speak about women being in subjection to men (Gen. 3:16)" and Ferguson (*Church of Christ*, 343) made essentially the same point: "1 Corinthians 14:34 supports the subordinate position of women in the assembly from the law (Gen. 3:16 would seem to be the passage in mind...)."

32   See Bruce, *1 and 2 Corinthians*, 136.

33   See Ferguson, *Women in the Church*, 19; Workman, "1 Corinthians 14:34-35," 38; and Allen Black, "Paul's Use of Genesis," 303.

34   See McGarvey, *Commentary*, 142 and Chism, "Woman's Work," 450-51.

Jewish interpretation of the OT[35] or some civil law in place in Corinth.[36] While it would be helpful to know exactly what Paul meant, we are just too far removed from the world of Paul and the Corinthians to arrive at an understanding with any level of certainty. Therefore, it is better to let this one remain a mystery for now and simply say that in Paul's mind something in "the law," whatever he means by that, supported his instructions for these wives.

But if there is something they want to learn, let them ask their own husbands at home (14:35a)

These few words offer the key to understanding what in these wives' behavior Paul wanted to stop when he silenced them. Interpreters have greatly complicated this by proposing numerous forbidden activities on these women's part, several of them quite out of sync with the development of Paul's argument in chapter 14.[37] However, Paul is fairly clear about

---

35   See Hutson, *Transforming Word,* 932 ("a traditional Jewish inter-pretation") and Robinson, *Community Without Barriers,* 78 ("the way the law was interpreted in synagogues").

36   See Frederick J. Long, "Christ's Gifted Bride," 98, n. 3 (Roman law) and Norman L. Parks, " Case Study," 19 ("the municipal law of Corinth").

37   Some of the questionable proscribed activities that have been imported into this passage include **praying** (Ferguson, *Church of Christ,* 17 and Garrell L. Forehand, "Girls Leading Public Prayers," 8), **addressing the assembly** or **preaching** (Sanders, "Are Women Limited," 35; Gary C. Hampton, "Keep Silence," 39; Highers, "Keep Silence," 24; Workman, "I Corinthians 14:34-35," 39; Edwin Broadus, "The Role of Women (3)," 7; and Lanier, Sr., "Woman's Liberty," 9), **assuming a leadership role in the assembly** (Warden, "Conduct of Christian Women," 11), **correcting their husbands in public** (Reese, *Bound & Determined,* 42), **teaching men in public** (Wayne Burger, "Women's Silence," 12**), prophesying in the presence of men** (Roy H. Lanier, Sr., "May Women Lead Prayer," 166), **leading men in thought** (Forehand, "Girls Leading Public Prayers," 8), and **chattering** (Anna M. Griffith, "Vision," 12). Curtis ("Women's Role," 15-16) even cites this passage and two others to prove that women may not **baptize**.

what he wanted to stop. These wives were repeatedly asking questions[38] in the assembly that they could get answered elsewhere more appropriately without damaging order in the assembly. Whether it was prophets' messages that were being interrupted by their questions or some other teaching (see "learn" in 14:35), if they had a husband present who could teach them what they wanted to learn, they should wait until they get home to get their questions answered.

A few writers have suggested that the use of *anēr* ("husband" or "man") here could refer to men other than husbands, thereby including more than just certain wives in the prohibition against speaking.[39] These efforts to extend what all English translations take as the meaning of *anēr* (see note 23 above) to other men fall under their own weight. Only assumptions imported from elsewhere would necessitate such a stretch. However, Paul is quite plain here. Had he written "*their*" husbands, he would have been clear enough. However, his words "their *own*" (*tous idious*) remove all doubt that all others are excluded.[40] Therefore, the effort to expand the application beyond this select group of wives and the conduct Paul specifically mentions does violence to the context and introduces matters that simply do not belong here.

For it is shameful for a woman/wife to speak in an assembly/church (14:35b)

Paul offers two reasons in support of his silencing of these wives: the law, as it relates to their submitting themselves

---

38   That this action was repeated does not come from the verb "ask" (*eperōtaō*) in this verse, because it refers to what the wives were to do at home. Rather, as noted in the section, **Speaking**, above, the present tense of "speak" (*laleō*) in both verses has this meaning.

39   Sanders, "Are Women Limited," 36; Olbright, "Speak in the Assembly," 38; and Allen Black, "Paul's Use of Genesis," 304.

40   See also the same phrase in I Cor. 7:2, where Paul is clearly referring to married couples.

(14:34), and custom (*aischron*, "shameful," 14:35). The first, if "the law" refers to something in the OT, presumably comes from God; the other from culture. We are concerned here with the latter. The repeated speaking of these wives (present infinitive of *laleō*, "to speak") in that setting was regarded as shameful (*aischron*). As is widely recognized in both the literature[41] and lexical tools,[42] this adjective carries the nuance of culture-related shame. It represents the conduct of wives in public presumably when their husbands were present. In this sense, then, it is not unlike the cultural shame of having their heads shaved or shorn (*aischron*, "shameful") or failing to wear their head covering when they prayed or prophesied (*kataischunō*, "dishonor") that we encountered in 11:5-6. Thus, this second of Paul's reasons for silencing these wives has no bearing on cultural settings, like our own, where such a practice is not shameful.[43]

---

41   On this cultural quality of *aischron* see, for example, Robinson, *Community Without Barriers*, 78; Ross W. Dye, " Culture," 28-29; Martin, "Orderliness," 181; Broadus, "Role of Women (4)," 7; Coffman, *1 and 2 Corinthians,* 241; and Parish, "Submission," 18. Ferguson's treatment of *aischon* in I Corinthians 11 and 14 is a curious one. He is quite clear in repeated writings that *aischron* refers to cultural shame ("Of Veils and Virgins (2014), 231, 241; *Women in the Church,* 23; "Assembly Part 2," 11-12; and *Church of Christ,* 342), but in the latter he retreats from this meaning in speculating that "here, given Paul's weighty declarations about the law and the command of God, it may be that the 'shame' is defined by God and not by society." (20) The reader can judge for himself whether this reasoning in sufficient to overturn the established meaning he assigns to *aischron* in Greek literature generally and specifically in the parallel usage in 11:6, where he refers to *aischron* as "the language of culture." (23)

42   Bauer (*Greek-English Lexicon*, 3rd edition, 29) calls *aischron* "a term esp. significant in honor-shame oriented society; gener. in ref. to that which fails to meet expected moral and cultural standards" and defines it as **"part. to being socially or morally unacceptable,** *shameful, base."* Rudolf Bultman ("αἰσχρός," 190) states that in the NT *aischros* has "the sense of 'that which is disgraceful' in the judgment of men."

43   McGarvey (*Commentary,* 143), having observed that "the customs of the age made it a shameful thing for a woman to speak in public," noted further that "the powers of woman have become so developed,

Excursus 9: I Cor. 11:5 and 14:34. Before summarizing the conclusions reached in this chapter on I Cor. 14:34-35, one final matter needs attention. Almost everyone who writes on both I Cor. 11:2-16 and 14:34-35 calls attention to a supposed conflict between 11:5 and 14:34. The issue has to do with the apparent approval of women speaking in the assembly by praying and prophesying in 11:5 and disapproval of speaking in the assembly in 14:34. Ferguson's treatment of this subject provides us with a good starting point.

As is frequently the case with Bible students whose serious studies of a passage or topic continue over time, Ferguson's views on this matter have evolved through the years. His entire development of this matter begins with his conclusion that I Corinthians 14 prohibits women from "prophesying or giving authoritative teaching in the assembly," which, he says, "would seem to contradict 1 Corinthians 11:2-16, where the women prayed and prophesied."[44] He suggests that either of two possibilities could remove the conflict. The first is that in 11:5 Paul discusses women praying and prophesying in theory but he later qualifies, namely prohibits, it in practice in 14:34[45] or that 11:5 is "descriptive, neither prescriptive nor approving" but that the practice was later disapproved in 14:34.[46] He argues this on the analogy of the way Paul treats eating meats sacrificed to idols in I Corinthians.[47]

Ferguson's second suggestion for resolving the apparent

---

and her privileges have been so extended in gospel lands, that it is no longer shameful for her to speak in public."

44   *Church of Christ*, 342.

45   "Assembly Part 2," 11.

46   *Women in the Church*, 28-29.

47   On whether or not this interpretation of Paul's argument about eating this meat is valid, see Wendell Willis, "I Corinthians 8-10," 103-110, especially 109-110, and Mark C. Black, "1 Cor. 11:2-16," 194, n. 11.

conflict between the two passages is to question whether the setting being address in 11:5 is the same as the assembly of the whole church in 14:34. Here his views have changed somewhat over time. Earlier he argued that 11:5 reflected activities in the regular assembly, if not other meetings as well.[48] Later he stated that "it is not certain that these activities occurred in the assembly."[49] However, in his detailed article on women's head coverings in 2014 he returned to his original suggestion in 1985 that this was a regular assembly but probably in a large home.[50]

What are we to make of Ferguson's proposed solutions to the presumed conflict between 11:5 and 14:34? First, it is important to note that he is not alone in his interpretation of these matters. He represents a common opinion that 14:34 is primary, so anything in 11:2-16 that does not agree with a specific interpretation of 14:34 must be made to harmonize with it. Most writers on the apparent conflict between 11:5 and 14:34 see the latter as primary, so the former must be interpreted in light of it.[51] Similar to Ferguson, the most common method of doing this is to argue that the setting in 11:5 is not the regular congregational assembly, thereby

---

48   "Of Veils and Virgins" (1985), 14-15. In 1990 he and his wife, Nancy, then published "New Testament Teaching on the Role of Women in the Assembly," *Christian Scholars Conference*: 12 and the same article in the *Gospel Advocate* ("Women in the Assembly," 30), making the same point. In *Women in the Church*, 26-27 he acknowledges this may have been a regular assembly if the other of his possible solutions is the correct one.

49   *Church of Christ*, 342.

50   "Of Veils and Virgins" (2014), 234.

51   Tom Yoakum ("Women at Prayer," 5, n. 3), who sees 11:5 as primary, is an exception, as is Bruce, (*Mind for What Matters*, 262). Here is a sampling of writers who believe 14:34 is primary. Roy Davison, "Response," 15; Broadus, "Role of Women (2)," 8 and "Role of Women (3)," 7; Hollis Miller, "Women (4)," 7; and George W. Knight, III, "Role Relationship," 89-90.

removing the contradiction.[52] This, of course, flies in the face of the evidence presented in chapter nine, **The Setting**, that the meeting where these women were praying and prophesying was, in fact, the regular Corinthian assembly.

Another line of reasoning, which also corresponds to Ferguson's other potential solution, is to maintain that 11:5 merely describes, without approval or disapproval, what some women were doing in the assemblies in Corinth, but in 14:34 Paul later disapproves of the practice.[53] The difficulty with this proposed solution is summed up in a question by Allen Black: "why should he specify the need of women wearing veils when they pray or prophesy if he intended to bring a halt to these practices?"[54] Robinson put it this way: "Paul's instructions requiring women to wear head coverings when they pray and prophesy becomes nonsensical if Paul was about to impose an absolute prohibition against women speaking at all."[55]

At least four other solutions to the apparent contradiction between the verses have been proposed to argue that the setting in the two verses is sufficiently different to remove any need for harmonization: (1) 11:5 relates to the regular assembly, but 14:34 does not;[56] (2) 14:34 relates to the regular

---

52   In addition to the references to Davison, Broadus, and Miller in the preceding footnote, see Alan E. Highers, "Praying and Prophesying," 11-12 and Lipscomb, "Women's Work," 6.

53   In addition to the references to Ferguson in footnote 45 and 46, see Sanders, "Are Women Limited," 36 and Lightfoot, *The Role of Women*, 34-35. Nichol (*God's Woman*, 121-22), with his characteristic directness, debunks the idea this way: "It seems to me that such a position would be disgusting to a man of reverence, if he knows the truth about the knowledge of the Holy Spirit. Paul was giving utterance to the words of the Holy Spirit in I Cor. 11:4, 5. The Holy Spirit did not reverse himself within a few minutes and make a statement in I Cor. 14:34, 35 contradicting what he had said in I Cor. 11:4, 5."

54   "1 Corinthians 14:34-35," 180.

55   *Community Without Barriers*, 75. See also Cukrowski, "Uncovered Prophets," 144 and Mark Black, "1 Cor. 11:2-16, 194. Also see Guin, *Buried Talents*, 95 and n. 99.

56   Nichol, *God's Woman*, 124.

assembly, but 11:5 does not;[57] (3) 11:5 is referring to praying and prophesying under the guidance of the Spirit, but 14:34 refers to ordinary speech;[58] and (4) the rule in 14:34 has exceptions, and 11:5 is one.[59]

But what if the conclusion of Ferguson and many others is faulty? What if Paul is not prohibiting all formal speaking in the assembly by these women in 14:34, namely making their silence absolute? In that case the suspected contradiction vanishes and there is no longer a need to harmonize 11:5 with 14:34. The evidence that this is, in fact, the case is quite compelling.

Perhaps recounting my own struggle with this matter may be helpful here. When I first studied I Cor. 11:2-16 in earnest, I was concerned primarily with women praying out loud in the assembly. From that study I came away with the conviction that, in fact, they did do that in first-century Corinth. Then my study moved to I Cor. 14:34-35, and I was immediately brought up short by the silencing of women in the assembly in 14:34. How could the practice of women praying and prophesying out loud in the assembly (11:5) coexist with the requirement that they remain silent? My initial reaction was to question my earlier conclusion about I Corinthians 11, but here I also stumbled on the question on which so many have stumbled—which is primary? Must my understanding of I Corinthians 11 be made to conform to my reading of I Corinthians 14 or the other way around? Or, was there no conflict at all and the problem was with me? Was it possible that I was not looking at one or the other passage correctly and that when I did the difficulty would go away? In my case, that is exactly what happened as further study confirmed my earlier understanding of I Corinthians 11. The problem lay

---

57   Olbright, "Speak in the Assembly," 36.
58   Lightfoot, *Role of Women*, 33, 35 and "Women in Religious Services," 135.
59   Martin, "Orderliness," 181 and McGarvey, *Commentary*, 142-43.

with my reading of 14:34 as a universal statement without a proper consideration of its context. I, as I later learned was true of so many others, was guilty of treating 14:34 as a proof text. It was humbling to realize how long it can take someone to notice the obvious in a passage.

So what does the context reveal about the meaning of 14:34? This is dealt with above in some detail in the critique of Fee's objection that 14:34-35 does not fit the context. For that, see the second through the fourth paragraphs in the section, **Placement of 14:34-35**, at the beginning of this chapter. The points made there are later summarized in the discussion of 14:34a in the section, **Let the women/wives be silent in the assemblies/churches**, by stating that the context is the need for order in the assembly (14:27, 31, 40) or, expressed another way, the lack of disorder (14:33a). The same corrective for disorder created by some of the tongue speakers and prophets—silence (*sigao*)—is prescribed for certain women who were interrupting the flow of the assembly with their persistent questions when they had a better alternative for getting them answered. In context, the silence required of these tongue speakers and prophets pertains to the point of order under consideration. Who would argue that they were also forbidden to speak in other respects in the assembly simply because of this requirement for silence? So why should the silencing of these women that follows immediately the silencing of tongue speakers and prophets be considered absolute, when it was not absolute for the other two? The inconsistency of tearing the silencing of the women from this context and treating it as absolute for every woman in every congregation for all time should be obvious.

There is, however, another feature of the context that is equally relevant to this discussion. If we take Paul at his word in his description of this Corinthian assembly, women did speak in it. As Robinson points out, the Corinthian assembly was "highly participatory."[60] One of the ways Paul's discussion in I Corinthians 14 reflects this is the repeated use of the plural personal pronoun, "you" (*humeis*, eleven times), and the plural adjective, "all" (*pantes*, nine times), with reference to the congregation. Twice (14:5, 18) he even combines the two words into "all of you," indicating that he is addressing the entire congregation.[61] Yet the way this chapter is read by many is to take most of the uses of "all" to mean "half" (men only). For example, "I want all of you [that is, men only] to speak in tongues" (14:5). In fact, in 14:31, where Paul uses "all" three times, by that interpretation "all" would mean "half" one time and it would mean "all" (men and women) twice—in the same sentence! Further, in 14:23 "the *whole* church" (*hē ekklēsia holē*) and "all" (*pantes*) refer to the same individuals as speaking in tongues. But according to this line of interpretation, flowing from the belief that 14:34 prohibits every woman from addressing the assembly in any formal way, "all" in this verse would mean "half" of the church, not the "whole" church.[62]

In view of all this, does it not seem strange that Paul would repeatedly express himself by such an inclusive word as "all" if he means "let the women be silent in the assemblies" to be exclusive and absolute? Many writers talk about an apparent conflict between 11:5 and 14:34. What about this inconsistency? Perhaps the problem is not with Paul but with the modern reader. What if Paul actually meant "all" to mean "all" earlier in the chapter? How might that call into question the common proof text interpretation of 14:34?

---

60   *Community Without Barriers*, 73.

61   The same expression, "all of you," is used only once elsewhere in I Corinthians, where clearly "all" means "all" of the congregation (16:24).

62   Note also 14:26, where Paul mentions five speaking activities in which "each" (*ekastos*) one engages: "each has a psalm, a teaching, a revelation, a tongue, an interpretation." On this see Philip B. Payne, "Use of οὐδέ," 248.

Conclusions

THE TRADITIONAL INTERPRETATION OF I COR. 14:34-35 has been that Paul is here forbidding all women in the congregation from speaking in any formal way in the regular assemblies. The result of this study has been to call that interpretation into serious question. Such a reading of 14:34a, "let the women be silent in the assemblies," as an absolute prohibition for all Christian women, in every congregation for all time is the result of wresting this verse from its context and treating it in proof text fashion. The passage in context, however, presents the careful reader with several clear points.

First, far from preventing any formal speech to the church, Paul only addresses some repeated disruptive questioning of other speakers. His solution is to silence that kind of speaking in the same way he did the disruptive practices of tongue speakers and prophets. In all three cases the required silence refers only to the point of disruption, not to all other vocal participation in the assembly. In fact, by Paul's repeated reference to "all" of the congregation or "the *whole* congregation" (14:23) as exercising various speaking gifts in the assembly, he is affirming that both men and women were thus engaged.

Second, the women in the passage are a limited group of wives who had Christian husbands in the assembly on a given day who were capable of enabling their wives' learning by answering their questions at home. No other women are addressed in this passage, so this is not a blanket prohibition of all women speaking in any way in these assemblies.

Third, Paul supports his prohibition in two ways. The first, an appeal to "the law" (14:34) in connection with these wives' submitting themselves turns out to be so general and ambiguous that no interpreter has been able to do any more than make an educated guess as to his meaning. It, therefore, is of little or no help in arriving at Paul's overall meaning in the passage. The other reason for forbidding this type of speaking in the assembly was local custom ("shameful," 14:35). Here Paul is reminding these Christian wives how they should conduct themselves around other people in the presence of their husbands. They should not be acting in a way that is regarded as shameful.

Finally, nothing in I Corinthians 14 suggests a modification of the picture of women in the assemblies presented in I Corinthians 11. Along with the men and with no distinction between them, save their head covering, women spoke in the assembly by praying and prophesying. In fact, as Paul repeatedly affirms in I Corinthians 14, "all," both men and women, were engaged in various types of speaking in the assemblies. How tragic it is that I Cor. 14:34-35 has been used by so many for so long to silence all women in every assembly in every place for all time!

CHAPTER ELEVEN

I Timothy 2:8-15

While I Cor. 14:34-35 has played a pivotal role in discussions about what women may or may not do in the assembly, I Tim. 2:8-15 has been more central to considerations of the wider question of women in the church. Not only has 2:8-10 been interpreted to prohibit women from praying out loud in the assembly, but 2:12 has been used to place women in general under men in general not only in the assembly but in all other areas of church life. Indeed, Carroll Osburn has remarked about 2:12 that "no biblical text has been so misused to legislate so many prohibitions that stifle so much service by so many people."[1] It is fitting, then, that our study of passages relevant to the matter of women in the church should conclude with I Tim. 2:8-15, where Paul is correcting the behavior of some of the men and women in the congregation.

Exposition

Prayer

*I desire that the men pray in every place, lifting up
holy hands without anger and arguing. Likewise
women to adorn themselves in appropriate attire
with modesty and moderation, not with braided hair*

---

1 *Reclaiming the Ideal*, 252.

and gold or pearls or expensive clothing, but what is
fitting for women professing piety, namely, through
good works. (2:8-10)

PAUL BEGINS THIS PARAGRAPH ON CONGREGATIONAL
prayer in 2:1, goes into an aside in 2:5 and returns to prayer
in 2:8. Quite predictably, depending on the views interpreters
bring to this text on women's participation in the assembly,
they are deeply divided on whether in 2:9-10 Paul is continuing his discussion of prayer or has changed the subject.
Even those who believe that 2:8-10 implies that women may
not pray out loud in the assembly actually treat 2:9-10 as
still referring to prayer. They just think that their implication *prevents* women from praying in the assembly, instead
of directing them to pray there. Thus, on either reading of
the verses, Paul does not end his discussion of prayer in the
assembly until 2:10.[2]

Men Praying (2:8). It is clear that by his use of the word *anēr*
("man") in 2:8 and *gunē* ("woman") in 2:9-10 Paul is giving
different instructions to the men and women of the congregation.[3] In fact, the concern about anger (*orgē*) and arguing or
verbal conflict (*dialogismos*) is more appropriate to men than
to women. This is an understandable corrective, given Paul's
charge to Timothy to put a stop to the unhealthy speech of
his opponents.[4] The posture of raising hands during prayer is

2   Taking 2:1-10 as a whole as a discussion of prayer, 2:1-2 identifies
the content and purpose of these congregational prayers and 2:8-10 the
way the desirable qualities of those who do the praying are expressed.
3   For a discussion of the gender-specific nature of these two words,
see the section, **The Man and Woman in 11:3b**, in chapter nine above.
Whether in these three verses Paul principally has in mind husbands
and wives, as appears to be the case in 2:11-15, or men and women in
general is not clear, nor does it seem to matter for the overall interpretation of 2:8-15.
4   Note these words that characterize these false teachers' speech
in Paul's charge to Timothy: divergent instruction (*heterodidaskaleō*),
useless speculations (*ekzētēsis*), empty talk (*mataiologia*), and dogmatic

widely commented on in the literature on this verse and generally has not been a source of disagreement among interpreters.

Women Praying (or not) (2:9-10). The literature on these two verses centers on two questions: (1) whether women are *included* in the discussion of prayer in the assembly or (2) whether they are *excluded*. For some of those who see women excluded from praying in the assembly a secondary concern is whether this prohibition extends to other settings as well. We will examine these three matters in order.

Included. This revolves around whether Paul ends his treatment of prayer in the assembly in 2:8 or 2:10. Those who argue that the discussion of prayer ends in 2:8 generally support their view in two ways. First, they cite the fact that a reference to prayer is not specifically repeated in 2:9. Second, they note that while the infinitive, "to pray" (*proseuchomai*), completes the thought of the verb "desire" (*boulomai*) in 2:8, a different infinitive, "to adorn" (*kosmeō*), is used to complete the thought expressed by "desire" in 2:9.[5] On the other hand, those who believe prayer is still under consideration in 2:9-10 note that the "likewise" (*hōsautōs*) at the beginning of 2:9 connects what these women were doing with what the men were doing.[6] They further point out that prayer has

---

speech (*diabebaioomai*) of those who do not know what they are talking about (1:3-7). The description of the toxic speech of the heretics is even more graphic in 6:3-5: divergent instruction (*heterodidaskaleō*), not sound words (*hugiainō*), teaching that is not godly (*eusebeia*), puffed up (*tuphoō*), sick with controversies (*zētēsis*) and disputes about words (*logomachia*), discord (*eris*), slanders (*blasphēmia*), and wranglings (*diaparatribē*).

5   See Ferguson, *Women in the Church*, 31 and Dave Miller, "I Timothy 2:11-15," 276.

6   See Geer, "Admonitions," 290. He also notes that a concern for women's dress when they pray provides a nice corollary to I Corinthians 11, a passage where how women were attired when they prayed and prophesied in the assembly is also under consideration. Also see Witherington, *Women in the Earliest Churches*, 263, n. 203.

been the overall topic under discussion since 2:1, so if it were not in 2:9-10, then these verses would represent a change in subject with no apparent reason in the context. Thus Paul's sense would be "likewise, I desire women, *when they pray*, to adorn themselves...." The Greek text allows either meaning, and which of the two options individual interpreters favor usually correlates with what they bring to the passage about their view of women's verbal participation in the assembly.

Excluded. It is one thing to conclude that Paul does not *include* women in his discussion of prayer in this passage and quite another to infer that he intends to *exclude* women from those who may pray in the assembly. The one should not necessarily follow from the other; yet some interpreters actually argue that it does.[7] The reasoning is that the mention of one (men) automatically excludes the other (women). Others, on the other hand, including C. R. Nichol,[8] reject the application of what some call the principle of exclusion to this passage.[9]

Let us examine the line of reasoning that leads some to the inference that women are prohibited from praying in the assembly. If "I desire that the men (*anēr*, adult males) pray" (2:8) means that women may not do so in the assembly, it should follow that "I desire that women (*gunē*, adult women) adorn themselves in appropriate attire with modesty and moderation" (2:9) means that men may not do that in the assembly. In fact, by that logic it is not just that Paul does not require men to dress that way, he *forbids* them to do so.

---

7   For example, see Webster, "Meaning of Galatians 3:28," 24; Burger, "Women's Silence," 12; and Roy Deaver, "Teaching and Praying," 676.
8   *God's Woman*, 147. Nichol writes, "No one should conclude that the passage is antithetic, and that because Paul says men are to pray in every place, the teaching is that women are never to pray." Although Nichol's comment is also addressing the question of the meaning of "in every place" here, it is clear from his denial that the passage is "antithetic" that he rejects the argument of exclusion here.
9   For excellent discussions of this point see James Casey, "Girls Praying," 104 and Bruce Terry, "Plea for Consistency," 6.

One more example from the Pastoral Epistles should suffice. In Tit. 2:2-8 Paul describes the character and behavior that are required of older men, older women, and younger men. As in I Tim. 2:9, the three are connected by the word "likewise" (*hōsautōs*, 2:3, 6). Is it reasonable to conclude that because a trait of one is mentioned the others may not exhibit that quality? For instance, older men are to be "sound in faith, love and perseverance" (2:2). Does this prevent older women and younger men from doing the same? Or older women are to be "teachers of what is good" (2:3). Does that preclude the other two from being that kind of teacher? Sometimes, when we read a passage we have read so many times before, it is easy to get so locked in by the unexamined presuppositions we bring to the text that we miss what is *actually* there. Surely the fact that Paul includes men in the praying does not mean that women are excluded from it. Certainly Paul does not say that.

Other Settings? The words "in every place" (*en panti topō*) in 2:8 provide the key to determining the setting Paul has in mind for these instructions. An article by Everett Ferguson in the *Restoration Quarterly*[10] is the definitive study on this matter. There he surveys an extensive array of Jewish and early Christian usages, many of them under the influence of Mal. 1:11, to show that "place" (*topos*) had become a technical term for a place of worship. Thus, "in every place" in I Tim. 2:8 refers to every place where the church meets to worship.[11] Just as was true in I Corinthians 11 and 14, Paul is here talking about what goes on in the regular Christian assemblies.[12]

---

10   "1 Timothy 2:8," 65-73.
11   Ferguson (Ibid., 65) actually applies the phrase to the entire discussion of worship in 2:1-15.
12   See also David Pharr, "Exercise Authority," 31, 33; Jack P. Lewis, "Analysis of 1 Timothy 2:8-15," 34; Tommy South, "Forbidding Women to Teach," 206, n. 2; Broadus, "Role of Women (3)," 7; Neil Lightfoot, *Role of Women*, 31 and "Women in Religious Services," 134; and

Failure to recognize this specialized meaning of "in every place" here has led to much speculation about the circumstances in which women are not allowed to pray. These include (1) in the presence of men,[13] (2) chain prayers in devotionals where men are present,[14] and (3) public praying.[15] One person even suggested that the passage on prayer also forbids women to preach.[16] It should be no surprise to anyone who looks closely at 2:8-10 that Paul put none of these restrictions in the text. He is talking about prayer in the assembly, period.

To sum up the conclusions reached above, nothing Paul wrote in 2:8-10 in any way restricts women's freedom to pray out loud in the assembly or any other setting. Such restrictions add elements to the text that are simply not there. Further, suggesting that this passage forbids women to pray out loud in the assembly would make the practice in Ephesus inconsistent with that in Corinth, where women did pray out loud in that setting (I Cor. 11:5). If we are using NT practice as our guide, limiting women's freedom to pray in our assemblies today is a grave departure from apostolic practice and needs to end.

Teaching

Let a woman/wife learn in quietness in all submissiveness. I do not permit a woman to teach or to have authority over/domineer a man/husband, but to be in quietness. (2:11-12)

Deaver, "Women and Prayer," 15.

13   See, for example, Webster, "Meaning of Galatians 3:28," 24; Burger, "Women's Silence," 12; Dave Miller, "Permit Not a Woman," 28, n. 11; and Guy N. Woods, "Questions Answered," (Aug. 1977), 516.

14   Charles A. Whitmire, "Girls Leading Prayers," 9.

15   David Lipscomb, *Commentary*, 142, 144.

16   Phil Sanders correctly identifies the setting as the church assembled for worship, but he adds, "If women are not to lead prayer, surely they are forbidden to preach." ("Women Preachers," 19).

THE OVERALL POINT PAUL IS DISCUSSING IN THESE VERSES
has to do with women teaching. However, three elements in
the context need attention before examining what Paul's point
is about women teaching: (1) the identity of the "woman"
(*gunē*), (2) the meaning of "quietness" (*hēsuchia*), and (3) the
requirement for "submissiveness" (*hupotagē*). For the larger
question of teaching (*didaskō*), did Paul's point about these
women teaching have to do with the fact *that* they were teaching, *what* they were teaching, and/or *how* they were teaching?
We will consider the three contextual elements first.

Three Contextual Elements

Identity of the "Woman" (**gunē***).* As was the case in both I
Corinthians 11 and 14, Paul's use of the word *gunē* twice in
these two verses begs the question of whether he has wives or
women in general primarily in mind. The threefold allusion
to the creation narrative in 2:13-15 is rather decisive evidence
pointing to the former. Paul refers here to Genesis 2 and 3.
As has been pointed out repeatedly in this book,[17] especially
in chapter four, everything in those chapters in Genesis is
about the relationship of a particular man and woman to each
other. The all-too-common application of the creation narrative to the relationship of men and women generically to each
other ignores this fact and inserts into the text what neither
the original author in Genesis nor any NT writer or speaker
does. Jesus even applies the more generic reference to "male
and female" in Gen. 1:27 to married couples (Matt. 19:4).[18]

Here in I Timothy 2, then, Paul's reference is to wives, not
to women in general in the assembly. The woman was formed

---

17   See chapter five in the section, **I Corinthians 11:8, 9**, and at the
end of the section, **I Timothy 2:13, 14**; chapter eight, n. 71; chapter
nine at the end of the section, **The Man and Woman in 11:3b** and n.
17; and chapter ten, n. 31.
18   See chapter four, n. 9 and the full discussion in the section, **Matthew 19:4, 5=Mark 10:6-8a**, in chapter five.

for a particular man, her husband (2:13). The woman sinned when she was deceived by the serpent in the presence of her husband (2:14). Among the consequences of the woman's sin was increased pain in childbirth (2:15), a result coming from an intimate activity between a particular man and woman. Thus Paul's triple use of the creation narrative in 2:13-15 is his clue that in his restrictions on women teaching in 2:12 he does not have in mind all the women in the congregation but rather some of the married women.[19]

***Quiteness* (hēsuchia).** Paul employs the word translated "silence" or "quietness" (*hēsuchia*)[20] only in II Th. 3:12[21] and the two instances here in I Tim. 2:11-12. However, he also uses the cognate adjective, *hēsuchios*, (I Tim. 2:2) and verb, *hēsuchazō* (I Th. 4:11) once each. While in certain contexts these words may refer to vocal silence, this nuance does not capture the essence of the word group. It has more to do with such conditions as quietness, lack of disturbance, tranquility, or good order.[22] This is well illustrated in Luke's use of

---

19   See Long, "Christ's Gifted Bride," 99.

20   Older English translations of 2:11-12 generally favor "silence" over "quietness," as do a few newer ones. Most newer English translations favor "quietness."

21   Here the persons to whom *hēsuchia* is addressed in 3:12 are acting in a disorderly manner (*ataktōs*, "**in defiance of good order, *disorderly*,**" Bauer, *Greek-English Lexicon*, 3rd edition, 148), are refusing to work and are busybodies (3:11). Thus Paul commands them to work for their own food "with quietness" (*hēsuchia*), that is, to stop acting in a disorderly manner.

22   Bauer (*Greek-English Lexicon*, 3rd edition, 440) defines *hēsuchia* as 1. "**state of quietness without disturbance, *quietness***" and 2. "**state of saying nothing or very little, *silence***"; *hēsuchios* as "**quiet, well-ordered**"; and *hēsuchazō* as 1. "**to relax from natural activity, *rest*,**" 2. "**to live a quiet life or refrain from disturbing activity, *be peaceable/orderly*,**" 3. "**to be free from being disturbed, *have rest*,**" and 4. "**to refrain from saying someth., *be quiet, remain silent*.**" From each of these definitions, which are completely borne out in their eleven uses in the NT, it is evident that the words have to do with a person's overall conduct, which may or may not involve his/her speaking.

hēsuchia in Acts 22:2, its only other occurrence in the NT. The setting is the mob violence, including beating Paul, that occurred when he had been suspected of taking a Greek into the Temple (21:28-36). Luke's description of the absolute chaos is riveting. They seized Paul, dragged him out of the Temple, and tried to beat him to death. The city was stirred up with people running all around. Luke uses four different words to describe the chaos before the tribune allowed Paul to speak.[23] Paul motioned with his hands, and the people greatly quieted down (*sigē*, 21:40). Then, when they heard him speaking in their native tongue (Aramaic), they got even quieter (*hēsuchia*, 22:2). From all of this it is evident that there can be a definite verbal element to the quietness expressed by *hēsuchia*, but the contrast with what was going on in the crowd before the *hēsuchia* shows that it is much more than that.

This meshes perfectly with what we find in I Tim. 2:11-12. Just as with the men who were told to behave themselves in the assembly (without anger and arguing, 2:8), whatever these women were doing was disruptive to the tranquility or quietness (*hēsuchia*) that should characterize Christian meetings. Thus *hēsuchia* in 2:11-12 refers to much more than speaking. It indicates quiet, well-ordered behavior, just as its cognate adjective (*hēsuchios*, "quiet") does earlier in the chapter (2:2).[24]

---

23   *Sugcheō*, "to be in confusion"; *epiphōneō*, "shouting"; *thorubos*, "disturbance"; and *bia*, "violence."

24   This is widely recognized by interpreters on both sides of the question of women in the church. For example, see Ken Cukrowski, "Women and Wealth," 36; Sellers S. Crain, Jr., "Women in Public Worship," 34; Ferguson, *Women in the Church*, 33; Soper, "I Timothy 2:8-15," 4; Lipe, "1 Timothy 2:11-15," 296; Howard, "Women's Role," 8; and Payne, "Libertarian Women," 169-70. Hollis Miller ("Women (3)," 11) sums up the meaning of *hēsuchia* here well "as having reference to women not disturbing the learning process with a dominant and authoritative spirit, but to be gentle and tranquil." See also Witherington, *Women in the Earliest Churches*, 120: "Paul is suggesting correct behavior for one who is learning; it is not a prohibition of speaking. The focus

Finally, note that the phrase "in quietness" (*en hēsuchia*) frames Paul's discussion of these women's learning and teaching in the assembly in 2:11-12. This suggests that what Paul writes between the two occurrences of this phrase all belongs to the same issue. Later in this chapter we will return to this point as it relates to whether the word translated "have authority" (*authenteō*) in 2:12 refers to the teaching that was taking place in the assembly or to something else beyond the assembly.

Submissiveness (hupotagē). The word translated "submissiveness" in 2:11 (*hupotagē*) is used only four times in NT, all of them by Paul.[25] Only in this current usage in I Tim. 2 does it relate to women, but the cognate verb, *hupotassō*, ("to submit") does five times in Paul. As discussed earlier in **Excursus 7: Hupotassō ("to submit") in the New Testament** in chapter eight, four of these relate to married women's voluntary submission to their husbands.[26] The fifth occurrence is in I Cor. 14:34, where the context ("their own husbands," *tous idious andras*, v. 35) clearly indicates that wives, not women in general, are in view. So here in I Timothy 2, where there are already other indications that Paul is discussing wives, it is reasonable to assume Paul is using *gunē* here as he does in all other "submission" passages where he is referring to men and women/wives.

The reference to these women's (wives') submissiveness while learning raises an additional question. To whom was their submissiveness to be addressed? Paul is not explicit about that. In fact, the situation here is the same as it was in I Cor. 14:34, where, as was noted in the excursus mentioned above,

---

is on how one should listen and learn, not on whether or not one may speak at all in worship."

25   II Cor. 9:13; Gal. 2:5; I Tim. 2:11 and 3:4.

26   In Eph. 5:22 and Tit. 2:5 it is "to their own husbands" (*tois idiois andrasin*), while in Eph. 5:24 and Col. 3:18 it is simply "to the/their husbands" (*tois andrasin*).

Paul does not tell us there either. In the literature, several possibilities have been suggested, including these wives' submission to their husbands, to the men in the congregation, to the leaders of the congregation, to the designated teachers of the congregation, or to the message being taught itself.[27] Without strong indicators in the context, perhaps it is best to say simply that these wives were to exhibit a submissive demeanor while learning and leave it at that.[28]

One final matter about the use of the word "submissiveness" here is its relationship with the word translated "have authority" (*authenteō*) in 2:12. In connection with the structure of 2:11-12, "in quietness" (*en hēsuchia*) frames 2:11-12, "learn" (*manthanō*, 2:11) balances out "teach" (*didaskō*, 2:12), and "submissiveness" balances out "have authority." The precise relationship between the two will be discussed in the treatment of *authenteō* below.

Paul's Point about These Women's Teaching

That *They Were Teaching*. Many interpreters seem to have missed the point that Paul is here correcting something that has already been going on.[29] He does not simply pull this out of the air. What this means is that women (wives) were teaching in the assemblies in Ephesus. Think about the significance of that. This is the most Pauline of all churches,[30] a congregation whose leadership would have been intimately

---

27   For the references, see chapter eight, nn. 36-38.
28   See Ferguson, *Women in the Church*, 33.
29   See Crain, "Women in Public Worship," 32 and Osburn, *Reclaiming the Ideal*, 239.
30   Paul spent three years with this church on his third missionary journey (Acts 20:31), longer than with any other church. During two of those years he used Ephesus as his base of operation to train other evangelists in the school of Tyrannus, with the result that "all the inhabitants of Asia heard the word of the Lord" (Acts 19:9-10). He had a particularly intimate relationship with the leaders of the church in Ephesus (Acts 20:36-38), training and working side-by-side with them (Acts 20:18-20).

familiar with any restrictions Paul placed on women's activities during the assembly. Yet, here they were, allowing women (wives) to teach during their assemblies. Not only that, but Timothy, one of Paul's closest evangelistic companions, was in Ephesus when he received this letter (1:3). If Paul's universal and inflexible practice was to prevent women from teaching during the assembly, why would Timothy, knowing this, have been allowing it? The answer is obvious. It was not the *fact* that these women (wives) were teaching during the assembly but something else. Something about the *content* of what they were teaching and/or the *manner* in which they were doing it was troubling Paul.[31]

What *They Were Teaching*. It is well known that opposition to false teaching is prominent in I Timothy. After a short salutation, Paul immediately launches into a charge to Timothy to confront false teachers (1:3). Numerous interpreters have inferred from this and the reference to "the woman's" deception in 2:14 that the women (wives) in 2:12 had likewise been deceived by false teachers and were therefore forbidden to teach their false message.[32] In particular it is argued that certain women were swept up into the opposition to marriage and traditional wifely roles alluded to in 4:3 and 5:14.[33] It must be acknowledged, though, that direct evidence that these women were guilty of false teaching is lacking. Such is certainly a reasonable reading of the situation, given the background of false teaching in the epistle and the reference to "the woman's" deception, but in the absence of concrete substantiation it is difficult to pin down precisely what the

---

31 See Osburn, *Reclaiming the Ideal*, 246 and I. Howard Marshall, *Pastoral Epistles*, 466.

32 See Osburn, *Reclaiming the Ideal*, 246; Geer, "Admonitions," 295-96; Harris, "Eve's Deception," 348-49; and Payne, "Libertarian Women," 190 and "Use of οὐδέ," 247.

33 See Robinson, *Community Without Barriers*, 93, 95; Marshall, *Pastoral Epistles*, 466; and Brauch, *Hard Sayings of Paul*, 259.

content of that teaching may have been. In fact, the suggestion that it may have had something to do with the attack on marriage is not without its own problems. On this see note 49 in chapter five earlier in the book. Perhaps our best course here would be to grant that Paul's reason for these women to stop teaching in the assemblies in Ephesus *may* have been his problem with *what* they were teaching. However, we will be on much firmer ground in examining the evidence that he was primarily concerned with *how* they were teaching. Before moving there, however, it is necessary to examine the meaning of the Greek word, *authenteō,* in 2:12, because it has a bearing on how these women were teaching.

Excursus 10: *The Meaning of* Authenteō *and Its Use in I Tim. 2:12*. Of all the Greek words that appear in Paul's key texts on women in the church, the one that has become the most critical, and therefore most controversial, to the overall discussion is *authenteō,* usually translated "have/exercise authority over" or "domineer."[34] The history of the interpretation of *authenteō* in this passage has been complicated by issues that go well beyond the matter of teaching and learning in the assembly that is discussed in 2:11-12. Among writers in the Churches of Christ are those who have broaden the application well beyond the assembly.[35] For them, any form

---

34   The ambiguity surrounding the precise meaning of this word is well indicated by the multiplicity of its English renderings. A survey of 35 English translations of *authenteō* in I Tim. 2:12 reveals a wide range of English words used to render the Greek word: "authority," "dominion," "control," "conflict," "leader," "lordship," "rule," and "domineer."

35   For example, see Whitmire, "Girls Leading Prayers," 9: "In addition to teaching, this would seem to cover any other situations in which the woman is placed in a position of superiority or leadership over the man." Contrary to this application, Ferguson (*Women in the Church,* 34) is certainly correct in limiting the locus of *authenteō* to the

of leading is seen as an exercise of authority and therefore a violation of 2:12.[36] Thus, for example, some see *authenteō* as forbidding the practice of teenage Christian girls or older Christian women leading able Christian boys and men in prayer,[37] teaching in a Bible class where men are present,[38] or even baptizing.[39] In the case of interpreters in the Christian community at large, the issue of ordination of women frequently looms in the background, a concern not shared in the Churches of Christ with our aversion to the later development of a clergy class. The matter of "authority" is real for these writers because of their concerns about the authority usually invested in those who are ordained. Remove these two concerns—the exercise of authority in other settings than the assembly and the matter of ordaining women—and the issue becomes somewhat easier to manage.

The Meaning of *Authenteō*. The first obstacle to defining *authenteō* is the fact that it is an uncommon word used in the NT only here in 2:12 and never in the Septuagint.[40] This is further complicated by the fact that there are very few known

assembly: "The prohibition of exercising authority over men, therefore, is not a general principle applicable to any situation, but has a specific reference to the assembled church."

36   For a discussion of the serious problem with this approach to Christian leadership, see the section, **2. Jesus' Approach to Leadership,** at the end of chapter seven of this book.

37   Forehand, "Girls Leading Public Prayer," 8. See also Dave Miller, "I Timothy 2:11-15," 286, who sees Paul here opposing women "audibly leading a man in prayer anywhere."

38   Miller, "I Timothy 2:11-15," 286 and Joe Hopper, "Women and the Classroom," 346.

39   Curtis, "Women's Role," 15-16.

40   Its cognate nouns are not used in the NT and in the Septuagint only in Wisdom 12:6 (*authentēs* – an adjectival use of the noun to mean "murdering") and III Macc. 2:29 (*authentia*). Only about 330 occurrences of *authenteō* and cognates, most of them after Paul, have been found in the approximately 3,000 Greek literary authors from Homer to about A.D. 600. On this see Leland E. Wilshire, "Reference to AYΘENTEΩ," 120-21and Scholer, "Headship," 45.

examples of the word's being employed prior to Paul's own use in 2:12. Most of the evidence is late, even centuries after the NT. There are more pre-Christian instances of the cognate noun, *authentēs*,[41] than the verb *authenteō*, but they are relatively rare as well. Until recently, lexicographers depended primarily on these late examples of the verb, uses of its cognate nouns, and speculation about the word's derivation to help them define *authenteō*. In the last few decades there has been renewed interest in precisely defining *authenteō*, perhaps because the matter of women in the church has become a topic of such great interest.

Beginning in the late 1970s, two articles on *authenteō* sparked renewed scholarly attention. The first was written by Catherine C. Kroeger, at the time a doctoral candidate in Classics at the University of Minnesota.[42] She posited a meaning of "engage in fertility practices," viewing Paul as opposing women acting as teacher-prostitutes common in Ephesus at the time who would offer sex to their students. Not surprisingly, the reaction against Kroeger's theory was swift and intense. Articles by Carroll Osburn[43] and others strongly denounced her conclusions. Later she, herself, seems to have abandoned this definition in favor of "represent herself as originator of man,"[44] a definition likewise uniformly rejected by the scholarly community.

The second article, one by George W. Knight III,[45] has had a more long-lasting influence on the debate over *authenteō*'s meaning in 2:12. Taking his cue from the dual definition of the word ("have authority, domineer τινός over someone")

---

41   Defined as "murderer," "perpetrator," "author," "doer," "master" in Liddell- Scott, *Greek-English Lexicon*, 275.
42   "Strange Greek Verb," 12-15.
43   "ΑΥΘΕΝΤΕΩ (1 Timothy 2:12)," 1-12.
44   *I Suffer Not a Woman*, 103.
45   "ΑΥΘΕΝΤΕΩ," 143-57. Also see a brief synopsis of his conclusions in his *Role Relationship*, 18, n. 1.

in the second English edition of Bauer's Greek lexicon,[46] he studied the examples supplied by Bauer and a few others, concluding that only the first half of the definition applied. He denied that *authenteō* had a negative connotation ("domineer") to it. He had thrown down the gauntlet, and others were ready to take it up, including those who agreed with him.

The most significant challenge to Knight's conclusion came four years later in an article by Leland E. Wilshire in which he for the first time presented results from an examination of 314 uses of *authenteō* and its two cognate nouns in the Thesaurus Linguae Graecae computer database.[47] He found that the word group had an overwhelmingly negative connotation.[48] This conclusion supports Bauer's second definition ("domineer over someone") rather than the more neutral nuance of the first ("have authority"). The battle lines were now drawn between the word meaning "have authority" (Knight) and "domineer" (Wilshire), with those affirming more traditional roles for women in the church favoring "have authority" and those arguing for an expanded role for women favoring "domineer." The reason it is important for Knight and others who support traditional limitations on women in the church that *authenteō* has a positive or neutral connotation ("have authority") is their belief that a negative meaning ("domineer") would leave open the possibility that this is not a general prohibition against teaching by all women for all time but rather specific inappropriate behavior by some

---

46   *Greek-English Lexicon*, 2nd edition, 121.

47   "Reference to AYΘENTEΩ," 120-34. Housed at the University of California, Irvine, this database, which at the time of Wilshire's article was nearly complete, provides much more evidence than the few citations in Bauer's second edition mentioned above. It encompasses the writings of about 3,000 authors of Greek literary works from Homer to A.D. 600 and also provides access to a database of papyrus documents at Duke University.

48   For an excellent discussion of Wilshire's article and its aftermath, see Scholer, "Headship," 45-50.

women in Ephesus. On the other side, "domineer" supports the belief that in 2:12 Paul is responding to a specific abuse in the Ephesian assemblies. Thus we have reached somewhat of an impasse, where prior theological conclusions seem to overshadow dispassionate biblical inquiry.

All of this, however, skirts a more fundamental point. For Christians, going back to Jesus' rejection of pulling rank or authority on one another (Bauer's first definition) (Matt. 20:25-28=Mark 10:42-45, Luke 22:24-27), the exercise of authority in the church is by its very nature negative and objectionable.[49] Even in relationships that are somewhat hierarchical, like elders and their congregations[50] or husbands and their wives, there is no justification for the exercise of authority. Note, for example, from points developed in chapter eight of this book, that Paul, while recognizing the wife's subordinate relationship to her husband, never encourages or authorizes husbands to assert their "authority" over their wives. Instead, he urges them to love their wives by modeling Jesus' love for his church. Further, of all the passages in which Paul discusses what should occur in Christian assemblies, the only place where he mentions authority is I Cor. 11:10. There

---

49   In Tit. 2:15 Paul does instruct Titus to "declare these things with all authority" (*epitagē*). However, elsewhere Paul uses this word, which is usually translated "command," only of God (Rom. 16:26; I Tim. 1:1; Tit.1:3), the Lord (I Cor. 7:25) or of himself (I Cor. 7:6; II Cor. 8:8). In the context of this epistle it is clear that any "authority" Titus may have had here was not his own but rather, as an apostolic legate, derived from Paul's own apostolic authority.

50   Some might view Paul's instruction to elders to expose (*elegchō*) false teachers as an exercise of authority (Tit. 1:9), though he does not treat it that way. More characteristic of congregational leaders' actions toward their flock are encouraging (*parakaleō*, Tit. 1:9), caring for (*epimeleomai*, I Tim. 3:5), shepherding (*poimainō*, Acts 20:28, I Pet. 5:2), and being an example (*tupos*, I Pet. 5:3). More to the point, Peter specifically forbids the exercise of authority in the form of lording it over (*katakurieuō*) the flock (I Pet. 5:3). Note that the only other NT examples of this word to lord it over someone is found in Jesus' rejection of that type of leading by his apostles (Matt. 20:25=Mark 10:42).

"authority" (*exousia*) has to do with the right women/wives have to pray and prophesy in the assembly given them by their head covering.[51] There is absolutely no justification in Pauline texts for anyone having or exercising authority over anyone else when Christians come together to worship. So, a*uthenteō*, by looking at the development of its cognate noun, *authentēs*, or its own limited history, is a strong enough word to refer to behavior that no Christian, man or woman, should exhibit in the assembly. Add to that the appropriate behavior expected of women/wives in that culture, and it is clear that whatever the nuance of meaning may have been ("have authority" or "domineer"), the behavior of these women in their teaching was negative and wrong.

The Use of *Authenteō* in I Timothy 2:12. In 2:11-12 we learn that in the teaching and learning activities in the assemblies in Ephesus Paul found the behavior of certain women/wives to be out of order. First, the phrase, "in all submissiveness," suggests that when someone else was teaching and they were the learners they were not exhibiting the proper respect. When the role was reversed, however, and they were the teachers, these women/wives were acting in an inappropriate authoritarian or domineering manner over men (*anēr*) (or perhaps their own husbands). Precisely what this behavior looked like is unknown, nor is it known what norms of appropriate behavior expected in this type of situation in Ephesus were being violated. What is clear is that Paul's use of this strong uncommon word (*authenteō*) from everyday vernacular[52] indicates that it was serious enough to be stopped. Both men and women needed to bring their behavior in the assembly in line with what was expected, either as proper Christian conduct and/or so as to be sensitive to what outsiders in

---

51   See the development of this point in chapter nine of this book in the section, **Activities and Restrictions on Them**.
52   See Archibald T. Robertson, *Word Pictures*, ad loc. and Moulton, *Vocabulary*, 91.

Ephesus regarded as proper behavior.[53] Where needed, men were to control their anger (*orgē*) and arguing (*dialogismos*) (2:8). Women were to dress appropriately (2:9-10) and conduct themselves in teaching-learning situations with proper submissiveness and restraint (2:11-12).

Thus, in the use of *authenteo* in 2:12 Paul is describing the kind or manner of teaching these women/wives were to stop. Many writers on the various sides of the issue of women in the church point this out.[54] For example, Roy H. Lanier, Sr., referring to a similar grammatical construction in Acts 4:18 where two infinitives for "speak" and "teach" are used together, argues that

> One verb limited, colored, the other so as to determine its meaning.... So in Paul's statement to Timothy, he does not forbid women to teach.... But Paul taught that women are not to teach in such situation, or in such disposition of mind, as will cause them to exercise dominion over men.[55]

Others, however, disagree and take *didaskō* ("teach") and *authenteō* as referring to two distinct activities unconnected to each other.[56] Their reasoning has to do with their interpreta-

---

53   Although Paul does not express concern with what outsiders thought about Christians here, he does so repeatedly in the Pastoral Epistles, including just a few lines into chapter three. A bishop is "to have a good reputation with outsiders" (3:7). Paul addresses the bad behavior of some young widows out of concern that "the adversary not be given an occasion for reviling" (5:14). Slaves were to regard their masters with respect "lest God's name and the teaching be maligned" (6:1). In Tit. 2:5 Paul expresses a similar concern about younger women's behavior—"lest God's word be maligned." Finally, younger men are to conduct themselves in such a way that "the opponent may be put to shame, having nothing bad to say about us" (Tit. 2:8).

54   Thompson, *Transforming Word*, 39; Osburn, *Women in the Church*, 246; Soper, "1 Timothy 2:8-15," 6; Geer, "Admonitions," 294, n. 40; Hugenberger, "Women in Church Office," 358; Deaver, "Woman and Prayer," 14-15; and DeHoff, *Sermons on First Corinthians*, 99.

55   "Teacher of Children," 12.

56   Lewis, "Analysis of 1 Timothy 2:8-15," 36; South, "Forbidding Women to Teach," 204-5; and Douglas J. Moo, "1 Timothy 2:11-15,"

tion of the second negative, *oude* ("nor"), in the words in 2:12, "not (*ouk*) to teach nor (*oude*) to have authority (*authhenteō*)." They are right that this double negative construction (*ouk... oude*) for these two verbs is key to deciding whether the verbs present one idea or two. So what is needed is an in-depth study of this grammatical construction in Paul' writings to see if it can shed any light on its proper interpretation in 2:12.

For that we turn to Philip B. Payne's groundbreaking study of *oude* ("nor") as a coordinating conjunction in Paul's writings.[57] He found that in the vast majority of passages where Paul duplicates the "*ouk...oude* (not...not)" construction found in I Tim. 2:12 the two negated elements express a single idea.[58] The case for a single idea becomes even more

---

68. While none of these three present evidence-backed reasoning to support their conclusion, Ferguson (*Women in the Church*, 32-33) briefly discusses the pros and cons of what writers have suggested as five possible interpretations of this grammatical construction. He believes that it should not be taken as "the prohibition of only one type of teaching."

57   "Use of οὐδέ," 235-53.

58   My own study of his Pauline examples produced slight disagreement on a few of them, but in general his findings are solid. The most serious challenge to Payne's conclusions came in a 1995 study by Andreas J. Köstenberger "Complex Sentence Structure," 81-103). It is a response to an earlier paper Payne read at the 1986 annual meeting of the Evangelical Theological Society, rather than to Payne's later, more extensive 2008 study. Payne's 2008 article rendered moot a number of Köstenberger's objections, but his main argument deserves consideration. Asserting that "there is only one close syntactical parallel to 1 Timothy 2:12 in the New Testament"—Acts 16:2--he then produces 52 NT and 48 Septuagint and extra-biblical examples of a grammatical structure similar to it. From these examples he maintains that when *oude* joins two verbs, they are both viewed by the writer or speaker as either positive or negative, never mixed. So, he concludes that since Paul views *didaskō* ("teach") throughout I Timothy as positive, so must *authenteō* be considered positive in I Tim. 2:12. Köstenberger's methodology, and therefore his results, are flawed at multiple points. First, he builds his whole case on one non-Pauline example. Second, although Acts 16:21 is a "close syntactical parallel to 1 Timothy 2:12," it is not a perfect match. The order of two key elements in the verses is different. Third, I was unable to find his distinction about positive/positive and

compelling when we examine the occurrences where Paul adds the contrasting "but" (*alla*) that replicates the full construction in 2:12. It reads, "not (*ouk*)... not (*oude*), but (*alla*)...." In eleven of the twelve[59] other examples of this combination in Paul, the "but" (*alla*) exhibits a strong contrast with the two negated elements preceding it taken together. If, as is reasonable to believe, here in 2:12 Paul is using this grammatical construction as he usually does, his point is made by what follows the "but,"[60] and it is a denial of the two negated elements taken together. It can be expressed as "not that (*ouk...oude*), but this (*alla*)." So when we read Paul's "not *that* (teaching and *authenteō*, taken as a combined contrasting thought), but *this* (*en hēsuchia*, 'in quietness')," we discover the point Paul is making. He was concerned with the tranquility (*hēsuchia*) of the assembly being disrupted by the way these women/wives were teaching.

How *They Were Teaching*. From this examination of the meaning of *authenteō* in 2:12 and its connection to these women/wives' teaching activities, it now seems reasonable to conclude that Paul is not forbidding women to teach in

---

negative/negative verbs joined by *oude* in any of twelve Greek grammars I consulted. Fourth, what he calls a "syntactical parallel" with I Tim. 2:12 misses the actual grammatical feature that reflects Paul's meaning. Köstenberger studies only examples of *ouk... oude* ("not... not"), not ones that also end with *alla* ("but"), as in I Tim. 2:12 and the 12 examples Payne discusses. This leads to the fifth and possibly most glaring of Köstenberger's omissions. Surprisingly, he never deals with Payne's thesis or his evidence for it, in effect allowing Payne's work to stand unopposed.

59   Rom. 2:28-29, 9:6-7, 16; I Cor. 2:6-7; II Cor. 7:12; Gal. 1:1, 11-12, 16-17, 4:14; Phil 2:16-17; I Thess. 2:3; and II Thess. 3:7-8.
60   See Ferguson, *Women in the Church*, 32.

the assembly but is concerned with the manner in which they were teaching. This would not be unlike the situation in Corinth, where there was nothing per se wrong with the Corinthians eating a regular meal when they got together. It was the *manner* in which they were doing it that Paul opposed so strongly (I Cor. 11:17-22).[61] There was a rift between the more well-to-do and the poor. The poor were being humiliated, and they were going home hungry, while the ones who had enough food to bring their own were leaving with full bellies. If you are going to abuse this common meal, it is better for you just to eat at home. So too, here in Ephesus, you women/wives who are upsetting the tranquility of the assembly during the teaching-learning activities should just stop teaching!

To summarize, just as in I Corinthians 14, Paul is here addressing disorder in the assembly. In Corinth it involved some tongue speakers (14:27-28), prophets (14:29-32), and women/wives (14:34-35). Here in I Tim. 2 it may have involved some men, as evidenced by Paul's concern about anger and arguing (2:8). In 2:11-12 it concerned the behavior of some of the women/wives that was detrimental to the tranquility (*hēsuchia*) of the assembly. The fact that in the Greek original *hēsuchia* frames (begins and ends) 2:11-12 shows that tranquility during the assembly is his major concern, and certain women/wives were at the heart of the problem. When others were teaching and they were learning (*manthanō*) they were not exhibiting proper submissiveness (*hupotagē*). When they were teaching (*didaskō*) they were exhibiting an aggressiveness or assertiveness (*authenteō*) either over the men present or their own husbands that upset the tranquility of the assembly. The immediate reference to Genesis 2-3 in 2:13-15

61   On this see, Köstenberger's ("Complex Sentence Structure," 89) comment about I Tim. 2:12 in this regard. "It remains a legitimate possibility for a writer to deny someone for certain reasons the exercise of activities he otherwise views positively."

strongly suggests that the offending women were, in fact, certain *wives*, since as was shown earlier in chapter four of this book, everything in Genesis 2-3 has to do with a specific married couple, not with women and men in general. So the behavior of these women (wives) not only would have been destructive to the tranquility of the assembly but also out of line with the way Ephesians would have regarded proper behavior of wives toward or in the presence of their husbands.

Two Additional Matters Addressed in the Literature. Before moving to 2:13-15, where Paul supports his point in 2:11-12, it is perhaps best to deal with two matters that have occupied much attention in the literature on 2:11-12. They have to do with (1) the setting and women to which 2:11-12 applies and (2) whether authority is inherent in the act of teaching.

The Setting and Women to Which 2:11-12 Applies. In much of the literature on women in the church it has become axiomatic that women may not lead men in any activity in the church, either in or out of the assembly.[62] Of course, no NT text teaches that. However, many writers find justification for this view in their interpretation of the two-word prepositional phrase, "*authenteō* man," in 2:12.[63] In fact, there is no other passage in the NT that could possibly be used to support this assertion. So, an interpretation of 2:12 is the *sole* biblical

---

62   For examples of limitations interpreters have placed on women outside the assembly, see the first paragraph in ***Excursus 10: The meaning of* authenteō *and its use in I Tim. 2:12*** and nn. 35 and 37-39 above.

63   Many interpreters make the faulty leap from their definition of *authenteō* as "exercise authority" to equating it with the act of leading. For example, Deaver ("Teaching and Praying," 676 and "Woman and Prayer," 15) in discussing leading prayer asserts that "such leading (or leading part) by the very nature of the case or situation inherently involves exercising authority." See also May, "Woman's Role," 247; Hopper, "Women and the Classroom," 346 and Dave Miller, "Permit Not a Woman," 27 and "I Timothy 2:11-15," 285.

basis for this highly questionable conclusion that has been so limiting to half the members of every congregation. This begs the question of whether this phrase is solid enough to bear the weight of such all-encompassing restrictions on women's activities, even out of the assembly.

There are several reasons to conclude that it is not. First, as discussed above in the section, **Other Settings?**, the phrase, "in every place," in 2:8 makes it clear that Paul is here referring only to regular Christian assemblies. Ferguson, who developed the evidence for this conclusion in an excellent article on the subject,[64] also sees 2:12 as referring to the assembly. In another place he states that "the prohibition of exercising authority over men, therefore, is not a general principle applicable to any situation, but has specific reference to the assembled church."[65] Thus in the introduction (2:8) to this whole section (2:8-15), Paul identifies the assembly as the setting to which his instructions apply.

Second, since the precise meaning of *authenteō*, a Greek word used only here in the NT, is highly disputed, using this word as the sole basis for such blanket limitations on women's service is risky at best. Such a far reaching application needs a much firmer foundation than this.

Third, as was shown above in the excursus on *authenteō*,[66] this Greek word in 2:12 should be taken with *didaskō*, "to teach." It does not introduce any additional types of activities in the assembly or out.

Finally, as was shown in the section, **Identity of the "Woman" (gunē)** above, Paul is not writing here about all the women in the congregation but about some wives who were conducting themselves in the teaching-learning activities in the assembly in a way that was detrimental to the tranquility that should characterize their meetings. To expand Paul's

---

64   "1 Timothy 2:8," 65-73.
65   *Women in the Church*, 34.
66   See **The Use of Authenteō in I Tim. 2:12** above.

prohibition to all women does not take adequate account of the context.

In view of all of this, there is simply no justification for broadening the application of the prepositional phrase "*authenteō* man" to all women in all settings where they might be "leading," both in and out of the assembly. *Authenteō* does not even mean "to lead." By any definition it is a stronger word than that. Further, according to Jesus, in the kingdom leading has nothing to do with the exercise of authority. When will we stop the destructive teaching, based on this prepositional phrase in I Tim. 2:12, that women may not lead men in the church either in the assembly or out? Whether it is hearing the beautiful prayers of our sisters in the assembly or benefitting from their almost limitless gifts in ministering more broadly in the activities of the church, congregations have been impoverished too long by the unbiblical limitations we have placed on our women.

Whether Authority is Inherent in the Act of Teaching. Some interpreters believe Paul is introducing the idea of authority into his discussion of women teaching in 2:12 not just in the word, *authenteō*, but in the word "teach" (*didaskō*) as well. They maintain that the exercise of authority is inherent in the act of teaching. For them, for a woman to teach men in and of itself is a wrongful failure to submit to the authority of the men of the church. Thus, for example, one writer states that "teaching by its very nature is an authoritative function."[67] Another asserts, "What needs to be understood is that 'to teach' is to 'exercise authority.' In the mixed assemblies of the church a woman is not permitted to exercise the authority of a teacher."[68] This reasoning is what Nichol wrote *God's Woman* to correct. For him, throughout the Bible women taught men with God's approval and even at his direction. Only when

---

67 Neil Lightfoot, *Role of Women*, 32.
68 Pharr, "Exercise Authority," 33.

they did it in a way that exerted authority over men did it cross the line. For Nichol, then, teaching men was not in itself an act of assuming authority over men.[69]

That for someone to teach is not inherently an assertion of the teacher's authority over those being taught is evident from another consideration. If a teenage boy teaches or gives a talk at church and his father is present, would he not be exerting authority over one to whom he is supposed to be submissive? When I did this the first time at about age 16, my father did not take me home and discipline me for insubordination. Instead, he played the role of a proud father. How hung up we get on this notion that acts of service when we come together somehow involve the exercise of our authority over the others present. Again, how completely this conflicts with Jesus' vision of how his disciples should lead.

Allusions to the Creation Narrative

For Adam was formed first, then Eve. And Adam was not deceived, but the woman, having been deceived, became a transgressor. But she will be saved through childbearing, if they remain in faith and love and holiness with self-control. (2:13-15)

IN THE ONGOING DISPUTE OVER WOMEN IN THE CHURCH, these three verses, especially the first two, have played a key role. For those who support traditional limitations on women in the church, 2:11-12 states *what* they should and should not do, and 2:13-15 offers the *why*. Certainly the introductory word, "for" (*gar*), shows that Paul connects the two. 2:13-15 provides support for his point in 2:11-12. Unfortunately, Paul merely makes these allusions to the Genesis creation narra-

---

69   See passim, especially pp. 148, 153. See also DeHoff, *Sermons on First Corinthians,* 99 and Payne ("Libertarian Women," 173), who observes that *didaskō* "in the NT is a general term which can apply to all sorts and levels of teaching."

tive without specifying *how* they support his instructions for women/wives during the teaching-learning activities in the assembly. Does the fact that Paul refers to the creation narrative suggest that he is laying down a rule for all women in every congregation for all time or is something else going on here? This question is dealt with in some depth earlier in chapter five of this book.[70] The reader is referred to that discussion, but for the sake of continuity in the present chapter, points made there will be summarized here.

Adam Formed First, Then Eve (2:13). This verse makes a verbal allusion to Gen. 2:7-8, 15 (*plassō*, "*to form*") and a non-verbal allusion to the fashioning of Eve from a part of Adam in Gen. 2:21-22. The traditional interpretation of 2:13 is that Paul is making a point of primogeniture, the higher status of the one who is prior in time. Its normal application in the OT is to the birth order of brothers, so applying primogeniture to this relationship would be strange to say the least.[71] More in keeping with the context of Genesis 2, where the formation of the woman ("then Eve") complements the man, is the view that Paul is here calling attention to the companionship of the first married couple. Thus it is more reasonable to conclude that in 2:13 Paul is pointing to the fact that the women here are married women, like the first woman, and that the offense being addressed in I Tim. 2:11-12 is to the way a wife should act in the presence of or toward her husband.

Adam Not Deceived but the Woman Was (2:14). This verse is a verbal allusion to Gen. 3:13, where the woman made the excuse that the serpent had *deceived* her (*apataō, to deceive,* Gen. 3:13; *exapataō, to deceive* or *deceive utterly,* I Tim. 2:14). Just as with 2:13, Paul does not tell us what his point is in verse 14. Until recently the rather uniform understanding

---

70   See sections titled *I Timothy 2:13, 14* and *I Timothy 2:15*.
71   On the problem of applying primogeniture to the creation narrative, see chapter four, **Order of creation,** and chapter five, n. 36.

of his meaning in this allusion to the Genesis 3 temptation story has been that Paul is arguing that woman's ability to resist temptation is weaker than man's. Thus she should not be allowed to teach or be in a position of authority over men (2:12). However, many modern writers, including a number who support the traditional limitations on women in the church, find this view of women's nature unacceptable and have sought other explanations of the verse. Although there are many variations, the literature has produced three general approaches to the meaning of 2:14, starting with the traditional one.

Full Traditional Interpretation. While the traditional interpretation is possible, for several reasons it presents the interpreter with more problems than it solves. First, it adds elements not found in the Genesis narrative, namely a hierarchical relationship between the man and the woman before the fall and the woman's greater susceptibility to deception. Second, it goes against the flow of the way women are viewed in the rest of the NT, beginning with Jesus himself. Third, if Paul's use of the creation narrative in 2:13-14 is proof that the prohibition of women teaching and having authority over men is a universal precept, why does it show up so late in the Bible? In the OT women did these things with God's approval and at times at his direction. Fourth, if women are more susceptible to deception than men, how can we explain the fact that Paul directs older women to teach younger women (Tit. 2:3-5) and speaks favorably of women who taught the Scriptures to a child (II Tim. 1:5, 3:15)? Is it reasonable to conclude that women may teach women and children, who are more vulnerable to deception, but not men, who are less so?

Modified Traditional Interpretation. Some who maintain traditional limitations on women in the church but reject the traditional interpretation of women's greater susceptibility to being deceived find support for their view in one or both of two alternative lines of reasoning. The first is that the woman was the first to transgress. Not only is it not clear how this detail supports their position, but it introduces an element into I Tim. 2:14 that Paul does not. 2:14 talks about the woman's deception in contrast with Adam, not who transgressed first. Inexplicably, here a key interpretation of 2:11-12 is based on something 2:14 does not even say. The other approach might best be described as role reversal and is based on the assumption that the woman was in a subordinate relationship to her husband at the time she ate the fruit. Thus her sin included stepping out of her subordinate role by eating without consulting her husband first. Not only does the Genesis text not support this interpretation, neither does I Tim. 2:14. That verse simply talks about who was not deceived and who was and the consequences of that deception.

Full Rejection of Traditional Interpretation. Many interpreters find, in the traditional understanding of Paul's allusions to the Genesis creation narrative in 2:13-14, a failure to properly recognize the role the specific circumstances in Ephesus may have played in Paul's choice of these two features of Genesis 2-3. Just what elements of the situation in Ephesus caused Paul to forbid these women to teach is unclear. As discussed above, it could have been either the content or the manner of their teaching, more likely the latter. So rather than the potential of deception being Paul's concern,[72] he would instead be using the woman in Genesis 3 as an analogy or cautionary biblical illustration to support his restriction on these wives' teaching.[73] "Trouble in Paradise" came when, through

---

72 This is certainly possible, because Paul specifically mentions the woman's deception. However, the application of the word "to deceive" (*exapaptaō*) alone is not enough to disqualify a person due to the potential of being deceived, because Paul uses the same word of himself in Rom. 7:11.

73 This is much like he does in the fourfold cautionary analogy in I Cor. 10:7-10 (v. 7 – idolatry; v. 8 – immorality; v. 9 – testing the Lord;

deception, the woman became a transgressor (Gen. 3:6, 13; I Tim. 2:14). This is analogous to the lack of submissiveness in the behavior in the assembly in Ephesus that was detrimental to the tranquility of those meetings. 2:13-15 taken together demonstrates that the offenders Paul has in mind here were wives, rather than women in general.[74]

Whatever the reconstruction of the relevant background in I Timothy 2 may be, the traditional interpretation of 2:14 that Paul's point is that women are more susceptible to deception or temptation should be rejected. Further, the notion that the woman's culpability came from being the *first* to sin is found in neither Genesis 3 nor I Timothy 2 and should thus be dismissed as an insight of no value for interpreting 2:14. Finally, the contention that the woman sinned because she was not submissive to Adam might have some merit because of the role of "submissiveness" in I Tim. 2:11. However, it is a totally without support in the Genesis creation narrative, so is of no value in interpreting 2:14. We are left, then, with a solution that rejects any form of the traditional interpretation and relies heavily on the context of I Timothy 2 to reconstruct the circumstances 2:14 was written to address.

Before leaving 2:13-14, one final point deserves mentioning. As is well known, it is axiomatic among those who hold to the traditional limitations on women in the church that the way Paul uses the Genesis creation narrative in 2:13-14 shows that his instructions in 2:11-12 are timeless and universal, going back to God's original intent for women. Therefore, rather than being a response to a particular situation in Ephesus, they apply to every woman in every congregation for all time. On

---

and v. 10 – grumbling). More to the point is II Cor. 11:3, where Paul uses Eve's deception (*exapaptaō*) as a cautionary analogy or illustration of what might happen to the men and women of Corinth if they listen to false teachers.

74   For a fuller discussion of this point, see *Identity of the "Woman"* (**gunē**) above.

the surface this line of reasoning may sound convincing, but let us test it against a similar use of the creation narrative in I Cor. 11:8-9. In that passage, Paul uses two allusions to Genesis 2 to support his point that "the wife is the glory of the husband" (11:7). That point, in turn supports Paul's instruction about women covering their heads when they pray and prophesy. Yet, many of the same interpreters who argue, based on Paul's use of Genesis 2-3 in I Tim. 2:13-14, that the prohibition of women teaching is for all time deny that his instructions about women's head covering need to be followed today. This is a glaring inconsistency and calls into question the force of their argument from creation in I Timothy 2.

Saved through Childbearing (2:15). This verse presents the modern reader with questions whose answers have eluded its interpreters. We do not know who the subject of the verb "saved" is, the precise meaning of that verb in this context, or who the subject of the verb "continue" is.[75] So the verse is a testament to how little we know about the actual situation in Ephesus at the time. What to us is a strange statement that no one has ever been able to explain adequately must have been clear to Timothy, because it is the capstone of Paul's whole argument. The most that can be said with confidence is that the verse appears to be an allusion to Gen. 3:16a, "she will bear children." Here once again Paul has in mind *married* women.

Conclusions

INTERPRETERS HAVE USED I TIMOTHY 2 TO LIMIT WOMEN'S Christian service more than any other text in the entire Bible.

---

75   Many English translations mask the fact that the verb "saved" is singular, but "continue" is plural. These include CEV, Douay-Rheims, JUB, NASB, NCV, NET, NLT, NLV, Phillips, and Wycliffe. The GNT, NIV and RSV alert the reader in a footnote. The ASV, CSB, Darby, ERV, ESV, Geneva Bible, ISV, KJV, MEV, NKJV, NRSV, WEB, Webster, and Young's Literal maintain the distinction in their translations.

Their prayer in the presence of men in Christian meetings has been restricted, their right to teach men in any formal setting has been abridged, and their leading of men in any ministry of the church has been squelched. In this chapter, the evidence for these conclusions has been examined and found wanting.

Among many who would staunchly defend Paul against the charge of contradicting himself are those who oddly maintain that women may not pray out loud in the assembly in contradiction to the clear teaching of I Cor. 11:5. Arguing that denying women the right to teach men is based on God's universal will going all the way back to the creation, these expositors lack an explanation of how their theory of this timeless and "universal" principle contradicts the God-approved and often God-prompted teaching of men by women in the OT. And by a deft redefinition of the word "authority" to mean "leading" of any kind, women have had their ability to serve tragically abridged, despite Jesus' instructions about how his disciples are to lead and serve.

Clearly I Timothy 2 is a complex passage, rendered all the more so by our lack of understanding of certain key features of the background. What is Paul's concern for the men's anger and arguing during their prayers all about? Was the heresy being combatted in I Timothy a factor in his instructions about women teaching, and if so, which of its elements? What exactly were these women doing during the teaching-learning activities of the assembly that caused Paul to put a stop to their teaching? However, these gaps in our knowledge of the background do not account for all the confusion that has been generated around this passage. Some of it is attributable to flawed exegetical methodology. Forbidding women to pray in the assembly is based on an inference, not what the text actually prohibits. Likewise, in the interpretation of the Genesis creation narrative at the end of the chapter, elements are introduced that are found in neither Genesis nor I Timothy. Perhaps most critical, both here and in other biblical texts on women, has been taking teachings that in context refer to married men and women and applying them to men and women in general. The multiple references in 2:13-15 to a husband and wife in Genesis 2-3 make it abundantly clear that in 2:12 Paul is not issuing a general prohibition against women in general teaching in the assembly. The time has come for serious students of the Bible to take another look as this crucial passage dealing with women in the church.

CHAPTER TWELVE

The End of the Matter

*T*his book has been an attempt to shed light on the biblical passages that are relevant to the question of women in the church. It has done this by using the tools of exegesis to answer the first two questions about the text, what does it say? and what did it mean? In the process certain reconstructions of other interpreters have frequently been challenged by noting when they have imported into the text elements that are not there. It is not that there is anything wrong with this practice, per se. Given the fact that the multitude of questions we want to ask of the text far exceeds the available evidence, the interpreter often must make educated guesses. However, these guesses are informed by the presuppositions we all bring with us to the study of an individual passage. This is unavoidable. Where we get into trouble is when we do not recognize the impact our assumptions are having on our conclusions about the meaning of the text or when the guesses we make in reconstructing the situation in a passage become "evidence" to support other conclusions.

Because I have tried as much as possible to limit this inquiry to the exegetical study of the first two questions, to this point the third question—what *does* it mean?—has often lingered in the background, begging to be asked. Further, my readers would be perfectly justified in asking what my "educated guess" is about the situation addressed in these passages, after having spent hundreds of hours over much of a lifetime investigating their meaning. As an exegete, this part of my task is more uncomfortable, but exegesis is not complete if it does not try to piece together or synthesize elements that have been analyzed to death. This synthesis cannot answer the third question about application in the modern church, because it still lives in the world of the original church. What it can do is try to make sense of the situation of the original speakers, writers, and readers so those insights can guide us as we attempt to apply God's eternal word to our vastly different time and place. So here goes my best guess.

Proposed Situation for Women in the Church and Home in the First Century

CHRISTIANITY WAS BORN INTO A WORLD IN WHICH THE normal spheres and expectations of men and women were very different. Albrecht Oepke in his article on *"gunē"* ("women") in the *Theological Dictionary of the New Testament* observes that in the world of the NT "the further west we go the greater is the freedom of women."[1] In chapter six we saw evidence of this in the significant limitations on Eastern women in rabbinic statements in the *Mishnah* and other writers who were roughly contemporaries of Jesus and Paul. As we move west we find, for certain women at least, growing freedom, even in public, during the Hellenistic period. This varied from place to place and time to time, but what did not vary was the norm that married women had a special role in the home and a particular obligation to their husbands. This mixture of diversity in the application of the growing freedom of women and uniformity about their role as wives and "managers of their household" (I Tim. 5:14) is the setting in which NT speakers and writers found themselves.

Enter Jesus of Nazareth. Under the influence of the Pharisees (rabbis), first-century Palestine was very conservative and

---

1 "Γυνή," 777.

traditional in its mores and customs on the position and conduct of women both in the home and in public. Yet time after
time Jesus demonstrated that he did not see himself bound by
them, even to the point of openly flaunting them. From this
it is clear that Jesus was ushering in a new way of looking at
and interacting with women. We know that Jesus picked his
battles. On certain matters he chose not to engage in conflict,
for the sake of his mission.[2] This was not one of those issues.
Chapter seven pointed to numerous examples of where Jesus
broke with prevailing traditions in his interactions with women
both privately and in public. Clearly a new wind was blowing,
and it was coming directly from the author of Christianity.

In spite of a few verses in Paul's writings that sound strange
to the modern ear, on balance we find in the NT, following
Jesus' example, an enormous leap forward for the status of
Christian women.[3] However, due to the natural aversion to
anything new in the Jewish, Greek and Roman settings,[4] the
first Christians had to be careful about their reputation with
outsiders. This pertained to the way Christians were viewed
by both local governments and the populace. They, like Jesus,[5]
picked their battles for the sake of the mission. Paul alludes
to this concern frequently in his writings.[6] Not surprisingly
it surfaces in his discussions about women, especially wives,
in the church.[7]

---

2   For example, he paid the Temple Tax that he as God's son did not
have to pay, so as not to give offense (Matt. 17:25-27).
3   This is discussed briefly in chapter eight of this book in the section
on **Paul and Jesus**.
4   Among pagan authors see Suetonius, *Nero* 16.2; Lucian, *Peregrinus*
11; and Celsus in Origen, *c. Cel.* I.14, 21, 26 and VI.12ff. For Christian
authors see Theophilus of Antioch, *ad Autol.* II.33, III.4, 23, 29 and
Epistle to Diognetus 9.
5   See n. 2 above.
6   In addition to passages in the Pastorals discussed in chapter eleven,
note 53, see I Cor. 10:27, 29a, 14:16, 23-25; I Thess. 4:12; and Col.
4:5-6.
7   This is probably best seen in the way Paul handles the matter of

Many have suggested a parallel between the way Paul treats women and slaves. In terms of unity in Christ, "there is neither Jew nor Greek… slave nor free…male and female" (Gal. 3:28), but the full working out of the Christian application of those relationships in the church has been an ongoing task. I need only cite race relations in the church in North America in the last two or three centuries as an example of how hard that work has been. There are hints in the NT (e.g., Phlm. 8, 16) about what ultimately happened in the attitude toward slavery in the West in more modern times, but Christians during the first few generations were in no position to challenge slavery.

In a similar way, it is my educated opinion and that of many who have worked intensely with the relevant NT texts on women in the church that the often-hostile situation in which the early Christians found themselves and/or their concern for outsiders' receptivity to the gospel are the reasons they at times needed to avoid upsetting local norms about women's, especially wives,' behavior. This is why, when we read those very few passages that seem to go against the flow of the significant elevation of women by Jesus and in the rest of the NT, we need to ask whether there was something in

---

women's head covering in the assembly. In I Corinthians 11 he argues strongly for a practice that fits well with the customs of Roman Corinth. However, when it came to women's attire in the assembly in Ephesus in I Tim. 2:9 his instructions appear to reflect a cultural setting that did not expect women to cover their heads in this situation. On this see Ferguson, "Of Veils and Virgins" (2014), 242 and the discussion in the section **How Widespread the Restrictions Were Applied** in chapter nine of this book. Although Paul's justification for his directives in I Corinthians 11 include theologically based arguments, as Ferguson observes (*Women in the Church*, 23-24), at multiple points they are cultural. One of those is the word, "shameful" (*aischron*), which as a nod to acceptable practice in Corinth, resurfaces about women speaking in the assembly (I Cor. 14:35). On this see the discussion in the section **"For it is shameful for a woman/wife to speak in an assembly/church"** in chapter ten of this book.

the specific situation in Corinth or Ephesus that can account for it. It gets back to the fundamental interpretive principles of rejecting proof texting and commitment to interpreting a passage in light of its various contexts (the passage, the book, the author, the NT, the Bible, as well as the cultural and historical contexts). When we do this, the two passages in I Corinthians 14 and I Timothy 2 that seem so out of sync with what the rest of the NT has to say about women in the church become much less restrictive on women generally and more understandable as Paul's instructions for specific situations on the ground in Corinth and Ephesus.

Two Largely Neglected Topics

IN MOST OF THE WRITING ON THIS TOPIC THAT HAS BEEN done in the Churches of Christ, two matters have not received the attention they deserve. The first is the extent to which the relationship between Christian husbands and wives is in play in the key Pauline passages in I Corinthians and I Timothy. The other is that most early Christian assemblies were in a house-church setting and the impact that has on the understanding of these passages. Let me address these two separately.

Husbands and Wives versus Men and Women

THE ENORMOUS CONFUSION THAT HAS BEEN GENERATED around this issue goes back to an unwarranted application of the Genesis creation narrative to men and women in general in the church, rather than, as is clearly the intent in the Genesis narrative, to husbands and wives. Some modern interpreters have even gone so far as to suggest, without producing any evidence, that Gen. 3:16, which is clearly about marital relations, is later expanded to the matter of men and women in the church. In point of fact, there is no NT evidence to produce. There is no clear passage in the NT that places women in subordination to men in any other relationship than at home. In all the subordination passages in the NT where it is clear whether men and women or husbands and wives are in view, the latter is always the case. So why is it that some interpreters, going against the flow, see I Cor. 11:3 as referring to women and men in general in the church, rather than to wives and husbands, as in all the unambiguous passages? Or why do they go against the flow of the whole Bible, since there is no passage in the entire Bible that places women in general in subordination to men in general? Or why do many interpreters apply the statement about women being silent in the churches to women in general, when the passage clearly identifies certain *wives* as those to whom Paul is referring (I Cor. 14:34-35)? Or why do so many writers understand the women being discussed in I Tim. 2:11-15 as all women, when the context from the two references to the Genesis creation narrative (2:13-14) and the mention of childbearing (2:15) make it clear that Paul is talking about *married* women?

After much reflection on these and other questions, it has become my considered opinion that in all three of the key Pauline texts (I Corinthians 11, 14, and I Timothy 2), what Paul is dealing with is an affront by certain wives to the way, in their social setting, they should conduct themselves as married women. Additionally, some of the key details of those passages, rather than referring to God's intent for all wives for every situation for all time, reflect instead their unique setting. They are Paul's application of God's will for husbands and wives (see, e.g., I Cor. 14:37—"what I am writing to you is a command of the Lord") to a specific situation.

Assemblies in House Churches

IN RECENT YEARS MUCH NEW INTEREST IN WHERE THE first Christians assembled has produced studies that have greatly advanced our knowledge. We twenty-first century Christians who every week sit in orderly rows of pews in our

comfortable church buildings find it difficult to place ourselves in the shoes of our early brothers and sisters who had
no church buildings. Although in larger cities they may have
been able to rent a hall for larger meetings when no home of
adequate size was available, their normal place of assembly was
in homes. When the congregation was of sufficient size and it
was able to meet in the more expansive Roman home of one of
the well-to-do members, the line between private and public
could become blurred.[8] This might cause a particular problem
for members of the household where the church was meeting.
Should the women in the home dress and adorn themselves
as they normally would at home or should it resemble more
their public attire, since so many guests would be present
and it technically was not a family event? This may sound
trivial to us, but it may very well be in the background of
Paul's concern with attire and adornment in the assemblies I
Corinthians 11 and I Timothy 2.

My own involvement as a member of two house churches,
one in Manitoba and one in Connecticut, has made it easier
for me to appreciate how different that setting is from what
most of us experience every week. In both cases, we were a
small group meeting in someone's living room. In one we were
fewer than ten and in the other just under twenty. Now in
that kind of intimate setting, in a home, would it have made
sense to enforce a hard and fast rule that during the Bible
lesson a woman could not quietly ask a question or make a
comment? If no man was capable of leading a song, would
God have been upset with us if a capable woman started
the songs and helped us get through them? Should we have
kept a woman from getting up out of her chair to pass the
communion elements to someone sitting on a nearby couch?
I can tell you that in both of those congregations we talked

---

8   On this, see *Excursus 11: Satire on the First Christian Assembly
in Philippi* below.

and interacted as people normally do in a living room, and no one thought that any of the women were out of line. If any woman had done anything that was disrespectful to her husband, we would have addressed it, even if outsiders were not present. But we would just as quickly have addressed a husband's being disrespectful to his wife or any other inappropriate behavior by anyone, male or female.

Would it have been any different in a house church in the first century? Does it not seem more likely that the reason wives were singled out in I Corinthians 14 and I Timothy 2 is that in those two cases they, not their husbands or other men, were causing the problems? Some of the men were out of order in Corinth (tongue speakers and prophets), and Paul addressed it. If men had been disruptive in the way certain wives were, do we have any doubt that Paul would have addressed that as well? After all, his goals for the assemblies were edification (14:3-5, 12, 17, 26) and order (14:27, 31, 33, 40), so it seems reasonable that whoever stood in the way of those two goals would receive his correction.

One other factor in Paul's approach to the wives' behavior in the three passages is the precarious nature of these two young congregations in their cities. In the West, we rarely have to worry, out of unease for our safety, about what the government or populace might think of us or do to us in the way these early Christians did. In many places in Africa and Asia today, Christians are like their earlier brothers and sisters either in concern for their own safety or for the effectiveness of their mission. They have to adjust their behavior in ways that never even cross our minds. As mentioned earlier, Paul frequently stresses the importance of an awareness of what outsiders think, and in the three key passages relating to women in the church his instructions take into consideration what was considered proper in those settings. In different situations, now as it was then, the appropriateness of our conduct in our local setting should still be a prime concern.[9] This is part, though not all, of the answer to the third interpretive question, what does it mean?

Excursus 11: Satire on the First Christian Assembly in Philippi. It is very difficult for us living in the twenty first century in North America, given our own worship experiences, to put ourselves into the shoes of the original Christian worshippers. We have our own church buildings with built in baptisteries, fixed pews, podiums and often seats up front, screens for projection, sound systems, aluminum communion trays, and ample lighting. I have often wondered if Paul were to show up at one of our typical American Sunday morning services, would he recognize what he saw as anything close to the worship experience he tried to create in the first century. This came home to me when I reflected on the fact that most assemblies in the first century were in homes—house churches--and when I remembered my own experience as a member of two different house churches. So much of what has been written about what women may or may not do in our assemblies is written from the perspective of our formal, public worship services. Yet this was not the norm for the early Christians. How different might our conclusions be about women in early Christian assemblies if we simply recognized this fact.

To drive this point home, let us consider one possible reconstruction of that first Christian assembly in Philippi (Acts 16). First of all, it occurred in the home of a business woman, Lydia, who was very familiar with being a woman in the public sphere of a man's world. Paul and company were staying in Lydia's home, so that Sunday morning before the

---

9   See Robinson, *Community Without Barriers*, 65-66, 80.

assembly the conversation between Paul and his new sister might have gone something like this:

Paul: I know this is your home, but there is one thing I need to explain to you before we get started with our service. In spite of the fact that we are greatly enjoying the hospitality of your home and have had some wonderful discussions about your newfound faith, once our service begins today, you will not be able to open your mouth, except for the occasional "Amen" or to sing.

Lydia: I don't understand what you mean—I can't say anything in this small company of friends in my own home?

Paul: That's right.

Lydia: What if I have a question about something you say? Can't I ask it? I've had many questions about your teachings since you began your stay, and you have always answered them.

Paul: You can only ask your question after we end the service with a concluding prayer. Then you can ask to your heart's content, but not during the service.

Lydia: Why?

Paul: Because someone might think you are not being submissive to the men present.

Lydia: Did you think I was not being submissive when I asked my questions of you last night?

Paul: No. Of course not. That was different. We were sitting around in your home in an informal discussion. This is a formal worship service we are about to have.

Lydia: What makes this so formal? It is occurring in the privacy of my home. And even if it were not here, didn't you say that we are the family or household of God?

Paul: Yes I did, and we are, but when we meet in a formal assembly to take the Lord's Supper and engage in other forms of worship together, the analogy of a family is suspended for that brief time. When we meet together in this way, no matter where it is, it is regarded by God as formal and public.

Lydia: But how can it be public? It is just a group of people who have found salvation in Jesus meeting in a home?

Paul: It just is. Just remember. Once the service starts and until the final Amen is said, you are not allowed to make an announcement, teach us a Psalm for our singing, pray out loud, ask a question, get up out of your seat and pass the communion elements to others across the room or anything else that might cause someone to think you were not submissive to the men present. If you do any of these things, God will regard our time together today as vain worship and will not accept it.

A Word to Fellow Elders

Safe course?

BACK WHEN I WAS YOUNGER, I USED TO HEAR IT ARGUED sometimes that when we are not sure of a course of action, we should err on the side of the safe option. While this has a certain reasonableness to it, in practice it is often difficult to apply. The reason is that it is not always easy to identify which course is the safe one. The issue of women in the church is one of those cases. It is argued, for example, that if we are not certain that a woman may do this or that in the assembly, the *safe* course would be for her not to do it. But is that the safe course? What if we state the matter a different way? If we are not certain that a woman may *not* do this or that in the assembly, how is it the safe course before God to abridge her freedom in Christ by not allowing her to do it? There is no safe course here. Either choice has the potential of being against God's will.

In fact, limiting the freedom of action of half of our adult fellow Christians is anything but a safe course. Note Paul's discussion of Christian freedom in Galatians. The issue is very different, but listen to what he writes. "For freedom Christ has freed us. Therefore stand fast, and do not be loaded down again with a yoke of slavery.... But the one who is troubling you will bear judgment, whoever he may be.... Would that those who unsettle you would mutilate themselves" (5:1, 10, 12). The seriousness of limiting another Christian's freedom in Christ is so great that it should give us pause to ensure that we are on absolutely firm ground biblically if we do it. As an elder, I do not want to have to answer for wrongly abridging anyone's freedom in Christ, male or female, when I stand before my Creator.

Why Now?

WE ARE BECOMING INCREASINGLY OUT OF STEP WITH OUR world. We are, of course, called to be separate, to be holy. The problem comes when we have no firm biblical basis for being different. The early church was trying to establish itself in a world that was suspicious of them, if not openly hostile. It had to address the impact of being culturally offensive on both their safety and the reputation of the gospel message. We too live in a culture in which we are becoming more and more marginalized. It is vital that we do not unnecessarily stand apart from our culture in ways that limit the receptivity of the gospel message. I have come to believe that we have limited women's participation in affairs of the church in ways that cannot be justified by Scripture. Assuming for the moment that this is true, here is why it matters and why the clock is ticking.

- The church is the only place in our Western society where women are limited. What does that say to the non-Christian or even to our own women and teenage girls?

- Our young people have already moved on, both in their views on this matter, and for many of them as soon as they have the freedom to do so, from our fellowship. If you do not believe me, ask them or ask your youth minister.

- While we should be leading our culture to do the right thing in matters of right and wrong, we have sometimes needed to be steered by our world. The issues of the use of the Bible to justify slavery in the American South in the nineteenth century and race relations in the church in America in the twentieth century are embarrassing examples. We should determine our conduct by what we believe the Bible to teach, not by what our world values. However, sometimes it has taken our world to wake us up to reconsider what we believe the Bible teaches. In my lifetime, the treatment of African American brothers and sisters by many White Christians has been a glaring case in point. The segregation of our Christian colleges is just one area where this unchristian behavior has been most blatant. The Christian college I went to as an undergraduate was segregated when I matriculated. Thankfully, by the time I graduated we were fully integrated. Were we among the first in our setting to do so? Sadly, no. To my knowledge, my "Christian" college was the *last* college or university in the state, public or private, to integrate. We should have been the first. It took the momentum of our culture to wake us up to restudy our Bibles, repent of our sinful behavior, and change!

I know how difficult tackling such a tough question as women in the church is for congregational leaders. It has the potential of being divisive. If the Bible study should lead to a change in practice in any way, people may leave and sister congregations will view us suspiciously at best. The topic is complex enough that a serious examination would probably take a great deal of time and energy from other vital congregational priorities. The list could go on and on. I know, because I have lived through it. For many years, knowing that there were no simple answers and that this topic was a "can of worms," I resisted our congregation's taking it on in earnest. We had dabbled around the edge for some time, but that did not satisfy the thirst the majority of our congregation had for searching for the truth on this matter, regardless of where our quest led us. Finally, after looking at what was happening to young people and to the impediment to the gospel our practice was increasingly creating, our elders decided that this was one area where we could not afford to get it wrong. Beginning with the elders and then with the whole church, we committed to an examination of the Scriptures until we came to consensus, regardless of where that inquiry led us. If we needed to change our practice we would do it, but we would not change any aspect of that practice until we believed we were on a firm biblical footing. It was not easy, took several years, and in some respects we paid a dear price for it. But because we did not cut corners, the one thing we did not lose was our unity.

I am not presenting what our leaders did as a model for others. What I am saying is that the matter of women in the church is one that will not go away. It will only intensify. At some point we will all have to face it head on. Given our Restoration commitment to patterning our practice on the Bible, what we ultimately do must be based on disciplined Bible study, not simply a rehashing of traditional interpretations and superficial study. Yes, the clock is ticking. Our world has moved on. Our young people are walking out the door. How much longer can we put off settling this once and for all? The results of your congregational study may be different than ours, and it will cause trauma, but at least you will have gotten your heads out of the sand, as we finally had to do. You will be able to face your congregation, especially your young people, and your community in the conviction that your practice rests on a biblical foundation that is the strongest you can make it.

Concluding Remarks

SADLY, I COR. 14:34 AND I TIM. 2:12 HAVE BEEN A PLAYground for biblical expositors. These verses have been isolated from their contexts and treated in proof text fashion to support some bizarre applications in our modern-day church. Women have been silenced in our assemblies to the point that speaking alone they dare not utter a word heard by men, even in a respectful spirit to ask a question, make a prayer request or mention that someone in their house is sick. In many places, not only have their voices never been heard in prayer in the assembly, but any time Christians get together, even for small social gatherings, only men are called on to pray. In some homes, husbands never experience the spiritual pleasure of hearing their wives or baptized teenage daughters pray. Once a boy is baptized he may no longer hear his mother's gentle prayers. Somehow these two verses are seen by some to prevent women from passing a communion or collection tray to more than just the person seated next to them. According to others, they may not sign for the deaf or interpret for someone speaking in a language unknown to the congregation. With a deft hand, many writers have transformed "*authenteō* a man" in I Tim. 2:12 into "*lead* a man" and applied it to all sorts of situations, even beyond the assembly. The most obvious example is women's exclusion from "men's business meetings." Even beyond this, they may not lead any congregational ministry that includes men as participants.

All of these and many other unwarranted and harmful attempts to silence our women and limit their service to the Master seem to stem from two unbiblical sources. The first is the belief that the Genesis creation narrative places women in general under men in general and that that applies to the church as well. As has been observed multiple times in this book, such a view is without biblical foundation. The other is the rejection of Jesus' view of leadership and authority as it applies to his disciples and the reversion to that of "the rulers of the Gentiles." Thus, for a woman humbly and quietly to lead a prayer in the assembly (in the same manner, by the way, that men usually pray) is somehow regarded as an act of authority over the men present. How Jesus must weep at our human interpretations and disregard of his words!

The impetus for this book has been C. R. Nichol's groundbreaking study of women in the church published some 80 years ago in *God's Woman*. This highly respected preacher, teacher, writer, and prolific debater took a courageous stand in reexamining cherished beliefs and practices that most in the Churches of Christ considered long closed. Although in this present book I have disagreed with Nichol at several key points, my debt to him is profound. His integrity and dedication to go where his extensive study of the Scriptures led him no matter how unpopular his conclusions might be is a model for all of us. As he stood on the shoulders of others whose insight and study contributed to his own, so in this book in grateful respect, I stand on the shoulders of C. R. Nichol.

GLOSSARY

Definition of Terms. For the sake of clarity, here is the way a few selected terms are used in this study.

- *Eisegesis* refers to the uncritical practice of reading the current situation or modern categories or terminology into a biblical passage. It is to be distinguished from *exegesis*, which seeks to interpret a text in its historical, linguistic, and cultural context without interjecting elements from a different place and time.

- *Excursus.* An *excursus* is a more detailed side discussion of a topic so as not to disrupt the flow of the narrative. Because most of them in this book address matters relevant to specific chapters, they have been embedded within the chapters, rather than appearing at the end as appendices.

- *Exegesis, exegetical,* and *exegete* refer to the practice and practitioners of that discipline of biblical studies that seeks to determine what the original writer actually wrote and meant. It is to be distinguished from *hermeneutics*, which refers to the modern-day application of the findings of exegesis.

- *Hermeneutics* is the application of the findings of exegesis in other than its original setting. The process of modern application of the teachings of a biblical passage is incomplete without both exegesis and hermeneutics.

- *Septuagint.* The Septuagint, abbreviated LXX, is the ancient Greek translation of the Old Testament. Although the differences are not usually that great, more often than not quotations of the Old Testament in the New Testament are closer to the Septuagint than to the standard Hebrew text.

- *Manuscript.* In biblical studies a *manuscript* is a handwritten document containing portions of the Old Testament or New Testament. It can be a copy in the original language, a translation into another language, or quotations of the biblical text embedded in another document. In the field of *textual criticism*, these three are commonly referred to more specifically as manuscripts, versions, and quotations from the church fathers. When used as an adjective, such as in the expression, "manuscript evidence," *manuscript* may refer to any or all of the three, not just copies in the original language.

- *Textual Criticism.* In biblical studies *textual criticism* is the discipline that studies the *manuscript* evidence for the text of the Bible in order to determine the most likely original reading or text of a passage.

- *Traditional*, as, for example, in the expression "traditional interpretation," usually refers to longstanding and widely affirmed beliefs and/or practices. When *traditional* is used in this book, no presumption is made about God's approval or disapproval of such beliefs or practices, either in the past or present. The term is used simply to identify a belief or practice without making any value judgment.

BIBLIOGRAPHY

Abbott-Smith. G. *A Manual Greek Lexicon of the New Testament.* Edinburgh: T. & T. Clark, 1937.

Alford, Henry. *Alford's Greek Testament.* Vol. 2. Chicago: Moody Press, 1958.

Bartchy, S. Scott. "Slave, Slavery." *Dictionary of the Later New Testament and Its Development.* Edited by Ralph P. Martin and Peter H. Davids. Downers Grove: InterVarsity Press, 1997: 1098-1102.

—. "Slavery: New Testament." *The Anchor Bible Dictionary.* Vol. 6. Edited by David Noel Freedman. New York: Doubleday, 1992: 65-73.

Barth, Marcus. *Ephesians.* The Anchor Bible 34A. Garden City, NY: Doubleday, 1974.

Batsell Barrett and M. Norvel Young's *Preachers of Today.* Vol. 1. Nashville: The Christian Press, 1952: 249-50 and Vol. 2. Nashville: Gospel Advocate Company, 1959: 316.

Bauer, Wlater, William F. Arndt, F. Wilbur Gingrich, and Frederick W. Danker. *A Greek-English Lexicon of the New Testament and Other Early Christian Literature.* Second edition, 1979 and third edition, 2000. Chicago: University of Chicago Press.

Beale, G. K. *Handbook on the New Testament Use of the Old Testament.* Grand Rapids: Baker Academics, 2012.

—. *John's Use of the Old Testament in Revelation.* JSNT Sup. 166. Sheffield: Sheffield Academic Cross, 1998.

Bedale, Stephen. "The Meaning of *kephale* in the Pauline Epistles." *Journal of Theological Studies* 5:2 (1954): 211-15.

Bellizzi, Frank. "The Principle of Submission." *Spiritual Sword* 27:2 (1996): 31-34.

Betz, Hans Dieter. *Galatians.* Hermeneia. Philadelphia: Fortress Press, 1979.

Bilezikian, Gilbert. *Beyond Sex Roles*. Grand Rapids: Baker Books, 1985.

Black, Allen. "Paul's Use of Genesis and The Role of Women." *Where Genesis Meets Life*. Harding University's 68th Annual Bible Lectures. Searcy, AR: Harding University, 1991: 299-310.

—. "The Women Should Keep Silence in Churches: 1 Corinthians 14:34-35." *ACU Lectures* 71 (1989): 177-86.

Black, Mark C. "1 Cor. 11:2-16—A Re-Investigation." *Essays on Women in Earliest Christianity*. Vol. 1. Edited by Carroll D. Osburn. Joplin, MO: College Press, 1993: 191-218.

Bloesch, Donald G. *Is the Bible Sexist?*. Eugene, OR: Wipf & Stock, 2001.

Blomberg, Craig L. *1 Corinthians*. NIV Application Commentary. Grand Rapids: Zondervan, 1995.

Boomsma, Clarence. *Male and Female, One in Christ*. Grand Rapids: Baker Book House, 1993.

Brauch, Manfred T. *Hard Sayings of Paul*. Downers Grove, IL: InterVarsity Press, 1989.

Brewer, G. C. *The Model Church*. Nashville: Gospel Advocate, 1957.

—. "Women Praying." *Gospel Advocate* 76 (Oct. 25, 1934): 1020.

Broadus, Edwin. "The Role of Women in the Church (2)." *Gospel Herald* 48:11 (1982): 8.

—. "The Role of Women in the Church (3)." *Gospel Herald* 48:12 (1982): 7.

—. "The Role of Women in the Church (4)." *Gospel Herald* 49:1 (1983): 7.

Brown, Colin. "Head." *The New International Dictionary of New Testament Theology*. Vol. 2. Edited by Colin Brown. Grand Rapids: Zondervan, 1976: 159-62.

Brown, Francis, S. R. Driver, and Charles A. Briggs, eds. *A Hebrew and English Lexicon of the Old Testament*. Oxford: Clarendon Press, 1966.

Bruce, F. F. *The Epistle to the Galatians*. Grand Rapids: The Paternoster Press, 1982.

—. *1 and 2 Corinthians*. New Century Bible. Greenwood, SC: The Attic Press, 1971.

—. *A Mind for What Matters*. Grand Rapids: Eerdmans, 1990.

Büchsel, Friedrich. "ἀλληγορέω." *Theological Dictionary of the New Testament*. Vol. 1. Edited by Gerhard Kittel. Grand Rapids: Eerdmans, 1964: 260-63.

Bultmann, Rudolf. "αἰσχρός." *Theological Dictionary of the New Testament*. Vol. 1. Edited by Gerhard Kittel. Grand Rapids: Eerdmans, 1964:189-191.

Burger, Wayne. "Culture, the Holy Kiss, and Women's Silence." *Rocky Mountain Christian* 27:12 (Nov. 1999): 12.

Busenitz, Irvin A. "Woman's Desire for Man: Genesis 3:16 Reconsidered." *Grace Theological Journal* 7:2 (1986): 203-12.

Bushnell, Katherine C. *God's Word to Women*. Self published, 1921.

Calvin, John. *Commentary on I Corinthians*.

—. *Commentary on I Timothy*.

Campbell, Alexander. *The Christian System*. Cincinnati: Standard Publishing Company, 1835.

—. "Woman and Her Mission." *Lectures and Addresses*. Nashville: Harbinger Book Club, 1861.

Campbell, Thomas. *Declaration and Address*. St. Louis: The Bethany Press, 1960.

Carlston, C. E. "Proverbs, Maxims, and the Historical Jesus." *Journal of Biblical Literature* 99:1 (1980): 95-97.

Caselman, Randall. "Bella Vista Church of Christ Lifelines." (Aug. 26, 2015).

Casey, James. "Girls Praying: In the Light of I Corinthians 14:34, 35, I Timothy 2:8-12 and Other Passages." *ACU Lectures* 59 (1977): 96-113.

Cervin, Richard S. "Does Κεφαλή Mean 'Source' or 'Authority Over' in Greek Literature? A Rebutta.," *Trinity Journal* 10, n.s. (1989): 85-112.

Chesnutt, Randall D. "Jewish Women in the Greco-Roman Era." *Essays on Women in Earliest Christianity*. Vol. I. Edited by Carroll D. Osburn. Joplin, MO: College Press, 1993: 93-130.

Chism, J. W. "Woman's Work in the Church." *Gospel Advocate* 45 (July 16, 1903): 450-51.

Chouinard, Larry. "Women in Matthew's Gospel: A Methodological Study." *Essays on Women in Earliest Christianity*. Vol. 1. Edited by Carroll D. Osburn. Joplin, MO: College Press, 1993: 425-444.

Coffman, Burton. *Commentary on 1 and 2 Corinthians*. Austin, TX: Firm Foundation Publishing Company, 1977: 179.

—. *Commentary on 1 & 2 Thessalonians, 1 & 2 Timothy, Titus & Philemon*. Austin, TX: Firm Foundation Publishing House, 1978.

Colson, F. H. *Philo*. Loeb Classical Library. Vol. 7. Cambridge: Harvard University Press, 1937.

Condren, Janson C. "Toward a Purge of the Battle of the Sexes and Return for the Original Meaning of Genesis 3:16B." *Journal of the Evangelical Theological Society* 60:2 (2017): 227-45.

Conzelmann, Hans. *1 Corinthians*. Hermeneia. Philadelphia: Fortress Press, 1975.

"C. R. Nichol Biographical Notes" (a resume) archived in the Center for Restoration Studies at Abilene Christian University.

Crain, Jr., Sellers S. "Prayer and the Role of Women in Public Worship." *Gospel Advocate* 146:9 (2004): 32-35.

Cukrowski, Ken. "The Problem of Uncovered Prophets: Exploring 1 Cor 11:2-16." *Leaven* 9:3 (2001): 138-145.

—. "Women and Wealth in 1 Timothy." *Leaven* 13:1 (2005): 35-41.

Culver, Robert D. *"Mashal* III." *Theological Wordbook of the Old Testament.* Vol. 1. Edited by R. Laird Harris. Chicago: Moody Press, 1980: 534.

Curry, Melvin D. "Male and Female in the Church." *In His Image: The Implication of Creation.* Florida College Annual Lectures. Temple Terrace, FL: Florida College Bookstore, 1995: 176-90.

Curtis, Burl. "Women's Role in the Church." *Carolina Christian* 37:10 (1995): 15-16.

Daley, M. O. *God's Woman,* "Introduction." In *God's Woman.* Clifton, TX: Nichol Publishing Company, 1938.

—. "News and Notes." *Gospel Advocate* 80 (Nov. 3, 1938): 1040.

Dalman, Gustaf. *The Words of Jesus.* Edinburgh: T. & T. Clark, 1909.

Danby, Herbert. *The Mishnah.* London: Oxford University Press, 1933.

Daube, David. "Jesus and the Samaritan Woman: The Meaning of συγχράομαι." *Journal of Biblical Literature* 69:2 (June 1950): 137-147.

Davidson, Richard M. "The Theology of Sexuality in the Beginning: Genesis 1-2." *Andrews University Seminary Studies* 20:1 (Spring 1988): 5-21.

—. "The Theology of Sexuality in the Beginning: Genesis 3." *Andrews University Seminary Studies* 26:2 (Summer 1988): 121-31.

Davison, Roy. "Response." *Gospel Herald* 49:2 (1983): 15.

Deaver, Roy. "Christian Women and Red Purses: Part Two." *Gospel Advocate* 113:51 (Dec. 23, 1971): 810-12.

—. "First Corinthians 14:26-40." *Contending for the Faith* 26:11 (Nov. 1995): 10-11.

—. "Woman and Prayer." *Spiritual Sword* 6:4 (July 1975): 13-15.

—. "Women Teaching and Praying." *Gospel Advocate* 114:43 (Oct. 24, 1974): 676.

DeHoff, George W. *Sermons on First Corinthians*. Murfreesboro, TN: The Christian Press, 1947.

Delling, Gerhard. "ὑποτάσσω." *Theological Dictionary of the New Testament*. Vol. 8. Edited by Gerhard Kittel. Grand Rapids: Eerdmans, 1972: 39-46.

van den Doel, Anthoine. "Submission in the New Testament." *Brethren Life and Thought* 31:3 (Spring 1986): 121-25.

Dudrey, Russ. "The Problem of the Unveiled Woman in I Corinthians 11:2-16 in Light of the Literary Structure of I Corinthians 8-11." *Christian Scholars Conference* 17 (July 1997): 1-9 on http://www.christianscholars.acu.edu/97/Papers/Dudrey.html.

—. "'Submit Yourselves to One Another': A Socio-Historical Look at the Household Code of Ephesians 5:15-6:9." *Restoration Quarterly* 41:1 (1999): 27-44.

Dye, Ross W. "Women, Culture and the Church."*Gospel Advocate* 138:6 (June 1996): 28-30.

Ellis, E. Earl. *Paul's Use of the Old Testament*. London: Oliver and Boyd, 1957.

—. *Prophecy and Hermeneutic in Early Christianity*. Grand Rapids: Eerdmans, 1978).

Evans, Mary. *Woman in the Bible*. Carlisle, Cumbria: Paternoster Press, 1983.

Fee, Gordon D. *The First Epistle to the Corinthians*. Grand Rapids: Eerdmans, 1987.

Ferguson, Everett. *A Cappella Music in the Public Worship of the Church*. Abilene: Biblical Research Press, 1972.

—. "The Assembly—1 Corinthians 14 Part 2: The Assembly." *Gospel Advocate* 135:9 (Sept. 1993): 10-12.

—. "The Breaking of Bread." *Gospel Advocate* 133 (June, 1991): 52-55.

—. *The Christian Chronicle* (Sept. 2001): 31.

—. *The Church of Christ*. Grand Rapids: Eerdmans, 1996.

—. "The Lord's Supper and Biblical Hermeneutics." *Mission* 10 (Sept. 1976): 11-14.

—. "Τόπος in 1 Timothy 2:8." *Restoration Quarterly* 33:2 (1991): 65-73.

—. "Of Veils and Virgins." *Christian Scholars Conference* (1985): 1-21.

—. "Of Veils and Virgins: Greek, Roman, Jewish, and Early Christian Practices." *Restoration Quarterly* 56:4 (2014): 223-43.

—. *Women in the Church*. Chickasha, OK: Yeoman Press, 2003.

Ferguson, Everett and Nancy, "New Testament Teaching on the Role of Women in the Assembly." *Gospel Advocate* 132:10 (Oct. 1990): 28-31.

Fitzmyer, Joseph A. *First Corinthians*. The Anchor Yale Bible. New Haven: Yale University Press, 2008.

—. "*Kephalē* in I Corinthians 11:3." *Interpretation* 47:1 (Jan. 1993): 52-59.

Foerster, Werner. "κυριεύω." *Theological Dictionary of the New Testament*. Vol. 3. Edited by Gerhard Kittel. Grand Rapids: Eerdmans, 1965: 1097.

Foh, Susan T. "What is the Woman's Desire?". *Westminster Theological Journal* 37 (1975): 376-83.

Forehand, Garrell L. "Girls Leading Public Prayers." *Firm Foundation* 92:19 (May 1975): 8.

France, T. R. *Jesus and the Old Testament*. Grand Rapids: Baker Book House, 1971.

Fung, Ronald Y. K. *Epistle to the Galatians*. Grand Rapids: Eerdmans, 1988.

Gasque, W. Ward. "Response to Galatians 3:28: Conundrum or Solution?." *Women, Authority & the Bible*. Edited by Alvera Mickelsen. Downers Grove: InterVarsity Press, 1986: 188-92.

Geer, Jr., Thomas C. "Admonitions to Women in 1 Tim. 2:8-15." *Essays on Women in Earliest Christianity*. Vol. 1. Edited by Carroll D. Osburn. Joplin, MO: College Press, 1993: 281-302.

—. "I Cor. 11:2-16 and 14:34-35: Situation-Specific Solutions or Church-Wide Rules?." *Christian Scholars Conference* 5 (1985): 1-21.

Gobbel, Clarence C. "Principle or Custom." *Gospel Broadcast* 2:29 (July 16, 1942): 7, 14.

Goppelt, Leonhard. *Typos*. Grand Rapids: Eerdmans, 1982.

Grasham, Bill. "The Role of Women in the American Restoration Movement." *Restoration Quarterly* 41:4 (1999): 211-239.

Grasham, William W. *Truth for Today Commentary: Genesis 1-22*. Searcy, AR: Resource Publications, 2014.

The Greek New Testament: SBL Edition. Edited by Michael W. Holmes. Atlanta: Society of Biblical Literature, 2010.

Griffith, Anna M. "Vision in the Maelstrom." *Wineskins* 2:1(May 1993): 11-14.

Groothuis, Rebecca M. *Good News for Women*. Grand Rapids: Baker Books, 1997: 139.

Grosheide, F. W. *The First Epistle to the Corinthians*. Grand Rapids: Eerdmans, 1953).

Grudem, Wayne. "Does *kephalē* ('head') Mean 'Source' or 'Authority Over' in Greek Literature? A Survey of 2,336 Examples." In George W. Knight III. *The Role Relationships of Men Women*. Chicago: Moody Press, 1985: 49-80.

Guin, Jay. *Buried Talents: In Search for a New Consensus*. Tuscaloosa, AL, 2007: 32-35.

Guthrie, Donald. *The Pastoral Epistles*. Tyndale NT Commentaries. London: The Tyndale Press, 1957.

Hailey, Jan Faver. "'Neither Male and Female' (Gal. 3:28)." *Essays on Women in Earliest Christianity*. Vol. 1. Edited by Carroll D. Osburn. Joplin, MO: College Press, 1993: 148-61.

Hampton, Gary C. "Keep Silence in the Churches." *Spiritual Sword* 46:3 (April 2015): 36-39.

Hardeman, N. B. "News and Notes." *Gospel Advocate* 80 (Oct. 20, 1938): 992.

Hardin, Joyce. "Women's Role in the Church." *Gospel Advocate* 130:12 (1988): 12-15.

Harris, Timothy J. "Why Did Paul Mention Eve's Deception?." *Evangelical Quarterly* 62 (Oct. 1990): 335-52.

Hatch, Edwin and Henry A. Redpath. *A Concordance to the Septuagint.* Second edition. Grand Rapids: Baker Books, 1998.

Hays, Richard B. "The Letter to the Galatians." *The New Interpreter's Bible.* Vol. 11. Nashville: Abingdon Press, 2000.

Hayter, Mary. *The New Eve in Christ.* Grand Rapids: Eerdmans, 1987.

Herford, Travers. *The Ethics of the Talmud: Sayings of the Fathers.* New York: Schocken Books, 1962.

Highers, Alan E. "I Corinthians 14:34, 35—Keep Silence." *Spiritual Sword* 27:2 (1996): 22-26.

—. "Understanding the Bible." *Spiritual Sword* 45:4 (July 2014): 1-3.

—. "Women Praying and Prophesying." *Spiritual Sword* 46:3 (April 2015): 9-12.

Highfield, Ron. "Man and Woman in Christ: Theological Ethics after the Egalitarian Revolution." *Restoration Quarterly* 43:3 (2001): 129-46.

Holladay, Carl. *The First Letter of Paul to The Corinthians.* Austin, TX: Sweet Publishing Company, 1979.

Holley, Bobbie Lee. "God's Design: Woman's Dignity, Part III." *Mission* 8:11 (May 1975): 10-17.

Holman, Silena. "A Peculiar People." *Gospel Advocate* (May 2, 1888).

Hopper, Joe. "Questions Relating to Women and the Classroom." *Women to the Glory of God*. Spiritual Sword Lectureship 19 (Oct. 1994): 340-51.

Howard, Oliver S. "Women's Role in the Church—A New Perspective." *Christian Scholars Conference* (1985): 1-11.

Hugenberger, Gordon P. "Women in Church Office: Hermeneutics or Exegesis? A Survey of Approaches to 1 Tim 2:8-15." *Journal of the Evangelical Theological Society* 35:3 (Sept. 1992): 341-60.

Hurley, James B. *Man and Woman in Biblical Perspective*. Grand Rapids: Zondervan, 1981.

Hutson, Christopher R. *The Transforming Word*. Edited by Mark W. Hamilton. Abilene: Abilene Christian University Press, 2009.

Jackson, Wayne. "May Women Translators Be Employed in the Church Assembly?." *Spiritual Sword* 26:3 (April 1995): 24-29.

Jeremias, Joachim. *Jerusalem in the Time of Jesus*. Philadelphia: Fortress Press, 1969.

Jewett, Paul K. *Man as Male and Female*. Grand Rapids: Eerdmans, 1975.

—. "No Male and Female." *Reformed Journal* 24:4 (May-June 1974): 24-26.

Jividen, Jimmy. "Glorious Woman." *Restoration Quarterly* 19:3 (1976): 148-54.

Johnson, B. W. *The People's New Testament with Explanatory Notes*. Delight, AR: Gospel Light Publishing Company, 1891.

Johnson, Luke Timothy. *The First and Second Letters to Timothy*. The Anchor Bible. New York: Doubleday, 2001.

Jones, Charles. "Genesis 2:18-25." *Spiritual Sword Lectures* 17 (Oct. 1992): 297-309.

Keener, Craig S. *Paul, Women & Wives*. Peabody, MA: Henderson Publishers, 1992.

Kenney, David R. "Nichol's Pocket Bible Encyclopedia." *West Virginia Christian* 13:4 (March, 2006): 8.

—. Http://drkenney.bolgspot.com/2008/02/nichols-pocket-bible-encyclopedia.html: 2.

Kittel, Gerhard. "ἀκολουθέω." *Dictionary of the New Testament.* Vol. 1. Edited by Gerhard Kittel. Grand Rapids: Eerdmans, 1964: 210-15.

Knight, III, George W. "ΑΥΘΕΝΤΕΩ in Reference to Women in 1 Timothy 2.12." *New Testament Studies* 30 (Jan. 1984): 143-57.

—. "The New Testament Teaching on the Role Relationship of Male and Female with Special Reference to the Teaching/ Ruling Functions in the Church." *Journal of the Evangelical Theological Society* 18:2 (1975): 81-92.

—. *The Role Relationship of Men & Women* (Chicago: Moody Press, 1985).

Köstenberger, Andreas J. "A Complex Sentence Structure in 1 Timothy 2:12." in *Women in the Church.* Edited by Andreas J. Köstenberger, et al. Grand Rapids: Baker Books, 1995: 81-103.

Kraemer, Ross S. *Her Share of the Blessings.* New York: Oxford University Press, 1993.

Kraus, George. "Subjection: A New Testament Study in Obedience and Servanthood." *Concordia Journal* 8:1 (Jan. 1982): 19-23.

Kretzer, Armin. *Exegetical Dictionary of the New Testament. V*ol. 1. Edited by Horst Balz and Gerhard Schneider. Grand Rapids: Eerdmans, 1990.

Kroeger, Catherine C. "Ancient Heresies and a Strange Greek Verb." *The Reformed Journal* 29:3 (March 1979): 12-15.

—. "The Classical Concept of *Head* as 'Source.'" *Equal to Serve.* Edited by Gretchen G. Hull. Old Tappan, NJ: F. H. Revell, 1987: 267-83.

—. "Head." *Dictionary of Paul and His Letters.* Edited by Gerald F. Hawthorne, Ralph P. Martin, and Daniel G. Reid. Downers Grove: InterVarsity Press, 1993: 375-77.

—. *I Suffer Not a Woman.* Grand Rapids: Baker Book House, 1992.

Lanier, Jr., Roy. "Galatians 3:28—Does It Teach Egalitarianism?." *Spiritual Sword* 27:2 (1996): 19-22.

—. "The Role of Women in the Church." *The Challenge of Christianity.* Fort Worth Lectures 16:1 (1992): 216-28.

Lanier, Sr., Roy H. "The Long-Hair Question Again." *Firm Foundation* 92:11 (1975): 9.

—. "May Women Lead Prayer In Worship?," *20 Years of the Problem Page.* Vol. 2. Abilene, TX: Quality Publications, 1984: 166-68.

—. "Woman—As Teacher of Children." *Spiritual Sword* 6:4 (July 1975): 11-13.

—. "Woman's Liberty in Christ (2)." *Firm Foundation* 95:4 (Jan. 24, 1978): 9.

Lard, Moses. "The Care of the Churches." *Lard's Quarterly* (Jan. 1868): 106-07.

Lavender, Earl. "Tertullian—Against Women?". *Essays on Women in Earliest Christianity.* Vol. 2. Joplin: MO: College Press, 1995: 331-56.

Lemmons, Reuel. "C. R. Nichol Passes Away at Clifton." *Firm Foundation* (July 18, 1961): 450.

Lewis, Jack P. "An Analysis of 1 Timothy 2:8-15." *Spiritual Sword* 27:2 (1996): 34-38.

Lewis, John T. "There Is Death in the Pot." *The Bible Banner* 1:12 (July 1939): 12-13, 19.

Liddell, Henry George and Robert Scott. *A Greek-English Lexicon.* Ninth edition. Oxford: Clarendon Press, 1940.

Life Links to God, Adult Study Guide. "Freed to Serve: Galatians, Ephesians." 21st Century Christian Study Book. Edited by Tom Tignor. 26:3 (March-May, 2016): 105-06.

"The Life of C. R. Nichol," on http://www.therestorationmovement.com/nichol.htm.

Lightfoot. J. B. *Saint Paul's Epistle to Galatians.* New York: MacMillan and Company, 1892.

Lightfoot, Neil R. *The Role of Women: New Testament Perspectives*. Memphis, TN: Student Association Press, 1978.

—. "The Role of Women in Religious Services." *Restoration Quarterly* 19:3 (1976): 129-136.

—. "Women, Headdress, Long Hair, etc.—I Corinthians 11:2ff." *I Am Not Ashamed of the Gospel*. Abilene Christian College Annual Bible Lectures. Abilene: Abilene Christian College Book Store, 1975: 132-43.

Lipe, David L. "1 Timothy 2:11-15: Women's Role—Then, Now and Future." *Great Texts of the Bible Revisited*. Faulkner University Lectures (Oct. 1993): 293-301.

Lipscomb, David. *A Commentary of the New Testament Epistles*. Vol. 5. Nashville: Gospel Advocate Company, 1942.

—. *A Commentary on the New Testament Epistles: First Corinthians*. Nashville: Gospel Advocate Company, 1964.

—. "Covered Heads." *Queries and Answers*. Cincinnati: F. L. Rowe, 1918: 113-15.

—. "Queries." *Gospel Advocate* 18:45 (Nov. 16, 1876): 1110-11.

—. "Should Women Preach Publicly?." *Gospel Advocate* 33:31 (Aug. 5, 1891): 486.

—. "Women Preachers." (originally published in the *Gospel* Advocate) *Queries and Answers*. Fourth edition. Cincinnati: F. L. Rowe, 1918: 450-454.

—. "Woman's Work," (originally published in the *Gospel* Advocate) *Queries and Answers*. Fourth edition. Cincinnati: F. L. Rowe, 1918: 446-450.

—. "Woman's Work in the Church." *Gospel Advocate* (March 14, 1888): 6-7).

Lockhart, Jay. "The Principle of Male Spiritual Leadership." *Spiritual Sword* 46:3 (April 2015): 13-17.

Loewe, Herbert. *A Rabbinic Anthology*. Edited by Herbert Loewe and C. G. Montefiore. Philadelphia: The Jewish Publication Society of America, 1963.

Long, Frederick J. "Christ's Gifted Bride." *Women, Ministry and the Gospel*. Edited by Mark Husbands and Timothy Larsen. Downers Grove: IVP Academic, 2007: 98-123.

MacArthur, John. *1 Corinthians*. Chicago: Moody Press, 2006.

McGarvey, J. W. *Commentary on Thessalonians, Corinthians, Galatians and Romans*. Cincinnati: Standard Publishing, 1916.

McKeon, Richard. *The Basic Works of Aristotle*. New York: Random House, 1941.

McKinnis, Rick. *Equally Yoked*. Xulon Press, 2009.

McQuiddy, J. C. "Women's Work in the Church." *Gospel Advocate* 52 (Nov. 17, 1910): 1265.

Malbon, Elizabeth. "Fallible Followers: Women and Men in the Gospel of Mark." *Semeia* 28 (1983): 29-48.

Marshall, I. Howard. *The Pastoral Epistles*. ICC, n.s. Edinburgh: T. & T. Clark, 1999.

Marrs, Rick. *Embracing the Call of God*. Webb City, MO: Covenant Publishing, 2003.

—. "In the Beginning: Male and Female (Gen. 1-3)." In *Essays on Women in Earliest Christianity*. Vol. 2. Edited by Carroll D. Osburn. Joplin, MO: College Press, 1995: 1-36.

Martin, Luther. "Orderliness in Using 1st Century Spiritual Gifts." *Gospel Light* 65 (1995): 180-81.

May, Cecil. "Woman's Role in the Church." *In Times Like These*. Faulkner University Lectures. 55 (March 1996): 243-52.

Meyers, Carol L. "Gender Roles and Genesis 3:16 Revisited." *The Word of the Lord Shall Go Forth*. Edited by Carol L. Meyers and M. O'Connor. Philadelphia: American Schools of Oriental Research, 1983.

Mickelsen, Berkeley and Alvera. "What Does *Kephalē* Mean in the New Testament?." *Women, Authority & the Bible*. Downers Grove: InterVarsity Press, 1986: 97-110.

Miller, Dave. "'But I Permit Not a Woman…'." *Spiritual Sword* 25:3 (April 1994): 25-28.

—. "The Exegesis of I Timothy 2:11-15." *Women to the Glory of God.* The Spiritual Sword Lectureship 19 (Oct. 1994): 273-97.

—. "The Role of Women in the Church." *Spiritual Sword* 24:1 (Oct. 1992): 20-24.

Miller, Hollis. "Women in Paul's Letters (3)." *Firm Foundation* 93:13 (1976): 7, 11.

—. "Women in Paul's Letters (4)." *Firm Foundation* 93:14 (1976): 7.

Montefiore, C. G. *Rabbinic Literature and Gospel Teachings.* New York: KTAV Publishing House, 1970.

Montefiore, C. G. and H. Loewe. *Rabbinic Anthology.* New York: The World Publishing Company, 1963.

Moo, Douglas J. "1 Timothy 2:11-15: Meaning and Significance." *Trinity Journal* 1 n.s. (1980): 62-83.

Moore, George Foot. *Judaism.* Vol. 2. Cambridge: Harvard University Press, 1966.

Morris, Leon. *The Gospel according to John.* Grand Rapids: Eerdmans , 1971.

Mosher, Sr., Keith A. "To Preach or to Teach? Biblical Positions for Women." *Women to the Glory of God.* The Spiritual Sword Lectureship 19 (Oct. 1994): 364-75.

Moulton, J. H. and G. Milligan. *Vocabulary of the Greek Testament.* Peabody, MA: Hendrickson Publishers, 1930.

Neller, Kenneth V. "'Submission' in Eph. 5:21-33." *Essays on Women in Earliest Christianity.* Vol. 1. Edited by Carroll D. Osburn. Joplin, MO: College Press, 1993: 243-60.

Nestle, Eberhard. *Novum Testamentum Graece.* 27th edition. Edited by Kurt Aland, et al. Nördlingen: Deutsche Bibelgesellschaft, 2001.

Neusner, Jacob and Bruce D. Chilton. "Paul and Gamaliel." *The Review of Rabbinic Judaism* 8 (2005): 113-162.

Nichol. C. R. *God's Woman.* Clifton, TX: Nichol Publishing Company, 1938.

Norman, Morris D. "The Role of Women in the Church: Work and Worship." *Florida College Annual Lectures*. Temple Terrace, FL: Florida College Bookstore, 1982: 115-19.

Oepke, Albrecht. "ἀνήρ." *Theological Dictionary of the New Testament*. Vol. 1. Edited by Gerhard Kittel. Grand Rapids: Eerdmans, 1964: 360-63.

—. "ἀπατάω." *Theological Dictionary of the New Testament*. Vol. 1. Edited by Gerhard Kittel. Grand Rapids: Eerdmans, 1964: 384-85.

—. "γυνή." *Theological Dictionary of the New Testament*. Vol. 1. Edited by Gerhard Kittel. Grand Rapids: Eerdmans, 1964: 776-89.

Olbright, Owen D. "Are Women Permitted to Speak in the Assembly?." *Truth for Today* 18:7 (Dec. 1997): 36-39.

—. "In the Beginning." *Truth for Today* 18:7 (Dec. 1997): 7-9.

—. "Women in the New Testament." *Truth for Today* 18:7 (Dec. 1997): 15-17.

Orr, William F. and James A. Walther. *I Corinthians*. The Anchor Bible. Garden City, NY: Doubleday, 1976.

Osborne, Grant. "Hermeneutics and Women in the Church." *Journal of the Evangelical Theological Society* 20:4 (Dec. 1977): 337-52.

Osburn, Carroll. "ΑΥΘΕΝΤΕΩ (1 Timothy 2:12)." *Restoration Quarterly* 25:1 (1982): 1-12.

—. "The Interpretation of 1 Cor. 14:34-35." *Essays on Women in Earliest Christianity.* Vol. 1. Edited by Carroll D. Osburn. Joplin, MO: College Press, 1993: 219-42.

—. *Women in the Church: Reclaiming the Ideal*. Abilene, TX: ACU Press, 2001.

—. *Women in the Church: Refocusing the Discussion*. Abilene: Restoration Perspectives, 1994.

Oster, Jr., Richard E. *1 Corinthians*. The College Press NIV Commentary. Joplin, MO: College Press, 1995.

—. "The Use, Misuse and Neglect of Archaeological Evidence in Some Modern Works on 1 Corinthians (1 Cor 7,1-5; 8,10; 11,2-16; 12,14-26)," *Zeitschrift für die neutestamentliche Wissenschaft* 83:1-2 (1992): 52-73.

—. "When Men Wore Veils to Worship: The Historical Context of 1 Corinthians 11.4." *New Testament Studies* 34 (1988): 481-505.

Paden, Jon. "Woman in Genesis 1-3." *Image* 6:4 (July-Aug. 1990): 18, 20, 31.

Padgett, Alan. "Wealthy Women at Ephesus: I Timothy 2:8-15 in Social Context." *Interpretation* 41 (Jan. 1987): 19-31.

Pape, Dorothy R. *In Search of God's Ideal Woman*. Downers Grove: Inter Varsity Press, 1976.

Parks, Norman L. "The State of Institutional Scholarship: A Case Study." *Mission* 12:5 (Nov. 1978): 17-20.

Parrish, David. "Submission: A Scriptural Concept for Christian Women." *Mission* 10:11 (May 1977): 17-19, 21.

Patterson, Nobel. "C. R. Nichol." *2004 Freed-Hardeman University Lectures*. Henderson, TN: Freed-Hardeman University, 2004: 341-45.

Payne, Philip B. "1 Tim 2.12 and the Use of οὐδέ to Combine Two Elements to Express a Single Idea." *New Testament Studies* 54:2 (April 2008): 235-53.

—. "Libertarian Women in Ephesus: A response to Douglas J. Moo's Article, '1 Timothy 2:11-15: Meaning and Significance.'" *Trinity Journal* 2 n.s. (1981): 169-197.

Pharr, David. "Do Not Exercise Authority over Man." *Spiritual Sword* 46:3 (April 2015): 31-35.

Http:www. ptc.dcs.edu/teacherpages/tthrasher/listings/n.htm.

Ramsey, William M. *The Cities of St. Paul*. Grand Rapids: Baker Book House, 1907.

Reese, Jeanene. *Bound and Determined: Christian Men and Women in Partnership*. Abilene, TX: Leafwood, 2010.

Roberts, J. W. *Letters to Timothy*. The Living Word. Austin, TX: R. B. Sweet Company, 1964.

—. "The Veils in I Cor. 11:2-16." *Restoration Quarterly* 3:4 (1959): 183-98.

Robertson, Archibald, T. *Word Pictures in the New Testament*. Grand Rapids: Christian Classics Ethereal Library.

Robertson, Archibald and Alfred Plummer. *The Epistle of St Paul to the Corinthians*. Edinburgh: T. & T. Clark, 1914.

Robinson, Thomas. *A Community Without Barriers*. New York: Manhattan Church of Christ, 2002.

Rowland, Robert H. *"I Permit Not a Woman…" to Remain Shackled*. Newport, OR: Lighthouse Publishing Company, 1991.

Sanders, Phil. "Are Women Limited as Leaders?." *Gospel Advocate* 157:3 (March 2015): 34-37.

—. "The Case Against Women Preachers." *Spiritual Sword* 46:3 (April, 2015): 17-21.

Sakenfeld, Katharine D. "The Bible and Women: Bane or Blessing." *Theology Today* 32:3 (Oct. 1975): 222-33.

Schlier, Heinrich. "κεφαλή." *Theological Dictionary of the New Testament*. Vol. 3. Edited by Gerhard Kittel. Grand Rapids: Eerdmans, 1964: 673-81.

Schmitt, John J. "Like Eve, Like Adam: *msl* in Gen 3,16." *Biblica* 72 (1991): 1-22.

Scholer, David M. "The Evangelical Debate over Biblical 'Headship.'" *Women, Abuse, and the Bible*. Edited by Catherine C. Kroeger and James R. Beck. Grand Rapids: Baker Books, 1996: 28-57.

—. "Galatians 3:28 and the Ministry of Women in the Church." *Covenant Quarterly* 56:3 (Aug. 1998): 2-18.

—. "1 Timothy 2:9-15 and the Place of Women in the Church's Ministry." *Women, Authority & the Bible*. Edited by Alvera Mickelsen. Downers Grove, IL: InterVarsity Press, 1986: 193-219.

Schreiner, Thomas R. "An Interpretation of 1 Timothy 2:9-15: A Dialogue with Scholarship." *Women in the Church.* Edited by Andreas J. Köstenberger, et al. Grand Rapids: Baker Books, 1995: 105-54.

Schürer, Emil. *A History of the Jewish People in the Time of Jesus Christ.* Div. II, vol. 1. Edinburgh: T. & T. Clark, 1898.

Smith, F. LaGard. *The Cultural Church.* Nashville: 20th Century Christian, 1992.

—. *Men of Strength for Women of God.* Eugene, OR: Harvest House Publishers, 1989.

Snodgrass, Klyne R. "Galatians 3:28: Conundrum or Solution?." *Women, Authority & the Bible.* Edited by Alvera Mickelsen. Downers Grove: InterVarsity Press, 1986: 161-181.

Soper, Matt. "I Corinthians 14: Women, Silence, and Order. Sermon #2" (June 1, 1997): 1-9 on http://moon.pepperdine. edu/culver/archives/sermons/1997/1060197.htm.

—. "I Timothy 2:8-15: Women Who Reverenced God." Sermon #3 (June 29, 1997): 3-9 on http://moon.pepperdine.edu/culver/ archives/sermons/1997/1062997.htm.

South, Tommy. "Paul's Motive for Forbidding Women to Teach." *ACU Lectures* 71 (1989): 203-14.

Speiser, E. A. *Genesis.* Garden City, NY: Doubleday & Company, 1964.

Stagg, Evelyn and Frank. *Woman in the World of Jesus.* Philadelphia: The Westminster Press, 1978.

Stendahl, Krister. *The Bible and the Role of Women.* Philadelphia: Fortress Press, 1966.

Stevenson, Jeffery S. *All People All Times: Rethinking Biblical Authority in Churches of Christ.* Xulon Press, 2009: chap. 15.

Http://stonedcampbelldisciple.com/2011/09/29/voices-on-female-deacons-in-the-stone-campbell-movement.

Strack, Hermann L. *Introduction to the Talmud and Midrash.* New York: Harper and Row, 1931.

Tarbet, David. "Involvement of Men and Women in the Public Assemblies of the Connecticut Valley Church of Christ: A Review." April 2013.

Taylor, Nell. "My God and I … A Woman's View." *Gospel Advocate* 136:6 (June 1994): 16-18.

Terry, Bruce. "A Plea for Consistency." *Firm Foundation* 93:13 (March 1976): 6, 11.

Thackeray, H. St. J. *Josephus*. Loeb Classical Library. Vol. 4. Cambridge: Harvard University Press, 1961.

Thompson, James W. *Equipped for Change*. Abilene: ACU Press, 1996.

—. *The Transforming Word*. Edited by Mark W. Hamilton. Abilene: Abilene Christian University Press, 2009.

Treat, Jay. "Woman in Genesis 1-3." *Mission* 10:7 (Jan. 1977): 5-8.

Underwood, Maude Jones. *C. R. Nichol: A Preacher of Righteousness*. Clifton, TX: Nichol Publishing Company, 1952.

—. *The Possibility of Apostasy*. Clifton, TX: Nichol Publishing Company, 1951.

Vermes, G. *The Dead Sea Scrolls in English*. Baltimore: Penguin Books, 1962.

Walden, Wayne. "Galatians 3:28: Grammatical Observations." *Restoration Quarterly* 51:1 (2009): 45-50.

Wallace, Jr., Foy E. "God's Women Gather." *The Bible Banner* 2:4 (Nov. 1939): 40.

Warden, Duane. "The Conduct of Christian Women." *Gospel Advocate* 130:10 (Oct. 1988): 10-11.

Watson, Paul L. "Are Women to Pray and Prophesy (1 Cor 11:5) or are Women to Remain Silent (1 Cor 14:34)? Some Pastoral Implications of an Exegesis of 1 Cor 14:34-35." *Leaven* 9:3 (2001): 160-64.

—. "Why Should a Man Leave Home? An Exegesis of Genesis 2:24." *Christian Scholars Conference* 1 (1981): 1-10.

Webb, William J. *Slaves, Women & Homosexuals.* Downers Grove, IL: InterVarsity, 2001.

Webster, Allen. "What Is the Meaning of Galatians 3:28?." *Spiritual Sword* 26:3 (April, 2015): 21-26.

Whitmire, Charles A. "An Objection to Girls Leading Prayers." *Firm Foundation* 92:19 (1975): 9.

Willis, Wendell. "I Corinthians 8-10: A Retrospective after Twenty-five Years." *Restoration Quarterly* 49:2 (2007): 103-112.

Willis, John T. "Women in the Old Testament." *Essays on Women in Earliest Christianity.* Vol. 1. Edited by Carroll D. Osburn. Joplin, MO: College Press, 1993: 25-39.

Willis, Mike. "The Role of Women As Revealed In the Old Testament." *Guardian of Truth* 38:3 (Feb. 2, 1995): 20-24.

Wilshire, Leland E. "The TLG Computer and Further Reference to ΑΥΘΕΝΤΕΩ in 1 Timothy 2.12." *New Testament Studies* 34:1 (1988): 120-34.

Wilson, Charles H. "Biography of Charles Ready Nichol." Archives of the Center for Restoration Studies at Abilene Christian University, July 20, 1962.

Wire, Antoinette Clark. *The Corinthian Women Prophets.* Minneapolis, MN: Fortress Press, 1990.

Witherington III, Ben. *Women in the Earliest Churches.* New York: Cambridge University Press, 1988.

Wolfson, Harry A. *Philo.* Vol. 1. Cambridge, MA: Harvard University Press, 1947.

Workman, Gary. "I Corinthians 14:34-35." *Spiritual Sword* 26:3 (1995): 35-46.

Woods, Guy N. "An Exposition of I Cor. 11:2-16." *Gospel Broadcast* 2:1 (Dec. 18, 1941), 6-7, 14.

—. "Open Forum." (1976). Reprinted in *Contending for the Faith* 26:10 (Oct. 1995): 2-4.

—. "'Principle or Custom'—Which?." *Gospel Broadcast* 2:30 (July 23, 1942): 6-7.

—. *Questions and Answers*. Vol. 1. Henderson, TN: Freed-Hardeman College, 1976: 106-12.

—. *Questions and Answers*. Vol. 2. Nashville, TN: Gospel Advocate Company, 1986: 42-44, 59-60, 98, 127, 160-61, 265-6.

—. "Questions Answered." *Gospel Advocate* 119:33 (Aug. 18, 1977): 516.

Yeakley Jr., Flavil R. *Why They Left*. Nashville: Gospel Advocate, 2012: 190.

Yoakum, Tom. "Moses E. Lard and 'Women at Prayer.' A Perspective for Current Discussion of 'Issues.'" *Image*. (March-April, 1996).

Zerwick, Max and Mary Grosvenor. *Grammatical Analysis of the Greek New Testament*. Vol. 1. Rome: Biblical Institute Press, 1974.

General Index

A

'Adam 81, 90, 132, 134

Adam 6, 53–54, 80, 85, 88, 93, 96, 100–104, 117–119, 125, 128, 134, 214, 287-288, 290

Agapētē 190

Aischron 233, 253, 298

Akatastasia 240

Akoloutheō 172–173

Allegorical 106, 108, 110, 113, 122

Allegory 111, 115

Anēr (andrasin, andras) 45, 72, 200, 222–223, 225–226, 245–246, 252, 263, 265, 271, 279

Anna 14

Anthrōpos 132

Apataō 118, 119, 288

'Arar 90

Archē 204

Aristotle 207–208

Arsen 116

Authenteō 39, 128, 201, 271–272, 274–276, 279–287, 310

Authentēs 275–276, 279

Authority 6, 13–14, 18, 22–24, 34, 39, 41, 44, 49, 53, 56, 60, 75, 96, 98, 115, 121, 123–124, 126, 128, 135, 147, 151, 186, 198, 201, 203–205, 207, 212, 220, 230–233, 249, 266–267, 271–272, 275–281, 284–287, 289, 293, 310

B

Baptize 27–28, 76, 216, 252, 310

Bara' 81

Barth, Marcus 197, 199, 200, 209, 213

Ben Azzai 148

Bērak 81

Bilezikian, Gilbert 93, 134, 137, 191

Bill of divorce 142, 146, 163, 189

Black, Allen 117, 122, 131, 205, 231, 239, 250, 252, 254, 256

Bogart, Ben 30

Boulomai 264

Brewer, G. C. 19, 24, 32

Brightwell, W. E. 20

Bruce, F. F. 176, 189, 191, 195, 233, 243, 250, 255

C

Calvin 120, 243

Campbell, Alexander 12, 24, 30, 62, 64, 73, 80, 180

Childbearing 19, 40, 60, 91, 93, 130, 132, 136, 140, 287, 292, 300

Children 15–16, 26, 42, 123–124, 130, 142, 145, 148, 158, 161, 198, 207–211, 214, 249, 280, 289, 292

Chism, J. W. 23, 246, 250

Christian colleges 3, 101, 308

Commanding 208

Complementarianism 51

Complementary 51, 81, 87, 120

Culture x, 3–4, 7–8, 11, 22, 34, 38–40, 49, 73, 77, 88, 99, 134, 143, 148, 208, 211, 216, 231, 235, 253, 279, 307–308

Curse 86, 89–92, 154

Custom 15–16, 19–20, 22–24, 38–39, 69, 84, 99, 149, 154, 176, 220, 222,

Scripture Index

OLD TESTAMENT

NEW TESTAMENT

45797131R00205

Made in the USA
Lexington, KY
19 July 2019